Technical Aspects of
Data Communication
Second Edition

John E. McNamara

DIGITAL PRESS

Documentation Number EY-AX018-DP-001
ISBN 0-932376-18-5

Library of Congress Cataloging in Publication Data

McNamara, John E.
    Technical Aspects of Data Communication.

    Includes index.
    1. Data transmission systems.   I. Title.
TK5105.M4 1982   621'.38   81-17433
ISBN 0-932376-18-5   AACR2

Trademarks

Digital Equipment Corporation: DDCMP, PDP-8.

American Telephone and Telegraph Company: Dataphone, Touch Tone, Transaction.

Teletype Corporation: Teletype.

Xerox Corporation: Ethernet.

Contents

23 Interprocessor Communication 188

Parallel transmission, serial transmission, error detection and clocking problems in serial transmission, use of microprocessor controlled network links.

24 Digital Transmission and Packet Switching Networks 193

Problems with analog telephone systems, analog amplifiers, digital transmission systems, T1 carrier systems, digital transmission service offerings, circuit switching, message switching, packet switching, benefits of packet switching, X.25, introduction to SNAP protocol.

25 Parallel Communication 203

Use of tones from the subscriber telephone set for various applications.

26 Special Problems 207

Connection of two pieces of data terminal equipment via null modems, clocking of synchronous modems and terminals, active and passive 20 milliampere devices, use of optical couplers.

27 CCITT Recommendations X.20 and X.21 215

Trends in quantities of interface leads; summaries of X.20, X.20 *bis*, X.21, X.21 *bis*.

28 Local Area Networks 222

Connecting terminals to computers via PBXs, patchfields, data switches, and local area networks; star, ring, and bus topologies; network access control via polling, tokens, ALOHA, and CSMA/CD; file servers, printer servers, and communication servers.

Appendices

A How Far—How Fast? 233

Speed vs. distance tables for various types of interface circuits.

Acknowledgments

The production of a publication of this size and complexity can be achieved only through the efforts and cooperation of several people. For helping to make the second edition possible, all of those who contributed to the success of the first edition deserve additional thanks, especially the personnel of Digital Press and Publishing Services, who were again of invaluable assistance. Frank Fritsch of Digital's Communications Subsystems group, and Mike Patton and Larry Allen of M.I.T., deserve special commendation for donating their time and expertise to reviewing the new chapters and appendix.

Many of the figures and charts in this book are reproduced from publications of American Telephone and Telegraph, Electronic Industries Association, Comite Consultatif International Telegraphique et Telephonique, and Trans Canada Telephone System. Their permission to reprint these items is gratefully acknowledged.

Introduction

This book is intended for those who are about to design a data communication system, are about to purchase or program data communication hardware, or are just interested in knowing more about data communication. It is intended to fit between the books that treat data communication solely on a system level, without reference to hardware and transmission features and problems, and those hardware manuals which specify in detail the function of each bit in each register. It presumes some technical inclination on the part of the reader, since some circuit diagrams are shown. It also presumes some software background, as some registers with bit functional assignments are also shown. But all such material is presented only as an example of how some manufacturers have approached the problems being discussed. The reader need not accept those particular solutions, but he or she will be given the background necessary to know what to look for in various hardware and software systems that are used in data communication. Specific computer hardware offerings are not described because they change rapidly.

This book will not teach anyone everything about data communication. Knowledge of data communication is acquired by a bootstrapping process in which one learns enough to read the next book or explore the next problem, from which one learns enough to go on further. This book is intended to fill a place in that process.

1

Asynchronous Communications

Bits of binary data are commonly transferred between electronic devices by changes in current or voltage. Data may be transferred in "serial" over a single line, or in "parallel" over several lines at once. The transfers may be "synchronous," in which the exact departure or arrival time of each bit of information is predictable, or they may be "asynchronous," in which case the data is transferred at non-uniform rates.

In parallel transmission, each bit of the set of bits that represent a character has its own wire. An additional wire called the "strobe" or "clock" lead notifies the receiver unit that all of the bits are present on their respective wires so that the voltages on the wires can be sampled. Figure 1-1 schematically depicts the parallel transfer of the eight bit character 11000001.

In serial transmission, the bits that represent a character are sent down a single wire one after the other.

Computers and other high-speed digital systems generally operate on parallel data, so data is transferred in parallel between these devices wherever they are in close physical proximity. However, as the distance between these devices increases, the multiple wires not only become more costly, but the complexity of the line drivers and receivers increases, due to the increased difficulty of properly driving and receiving signals on long wires.

Serial transmission is generally used where the cost of the communications medium is high enough to justify a relatively complex transmitter and receiver system that will serialize the bits that represent the character, send them over a single line, and reassemble them in parallel form at the reception end. Conversion from parallel to serial and from serial to parallel is typically done with shift registers.

In most data communications applications, serial transmission is preferable to parallel transmission.

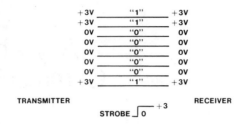

Figure 1-1. Parallel Data Transfer

Because of the mechanism design in early teleprinters, and to facilitate fail-safe operation, serial teleprinter systems have adopted the convention that an idle line (no data being sent) is one in which current is flowing. Data transmission occurs when the current in the line is interrupted in a specified fashion. By convention, the idle (current flowing) state is called the "1" state or "MARK" condition, and the lack-of-current state is called the "0" state or "SPACE" condition. To start the mechanism of the receiving teleprinter, the line is brought to the "0" state for one bit time; this is called the "START" bit. For the next eight successive bit times (see Figure 1-2 in the case of eight bit code), the line is conditioned to a "1" state or "0" state as required to represent the character being sent. To allow the mechanism of the receiving teleprinter to coast back to a known position in time for the beginning (START bit) of the next character, one or more bit times of "1" state (idle) are sent. This period is called the "STOP" bit interval.

Except for the requirement that the line be idle for at least the STOP bit interval, the transmission of the next character can begin at any time. The lack of a continuous synchronous agreement between the transmitter and the receiver—specifically, the lack of a clocking signal within or accompanying the data channel—causes this type of transmission to be called "asynchronous," literally "without synchronization." The asynchronous character format is shown in Figure 1-2.

Before discussing the details of electronic means of sending and receiving asynchronous serial data, a brief discussion of codes is in order.

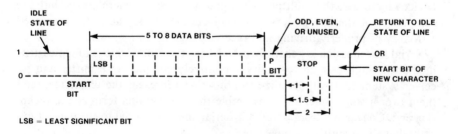

Figure 1-2. Asynchronous Data Character Format

While it is true that precise synchronism between transmitting station and receiving station is not necessary in asynchronous transmission, the receiving station must have a fairly good idea of what rate the transmitting station is using to transmit the bits in order to sample the received bits at the proper times. In countries where power grid networks do not keep the voltages and frequencies of the power lines in various communities in relative agreement, even the use of synchronous motors cannot insure that teleprinters in diverse locations are operating at exactly the same speed. This problem is partially solved by re-timing the reception of each character from the edge of the START bit, but, nevertheless, the sampling of the last received data bit in the character can take place off-center if the difference in motor speeds is too great. For this reason, the number of bits that represent each character is usually five under these circumstances. Five bit code, also called five-level code, is named "Baudot code" after Emil Baudot, who invented the first constant length teleprinter code in 1874. In theory, five bits can be used to represent 32 different characters. Since that is not enough to represent both all alphabetic characters and the numerals 0–9, a shifting character called "Figures Shift" is used to place the reception station in figures mode, after which all subsequent code combinations will be interpreted as numbers. The station may be returned to letters mode by sending "Letters Shift." Appendix C lists some versions of the Baudot code.

While ordinary message text can be transmitted and received quite well with five-level code, the newspaper industry found the lack of differentiation between upper and lower case letters to be a problem. A six-level code, which is basically similar to the five-level code, uses the shift feature to designate the difference between upper and lower case letters and uses a sixth bit to increase the number of available symbols. Appendix C also lists a version of this code.

The most widely used code today is the ASCII code, also listed in Appendix C, which is essentially a seven-level code. It is almost always transmitted with a parity bit (see Chapter 13) which makes a total of eight bits per character. Since the eight bit codes are so widely used for data communications, the remainder of this chapter will describe hardware methods for transmitting and receiving eight bit characters. The reader is cautioned, however, that a substantial amount of international data communications traffic uses five bits per character.

A simplified circuit for receiving asynchronous serial data is shown in Figure 1-3. The circuit contains a "16× clock" which samples the incoming data line at 16 times the anticipated bit rate. The line is sampled at such a rapid rate in order to detect the 1-to-0 transition (when the START bit begins) as soon as possible after it occurs. The circuit which detects the 1-to-0 transition enables a "spike detection" circuit which counts eight ticks of the 16× clock (one half a bit time) and checks the line to see if it is still in the "0" state. If it is, a valid START bit has presumably arrived; if the line has

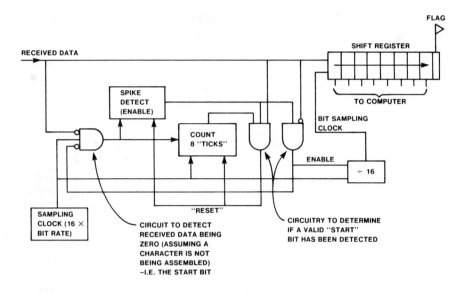

Figure 1-3. Asynchronous Serial Data Receiver

returned to the "1" state, it is assumed that the initial 1-to-0 transition was due to noise on the line and no further action is taken. If the "spike detector" circuit determines that a valid START signal has arrived, it enables a counter which divides the 16× clock by 16 to produce a sampling clock which ticks once per bit time. This "tick" occurs roughly at the center of the bit being sampled; the circuitry just described does not detect the initial 1-to-0 transition exactly when it occurs. This error can be made smaller by sampling at 32 times the bit rate, and even further minimized by sampling at 64 times the bit rate. When higher sampling rates are used, the counter in the spike detect circuit and the counter in the bit sampler circuit must both be made larger. In addition, for high speeds like 9600 bits per second,* the sampling rate may exceed the capabilities of the circuitry if certain types of MOS (metal-oxide semiconductor) materials are used.

The bit sampler circuit strobes the state of the line eight times (in the case of eight bit characters) and then generates a signal to the computer or controller with which it is associated. This signal is called a "flag," and announces that a character has been received. The computer can then parallel

*The serial transfer of data within a terminal or computer interface is described in terms of bits per second. The signaling rate of transmission facilities is described in baud (see Glossary). Bits per second and baud are equivalent if each signaling element on the transmission facility conveys one bit of information. Since this is most often the case, many advertisements and some data communications literature use the two terms interchangeably. In this book, an effort has been made to use the two terms correctly except where the application is unclear; in the latter case, baud has been used.

transfer the character from the register into which it was shifted by the receiver.

In the example cited above, a single register has the received data shifted into it from the line and that register is also used to store the character until the computer is ready to read it. The problem with this "single buffered" interface is that the computer has only the length of time during the STOP bit to read the character before another arrives. A simple but powerful alteration to the circuit provides a second register into which the received character can be parallel transferred as soon as the eighth bit has been sampled (see Figure 1-4). The flag is generated when the parallel transfer occurs and the buffer used for assembling the characters by shifting bits in off the line becomes immediately available for the next character. The computer thus has the entire time of the assembly of the second character to read the first one. This provision of a "holding buffer" characterizes a "double buffered" receiver. The only possible congestion occurs when a character has been assembled and transferred to the holding buffer, and a second character also gets completely assembled.

In either the single buffered or double buffered case, the arrival of a character which cannot be handled because the previous character has not been read is called a "Data Overrun." In the case of an overrun, most asynchronous receiver circuits use the newly arriving character to overwrite the character stored in the holding register and provide an error signal on a separate lead to indicate that a character has been lost.

Because the STOP bit arrival time is no longer the sole time available to the computer for reading the character in double buffered interfaces, there is time for circuitry to check the "ninth bit," i.e., the STOP bit, to confirm that it is a 1. If it is not a 1, one of the following conditions exists; communications line continuity is broken, receiver timing is confused, or the transmitting station is sending a special signal of some sort. The existence of one of these conditions typically provides an error lead in the asynchronous receiver in addition to the "Overrun" lead just described. This error generally results when the receiver has lost track of which zeros in the transmission are

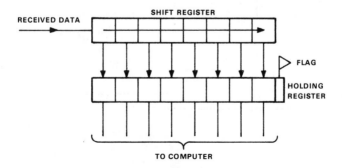

Figure 1-4. Double Buffered Asynchronous Receiver

the START bits and which are just zeros in the data. If, for some reason, the receiver treats a data bit as a START bit, it will assemble the next eight bits as a character. Since these eight bits are really parts of two characters (the end of one and the beginning of another) the ninth bit to arrive will not be the STOP bit but rather a data bit from the second character. If it is a zero, the error checking circuit will detect an error. "Framing" is the process of deciding which groups of eight bits constitute characters; since this error is due to a failure in that process, it is known as a "Framing Error."

Failures in the framing process can generally be avoided. The idle line condition is a MARK (ones) condition, for both current loop transmission and transmission involving modems, and any amount of idle time more than a character time in length will correct this condition. Also, for random received characters, the receiver will eventually become re-aligned and use the correct zeros as START elements. You can check this by writing down a few dozen characters and prefixing the START bits and suffixing the STOP bits. Then choose a zero in the first character as a START bit, count out eight bits, call the next bit STOP (even if it is a zero), look for the next zero, and call that the START of the next character. Since some ones will intervene before you find that zero, you will have moved the starting point of the framing process. Eventually you will repeat these steps and choose an actual START bit. From there on, you are back in proper framing. Loss of framing is not a common problem but gibberish can occur and it is important that modems are arranged for "MARK HOLD," i.e., the presentation of MARK on the received data lead when the line has not yet been established.

Asynchronous transmitters are also implemented with shift registers. A simplified circuit is shown in Figure 1-5. The computer parallel loads a character for transmission into the shift register. The circuitry can easily be ar-

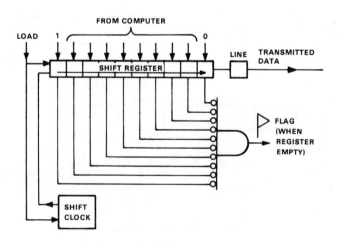

Figure 1-5 Asynchronous Serial Data Transmitter

ranged so that the parallel load automatically loads a zero at one end of the character to serve as a START bit and a one at the other end to serve as a STOP bit. The parallel loading of the character starts the shifting circuitry which successively shifts out the START bit, the eight data bits, and then the STOP bit to a flip-flop called "Line," while shifting zeros into the shift register. The Line flip-flop is connected to the communications line. When all of the shift register bits are zeros, the STOP bit is being applied to the communciations line by the Line flip-flop, the shifting process is stopped, and a zero-detector circuit signals the computer that another character may be parallel loaded. If the computer has another character available, it parallel loads that character into the shift register, a timer assures that the Line flip-flop has been asserting the STOP bit for at least a bit time, and the shifting process begins again. If the computer does not have a character available, the Line flip-flop merely applies the STOP bit (MARK or "1") to the line for a while until the computer does have another character available. As in the receiver case, the computer has one bit time, the STOP bit time, to respond to the flag. In contrast, however, the unavailability of the computer in time does not have fatal consequences; only efficient use of the line is lost, not any data.

Because it is desirable to keep the communications line running at full speed, and because the computer may have crests and valleys of activity, double buffering may also be used in transmitters. The simplified circuit is shown in Figure 1-6. Here, the computer loads a transmitter holding buffer whenever the flag signal indicates that the buffer is available. The transmitter circuitry automatically loads the shift register from the holding register whenever the shift register is available and there is a character in the

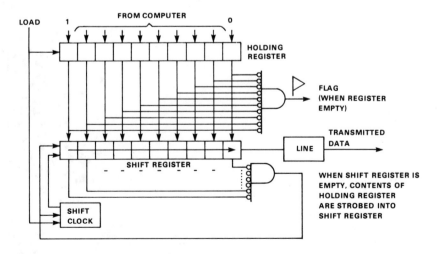

Figure 1-6. Double Buffered Asynchronous Transmitter

holding buffer. In this way, the computer has an entire character time (during the shifting out of a character) to refresh the transmitter holding buffer without the line going idle unnecessarily.

One interesting consequence of double buffered transmitters is that while they smooth the load on the computer, they can pose a problem when the communications line has control signals associated with it. If a line is equipped with modems whose transmitter units are turned off and on by means of a "Request-to-Send" lead, the program that controls that lead must not turn it off immediately upon loading the holding register of the transmitter, as the character loaded into the holding buffer has not yet been transmitted. In fact, the program controlling the Request to Send lead must not turn it off until *two character times* have elapsed—one for the character being shifted out when the holding register was loaded, and one for the character just loaded into the holding register.

In Chapter 2, a simple version of a single line asynchronous interface will be discussed in detail, including programming information.

2

A Single Line
Asynchronous Interface

It is possible to buy a single LSI chip which does all of the double buffered reception and transmission tasks described in Chapter 1. This device, the Universal Asynchronous Receiver/Transmitter (UART), has eight leads that are used to deliver the received characters to the computer and eight leads upon which the computer can place characters for transmission onto the communications line. There are, in addition, leads which indicate that a received character is available for reading by the computer and that the transmitter is available for the computer to load with a character for transmission. Additional leads provide Overrun and Framing Error indications (see Chapter 1) and Parity Error indication (see Chapter 13) and permit the selection of various character lengths (5, 6, 7, or 8 bits per character), various types of parity (odd, even, none), and various STOP bit arrangements (1 bit time, 1.5 bit times, or 2 bit times). Appendix D contains a more detailed description of the UART, including a listing of the pin assignments. The main function of this chapter will be to describe how a UART is typically interfaced to a computer.

Figure 2-1 shows a block diagram of a single line asynchronous interface using a UART. The "bus" is the computer input/output bus, including the address selection lines which permit the computer to select individual registers within peripheral devices for the purpose of reading or writing those registers. When a register is to be read, the address selection logic gates the contents of the receiver buffer, the receiver status register, or the transmitter status register onto the leads labeled "parallel data" at the top of the figure. This enables the "bus drivers" to place the data that has been read onto the computer I/O bus data lines. When a register is to be written, data on the computer I/O bus data lines is received by the "bus receivers" and presented to the receiver status register, the transmitter status register, and the trans-

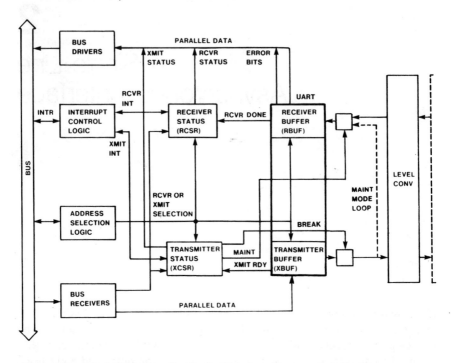

Figure 2-1. Block Diagram of a Single Line Asynchronous Interface

mitter buffer register via the "parallel data" leads at the bottom of the figure. The address selection logic strobes the data from the parallel data leads into the selected register.

The bit assignments for these registers are shown in Figure 2-2 and the discussion following that figure will clarify the function of the leads labeled "Break" and "Maintenance Mode."

The one remaining block to be explained is labeled "level converters." Data communication is seldom done at the same voltage and current levels as those used within a computer, since the computer's transistor-transistor-logic (TTL) levels are too sensitive to noise, ground potential differences, damage from short circuits to lines carrying higher voltages, etc. to be practical for transmissions over distances greater than a few feet. Thus, single line asynchronous interfaces typically contain level converter circuits which convert the TTL logic levels to 20 milliampere current loops or EIA RS-232-C voltage levels. The 20 milliampere signaling system is explained in Chapter 3 and the EIA voltage interface is explained in Chapter 5.

The receiver status register need only consist of two bits: a received character available bit (Receiver Done) and a bit which will enable the setting of the Done bit to generate an interrupt. (There are some occasions when the computer program will not want to be interrupted by arriving characters; in

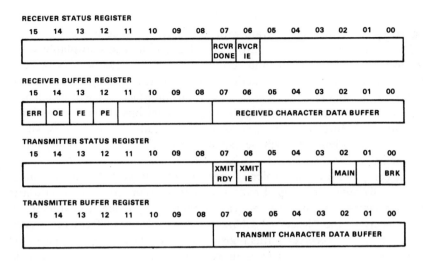

Figure 2-2. Sample Bit Assignments for a Single Line Asynchronous Interface

these cases the interrupt enable bit (RCVR IE) is cleared by the program to insure that no interrupts occur.)

The receiver buffer register has eight bits (07–00) for presenting the received characters for the computer to read, and three bits to report the Overrun Error (OE) and Framing Error (FE) described in Chapter 1 and the Parity Error (PE) described in Chapter 13. For the convenience of the program, these error bits can be logically combined to produce a single ERRor bit that will be set whenever one or more of the three error bits are set. In this way, the computer program can check for errors by testing a single bit, which in most cases will be clear. In the unlikely case where it is set, the program can then test all three error bits to determine the type of error.

Like the receiver status register, the transmitter status register really needs only two bits—one to say that the transmitter is available for loading (XMIT RDY), and one to enable and disable the ability of the Ready bit to generate interrupts to the computer. The Transmitter Interrupt Enable bit is abbreviated XMIT IE. The two other bits shown are MAIN and BRK. The MAINtenance bit loops the transmitter's output, which is a serial communications line, to the receiver's input, also a serial communications line. This permits the transmitter to send to the receiver, a feature handy in trouble situations when it is desirable to determine whether the various elements of the data communications system are functioning correctly. The BRK bit, when set, brings the transmitted data line to the SPACE ("0") state for as long as the bit is set. This permits the sending of a special signal, called "Break." The Break signal is used by some terminals as a special control character.

The transmitter buffer register provides eight bits (07–00) which can be loaded by the computer program with the character to be transmitted.

The bit assignments shown are those of a commercially available single line asynchronous interface, and certain bit positions have been assigned to make optimum use of the instruction set of a particular computer. The manufacturer makes a number of variations of this interface, some of which have extra features which make use of the large number bits shown as unassigned in Figure 2-2. In future chapters some of these additional features will be discussed and Figure 2-2 will be expanded to include the additional bit assignments.

The computer program typically operates with bit 06 of the receiver status register (Receiver Interrupt Enable) set, and with bit 06 of the transmitter status register (Transmitter Interrupt Enable) set. When a character has been received, the "Received Character Available" lead from the UART sets bit 07 of the receiver status register (Receiver Done) and this generates an interrupt. The computer program responds to the interrupt and reads the receiver buffer register. A lead called "Reset Data Available" then assures the UART that it is safe to replace the data in the UART's received data buffer with new data. Should the UART need to use its data buffer for new received data without having first received a "Reset Data Available" signal, it would know that an overrun condition was occurring and would assert that error lead (see Chapter 1). After reading the character from the receiver data buffer, the computer program checks for errors and then stores the character in memory.

Similarly, when a line's transmitter is available for transmitting a character, bit 07 (XMIT RDY) of the transmitter status register sets. The setting of XMIT RDY causes an interrupt to the computer program, which checks to see if it has anything to send on this line. If so, it loads that character into the transmitter data buffer and this automatically clears the XMIT RDY bit.

Additional control and status bits for single line asynchronous interfaces are, in general, dependent on the type of transmission facility used. The simplest facility is the 20 milliampere current loop discussed in detail in Chapter 3. Readers not of a technical inclination are encouraged only to skim Chapter 3. For distances beyond the capabilities of the 20 milliampere loop, MOdulator-DEModulators (modems)* are required. These are reviewed in Chapter 4. For single line asynchronous interfaces with more features, refer to Chapter 6. For multiple line asynchronous interfaces, refer to Chapter 7.

---

*Bell System literature refers to modems as "data sets," a term used in this book only in conjunction with signal names such as "Data Set Ready."

3
The Twenty Milliampere Loop

Twenty milliampere currents have historically been used for the transmission of binary serial asynchronous data; their use is widespread, largely due to their suitability for a wide range of applications. There are several parameters of such systems that can be varied to meet operational requirements.

The use of twenty milliampere currents for data communications began with mechanical teleprinters, such as the Teletype Corporation Models 28, 33, and 35 Teletypes ®, the operation of which is reviewed here for historical background. In a mechanical teleprinter, the line current is switched off and on to transmit information from the keyboard to the line. This switching is done by carbon brushes rotating over a copper etch commutator. This arrangement has two consequences. One is that there is substantial electrical noise introduced on the line from contact imperfections between the brushes and the commutator; the other is that a certain minimum current, generally about 18 millamperes, must be maintained to keep the contacting surfaces reasonably clean.

Any interface designed to work with a mechanical teleprinter must include circuitry to suppress the noise generated by the carbon-copper contact system in the teleprinter. In addition, the contact bounce that occurs when some teleprinters are switched from local mode to line mode must be filtered. Unfortunately, a circuit designed to filter noise from a 110 bits per second signal such as that generated by a mechanical teleprinter is also very effective in eliminating a 1200 bits per second information signal. Therefore, two different kinds of circuits are required to handle the low speed teleprinter and the higher speed data transmission schemes. The difference between the two

® Registered trademark of Teletype Corporation.

circuits may, however, be quite small; generally, a filter capacitor that can be optionally in or out of the circuit will suffice.

As stated above, a minimum current of 18 milliamperes must be maintained through the commutator contacts of a mechanical teleprinter. The interface that deals with the teleprinter usually generates the line current by means of a voltage source and a resistor; the available voltages and resistor dissipation usually limit the desirable upper current to about 25 milliamperes.

If the interface mentioned above is located in a computer, the voltages available to create the line current are usually +5 and −15, but others can be, and are, used. Since there is about one volt dropped at various points in the keyboard loop, let us assume that of the 20 volt difference between +5 and −15, only 19 volts are available to generate the line current. If the interface contains a 750 ohm resistor, or a combination of resistors giving this effective value, the line current will be slightly over 25 milliamperes, assuming that the wire from the interface to the teleprinter and back has no resistance. Note that a simple application of Ohm's Law (current equals the voltage divided by the resistance) indicates that an additional 300 ohms of wire resistance may be added to the circuit before the lower limit of 18 milliamperes is reached. Three hundred ohms is equivalent to 7300 feet (2220 meters) of 26AWG copper wire. Since this is a loop resistance, the teleprinter could be located 3650 feet away, assuming that distortion and crosstalk limits could also be met.

If the interface has 80 volts available, and uses a 3300 ohm resistor, slightly less than 25 milliamperes will be present when the wire resistance is zero, and an additional 1100 ohms of wire resistance can be added to the circuit before the 18 milliampere point is reached. In short, if the voltages being used are raised by a factor of four, about four times as much wire can be used. This is because the presence of a high voltage and a high resistance in the interface makes the resistance of the wire a less significant contributor to the total resistance of the circuit. In practice, the wire resistance can be even greater because high voltage systems usually are capable of lowering the resistance within the interface (the 3300 ohms in this case) when long lines are being used, thus preserving the loop current at a desirable value.

The high voltage approach is used by common carriers and others desiring to cover substantial distances. The hardware to support such a scheme is called "telegraph hardware." Telegraph hardware, and the communications facilities used with it, are usually limited to rates below 150 baud*; it is cus-

---

*The serial transfer of data within a terminal or computer interface is described in terms of bits per second. The signaling rate of transmission facilities is described in baud (see Glossary). Bits per second and baud are equivalent if each signaling element on the transmission facility conveys one bit of information. Since this is most often the case, many advertisements and some data communications literature use the two terms interchangeably.

tomarily used with teleprinters for which such speed restrictions are not a problem, and higher rates would increase the amount of crosstalk caused to adjacent circuits.

When telegraph hardware is used, a number of variables affect the system configuration. In some countries, the common carriers provide the loop current and the telegraph hardware at the computer site merely switches or detects it. In other countries, the computer site provides the loop current and must have the capability of adjusting it and must also have fuses. In either case, there are two variations: "polar working" and "neutral working." In polar working, a MARK is current flow in one direction while a SPACE is current flow in the other direction. In neutral working, a MARK is the presence of current and a SPACE is the absence of current. The currents used in telegraph hardware systems are typically 20 milliamperes or 60 milliamperes.

Most computer-to-teleprinter interfaces intended for use with teleprinters that will be located no more than 1800 feet (or, more conservatively, 1500 feet) away from the computer use the low voltage approach because the necessary hardware is much cheaper and easier to maintain. No special power supplies or high voltage components are necessary if only the power available in the computer system is used.

In low voltage interfaces for teleprinters, it is important to consider "active" interfaces and "passive" interfaces. Any current mode transmission scheme requires three components: a current source, a current switch, and a current detector. A typical teleprinter/computer interface system consists of two such arrangements—one called the "keyboard loop" and one called the "printer loop" (see Figure 3-1). In each loop, the current switch *has* to be

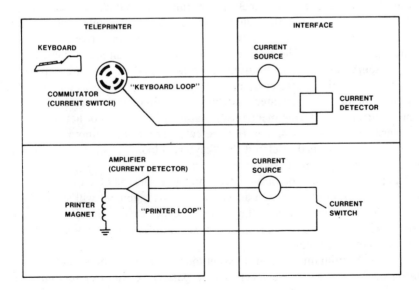

Figure 3-1. 20 Milliampere Keyboard and Printer Loops

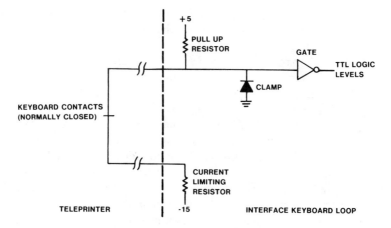

Figure 3-2. Teleprinter Interface—Keyboard Loop

located in the transmitter, and the current detector *has* to be located in the receiver. However, the current source can be located in the transmitter, in the receiver, or in the line connecting the two. If the current source is located in the transmitter, the transmitter is called an "active" transmitter and is used in conjunction with a "passive" receiver, where "passive" refers to something which does not contain a current source. Alternatively, if the transmitter has no current source it is "passive," and is used with a receiver which contains a current source and is therefore "active."

An interesting case is the typical teleprinter. It has a passive transmitter (a commutator) and a passive receiver (an amplifier that drives magnets but does not put current on the communications line). The teleprinter is connected to the computer by an interface that has both an active receiver and an active transmitter. The receiver section of such an interface consists of a voltage source and current limiting resistors. Together these are capable of creating a 20 milliampere current which will be switched off and on by the commutator in the teleprinter's keyboard circuitry. The receiver also contains a current monitoring mechanism that detects whether or not the 20 milliampere current is flowing and thus detects whether the remote device (the teleprinter) has opened or closed the "keyboard loop." A simplified diagram of the "keyboard loop" is shown in Figure 3-2.

The transmitter section of an active interface consists of a voltage source, a current limiting resistor, and a switch. This arrangement will send 20 milliamperes of current through the printer magnet driver circuit of the teleprinter whenever the switch is operated. A simplified version of the "printer loop" is shown in Figure 3-3.

For any 20 milliampere transmission loop, there must be an active transmitter sending to a passive receiver or a passive transmitter sending to an

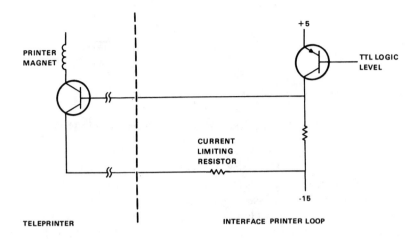

Figure 3-3.   Teleprinter Interface—Printer Loop

active receiver. In general, there cannot be an active transmitter sending to an active receiver because the voltage sources will fight each other. There cannot be a passive transmitter sending to a passive receiver, as there will be no source of current to switch or to detect.

Twenty milliampere current loop transmission offers the benefits of economy and simplicity, but it has some disadvantages. In addition to the previously mentioned circuit design problems concerning noise filtering and active/passive, system design is hindered by a lack of standardization. A 20 milliampere current loop can be made with a 20 volt voltage source and a 1000 ohm resistor. It can also be made with a 20,000 volt voltage source and a 1,000,000 ohm resistor. No one would want to simply plug these two "20 mil" circuits together. Another disadvantage is that 20 milliampere current transmitters and receivers cannot drive long lengths of wire without introducing crosstalk into other wires.

The invention of the "optical coupler" has been a boon to users of 20 milliampere loops. It consists of a light emitting diode (LED) and a phototransistor encased together in an enclosure into which no outside light can enter. When current flows through the light emitting diode, it emits light which is sensed by the phototransistor, causing the phototransistor to conduct. Thus LED current flow causes transistor current flow, but the only connection between the two current loops is a beam of light in a light-tight box. Therefore, it does not matter what voltages are used to derive the currents in the current loops, nor does it matter that those voltages are referenced to different grounding points (a topic discussed more fully in Chapter 5 on EIA interfaces).

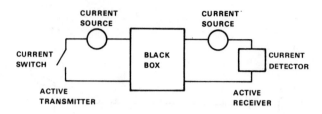

Figure 3-4.   Connection of Active Transmitter and Active Receiver by Optical Coupler

The circuit shown as a black box in Figure 3-4 permits a current loop containing an active transmitter to communicate with a current loop containing an active receiver by being essentially a passive receiver coupled to a passive transmitter. Figure 3-5 is a close-up look at the interior of the black box. Diode D4 limits the voltage across R1 and the diode part of Q2 to 2.4 volts. It also insures that, if the black box is connected in backwards, the current flow (which would be in the wrong direction) will go through D4 and not through the diode part of Q2. With such a backward hook-up, the current flow could blow out the diode part of Q2 if it were not so protected.

If the box has been installed correctly, the voltage between pins 1 and 2 of Q2 is about 1.4 volts (a typical voltage drop across this type of diode) and the voltage across R1 is therefore 2.4−1.4 or 1.0 volts. This will produce a current of 33 mils. Thus zener diode D4 insures that the current through the diode section of Q2 is never more than 33 milliamperes and thus protects it from excessive current. As stated above, the actual current will probably not exceed about 25 milliamperes due to the construction of the typical active transmitter circuits. The flow of current through R1 and from pin 1 to pin 2 of Q2 will cause the light emitting diode to light and induce base current in the transistor section of Q2. This in turn will cause the transistor to conduct and current will flow from pin 5 to pin 4 (positive current flow convention). That current flowing through R3 will cause a voltage drop across R3 sufficient to exceed the turn-on voltage of Q1 and current will flow through Q1.

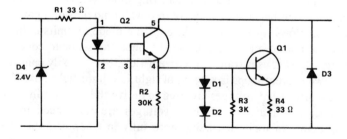

Figure 3-5.   Typical Optical Coupler Circuit

Note that most of the current flow will be through Q1, not through Q2. This is typical of optical coupler circuits, as the transistor sections of optical couplers are not rated as high as 20 milliamperes. Thus they can only be used to turn on an auxiliary transistor circuit that handles the actual loop current. Diode D3 on the right-hand side of the circuit protects transistor Q1 and the transistor part of Q2 from backward current should this side of the black box be incorrectly connected.

It should be noted that an optical coupler circuit is not a cure-all; the voltage difference between the two current loops should not exceed about 1000 volts or breakdown will occur in the coupler. Also, the interfacing of such a circuit with telegraph hardware must be done with great caution, as the voltages used may exceed the ratings of Q1. In that case, some additional components will be required to protect the transistor part of Q2.

The other 20 milliampere problem, how to drive substantial distances with low crosstalk generation on the transmitter and good crosstalk rejection on the receiver, can be attacked with the following circuits. Figure 3-6 shows a transmitter circuit which uses a single driver transistor Q101 to establish a current flow of 4 milliamperes from +5 through R103, R104, and R105. This current flow causes a 4 volt drop across resistors R103 and R105 which in turn causes points A and B to reach +1 and −11 volts respectively. The impressed voltage across these two resistors causes Q102 and Q103 to turn on, permitting current to flow through R106 and R107. Because the base-emitter drop of the transistors is about 0.7 volts, and because 4 volts were applied across the combination of R106 and Q102, 4−0.7 or 3.3 volts exist across R106, which is a 150 ohm resistor. Thus a current of 22 milliamperes is all that can flow. What is important about this circuit is that the Q101 switch turns on two current sources, Q102 and Q103, which are equal and

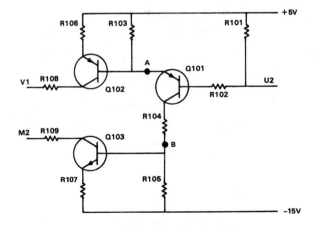

Figure 3-6. Active 20 Milliampere Transmitter Circuit

opposite, producing a "pseudo-differential" operation in which the current flow rises in each wire independently, but never exceeds 22 milliamperes. Even if the wire pair is highly capacitive, which normally causes current flow to begin at a very high value and then to reach an equilibrium value, this circuit merely charges such a capacitance at a controlled rate and high transients of current are absent. This is important in reducing crosstalk to adjacent circuits.

A companion receiver circuit has been designed and it is shown in Figure 3-7. Here, a current of 2.6 ma flows continuously from +5 through R114, R115, and R116. This causes voltage drops of 2.6 volts across R114 and across R116. These are sufficient to turn on Q104 and Q105 and to produce 1.9 volt drops across R117 and R118, which are 68 ohm resistors. This produces a current of 28 mils from +5 through R117, Q104, the line, Q105, and R118 (assuming that the line includes teleprinter keyboard contacts that are closed or an optical coupler that is conducting). Whenever that current exceeds 10 milliamperes, the voltages across R117 and R118 become large enough to cause their associated transistors, Q106 and Q107, to turn on, thus conditioning the inputs of the 11380 latch circuits to assert a TTL low signal at the output pin. An important feature of the latch circuits is that the state of the output pin will not change until both Q106 and Q107 have changed state.

The function of resistors R110, R111, R112, and R113 is to match the line impedance and to function with the capacitor C102 to filter the commutator noise in mechanical teleprinters, which was described in the early paragraphs of this chapter. With the exception of the optional filter capacitor, C102, there are no speed limiting components in either the circuit of Figure

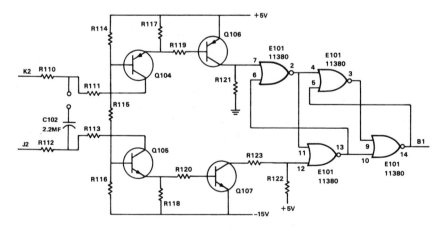

Figure 3-7. Active 20 Milliampere Receiver Circuit

3-6 or that of Figure 3-7, and these circuits have been tested over considerable distances at substantial speeds. The results of these tests are summarized in Appendix A: "How Far—How Fast." The tests were conducted on cable which was strung out around a building, rather than cable left on a reel. This is an important consideration, as noise from fluorescent lighting and the operation of heavy machinery can influence the results. In tests of voltage interfaces such as EIA RS-232-C differences in ground potential become important; this will be discussed in Chapter 5.

Since both of the circuits shown are "active," it was necessary to employ optical coupler circuits in the tests. The criteria of acceptability was that there be no more than 10 percent mark-space distortion (refer to Appendix A). Degradation of the performance of this circuit occurs as the capacitance of the cable increases, since the current limiting feature requires that a longer time be spent charging a high capacitance cable than a low capacitance (short) cable. In the tests, the results were worse for shielded (high capacitance) cable than for unshielded (low capacitance) cable. If the cable is to be run through a noisy environment, however, the use of the shielded cable might well be warranted, despite the loss of speed.

It should also be noted that the tests conducted on the unshielded wire did not employ additional signals on adjacent wires in the cable. Thus no crosstalk effects were measured, other than the "near-end crosstalk" caused by the transmitter of the unit under test affecting the receiver under test. This latter effect was noted when transmitters similar to those shown in Figure 3-3 were used, because such transmitters do not have the current limiting features of the Figure 3-6 circuit. The amount of crosstalk is directly proportional to the strength of the interfering signal, directly proportional to the length of wire exposed to that signal, and inversely proportional to the square of the distance between the interference source and the wire. Thus, crosstalk to and from adjacent wire in a cable has more of an effect than interference from lighting or machinery because the wires run close together for a long distance. A wire passing near a noisy machine, for example, is near it only briefly and is relatively far away from it, compared to its spacing from other wires in the same cable. For this reason, it is recommended that 20 milliampere circuits be kept out of cables containing stronger signals.

For transmission over distances in excess of 1500 feet, it is usually more satisfactory to use modems. Additional costs and lower speeds are often a consequence, however, as will be discussed in Chapter 4.

4

Asynchronous Modems For Private Lines

As any electrical signal travels along a communications cable, it becomes progressively weaker due to the resistance, capacitance, and inductance of the cable. Eventually, the signal becomes so weak that the information which it contains cannot be recovered. This is because the signal level is too low to compete with the noises that have been picked up by the cable and the noises in the apparatus being used to measure the signal. In order to transmit information over substantial distances, it is thus necessary to periodically strengthen the signals on the cable by some repeating process.

Early telegraph systems operated with circuits similar to that shown in Figure 4-1. When it was necessary to send information further than the wire resistance would permit, the arrangement shown in Figure 4-2 was used. The message was sent first from point A to point B, and then repeated by the operator at point B on to point C. Eventually a clever operator at point B added a contact to the telegraph sounder and used it to control the circuit on to point C, thus eliminating the need to repeat the messages. This circuit is shown in Figure 4-3.

Because voice communication involves frequencies which are too high for relays to respond to, this same technique cannot be used successfully for telephones. Some efforts, however, were made to build telephone repeaters which used an earpiece mechanically coupled to a mouthpiece to capitalize on the gain provided by carbon microphones.

Early telephone circuits accomplished long distance transmission by using exceptionally large gauge wire. When one considers the cost of such a line, it is not surprising that telephone calls over this line were very expensive. The advent of the vacuum tube and later the transistor permitted the design of amplifiers which could rejuvenate voice frequency signals and make truly

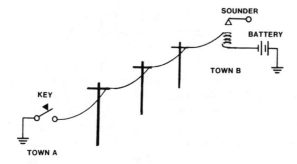

Figure 4-1. Simple Telegraph Circuit

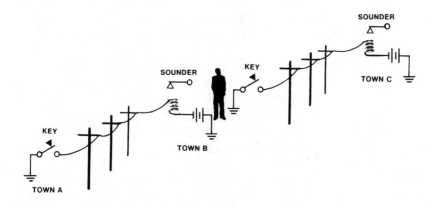

Figure 4-2. Simple Telegraph Circuit with Operator Relay

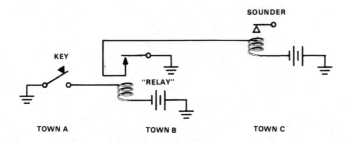

Figure 4-3. Simple Telegraph Circuit with Automatic Relay

world-wide long distance telephoning possible. For various technical reasons, including the presence of most of the important frequencies for voice communications in the 300–3000 Hertz frequency range, the repeating amplifiers have useful frequency response only in this range.

Eventually, it became desirable to extend data communications capability over distances that could not be accommodated by 20 milliampere loops or similar schemes. (Although high voltage, high current loops can be used over substantial distances, as noted in Chapter 3, these are generally limited to rates of less than 150 baud.) The possibility of using the facilities that had been set up for handling voice communications was naturally an attractive one, particularly because of the pervasiveness of the service.

While a great deal of the data communications traffic in the world takes place over the switched telephone network, this chapter will concern itself only with the use of voice frequency channels that are fixed in place between two end points—i.e., private lines.

The phrase "private line" at one time meant a single party telephone line as opposed to a "party line," but now it refers to a circuit permanently in place between two end points. While the circuit may be accomplished by wires, it can also be accomplished by microwave, light beams, satellite links, etc.

The simplest case of a private line is one which a person or company owns and installs without the assistance of a common carrier such as the telephone company. Generally speaking, such lines can easily be installed within the same building or on the same continuous property, where "continuous" usually includes property pieces directly across from each other on opposite sides of a public right of way. With appropriate licensing arrangements, it can also include microwave towers or satellite earth stations.

The more common case is that where a person or company rents a line from the local common carrier. This is usually the telephone company, but may be one of the specialized common carriers; in many countries, it is the government post and telegraph authority.

When customer owned wire is used, the electrical characteristics of the wire, the electrical interference presented to the wire by outside sources, and the possibility of the wire creating interference are the limiting factors on the speed and distance of transmission. For licensed, customer-owned facilities (microwave, etc.) maximum signal rates and signal powers are determined by the equipment and the licensing restrictions. For channels provided by common carriers, the common carrier tariffs specify the operating restrictions as well as the rental rates for various services.

While digital transmission (see Chapter 24) offers transmission speeds up to 1.544 million bits per second and while the analog offerings of the telephone companies can be subdivided into chunks larger than those required for voice grade transmission, the most common size channel used for data communication is the "voice grade" channel. This facility has a frequency response of roughly 300–3000 Hertz. The equipment used to construct voice grade private lines is somewhat different from that used to construct dialed network calls. As mentioned earlier in this chapter, amplifiers are used to repeat or regenerate the audio signals on a telephone transmission medium.

While some of these amplifiers have been designed to operate on a "two-wire" basis, most of them operate on a "four-wire" basis. The remainder of this book will assume that all transmission facilities containing amplifiers are four-wire transmission facilities. A simple connection between two telephones is shown in Figure 4-4. Note that only two wires are required for the connection and that the signals from party A to party B and those from party B to party A are therefore present on the line simultaneously. If a substantial distance separates the two parties, it may be necessary to add amplification (repeaters). Since amplifiers are essentially uni-directional devices (i.e., have an INPUT side and an OUTPUT side), it is necessary for the transmission facility to be divided in half. The east-west transmission facility contains an amplifier for party A to transmit more loudly to party B, and the west-east transmission facility contains an amplifier for party B to transmit more loudly to party A. Such an arrangement is shown in Figure 4-5. Note that in this case the telephone instruments do not contain circuitry to permit signals from the transmitter and the earpiece to be simultaneously present on a single wire pair. Rather, the transmitter of each telephone runs through the amplifier to the earpiece of the other telephone.

In the nationwide telephone network, amplifiers are also used, but the telephone switching systems used at the ends of the connection are precisely those used for local calls. Since local calls have traditionally been switched on a two-wire basis, without amplifiers, the local switching equipment and the "local loops" (the wires to people's homes and businesses) are designed for only two-wire operation. Thus, a conversion must be made between the two-wire circuits used locally and the four-wire circuits used for long distance transmission. This is accomplished by a hybrid coil, which is shown as a simple rectangle in Figure 4-6. The "rules" of the hybrid coil are that signals

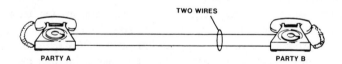

Figure 4-4. A Simple Connection Between Two Telephones

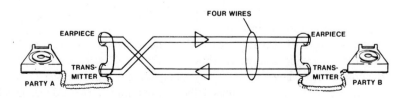

Figure 4-5. A Four-Wire Connection Between Two Telephones

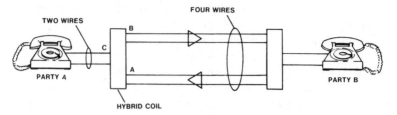

NOTE: FOR SIMPLICITY, POWER SUPPLIES HAVE BEEN LEFT OUT OF THESE FIGURES

Figure 4-6. A Connection Between Two Two-Wire Telephones over a Four-Wire Transmission Facility

entering at A go to C, but not to B, while signals entering at C go to B, but not to A. In some ways, the hybrid coil may be likened to a divider strip down the center of a highway at the point where a divided highway becomes an undivided highway. Figure 4-7a shows how hybrid coils fit into a typical telephone call. Note that most, but not all, of the switching equipment interspersed between the "local offices" is capable of switching all four wires simultaneously.

Figure 4-7b shows a two-wire private line as it is usually implemented over a substantial distance, and Figure 4-7c shows a four-wire private line. Note that the only difference between the two-wire (4-7b) and four-wire (4-7c) private lines is that the local loop in the latter case consists of two pairs rather than one. For this reason, the cost of a four-wire private line is usually only slightly more than that of a two-wire private line for the distance between local "rating points" (usually the local switching centers), plus the cost of an additional local loop pair at each end. Thus, for a small additional investment, the customer gets two complete circuits of voice grade quality—one from east to west and one from west to east. Essentially the only reasons one would ever want a two-wire private line for data transmission are that over shorter distances (sometimes within the same state) four-wire is exactly twice the price of two-wire, or that the application permanently calls for transmission in only one direction. Even half-duplex transmission can benefit from four-wire facilities because of the lack of turn-around delay. Usually, however, people with four-wire facilities make the most of them by using full-duplex.

In summary, private lines offer the benefit of obtaining four-wire service for only a modest increase in cost over two-wire service.

A second feature of private lines is that the same transmission facilities are used for the connection at all times. In Figure 4-7a it should be noted that the connections shown between switching centers could consist of different transmission facilities on various calls. The common carriers do their best to keep the electrical characteristics of the transmission facilities consistent. It is possible, however, for calls from one point to another to go through en-

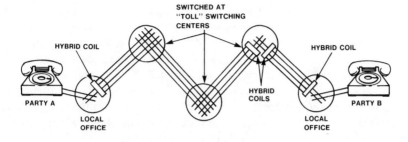

Figure 4-7a. Typical Telephone Call

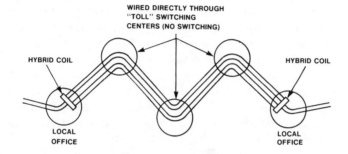

Figure 4-7b. Typical Two-Wire Circuit Implementation

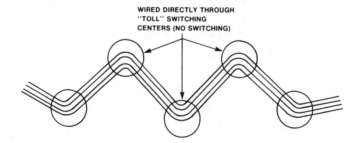

Figure 4-7c. Typical Four-Wire Circuit Implementation

tirely different cities at different times of day, so understandably there is considerable variation. The "Switched Network Connection Survey 1969–70" (Bell System Technical Reference PUB 41007) is a tabulation of the results from a survey of these variations. On private lines the facilities are fixed, with the exception of microwave protection switching which uses different routes due to atmospheric problems. As a result, the electrical characteristics of the circuit are less variable with time. Additional circuitry can be added to correct for the various degradations that do exist. This process is called "conditioning." When done by the common carriers, there is usually a one time charge and a monthly charge. AT&T prepares its data circuits with six different degrees of conditioning, each successive grade costing more and holding the line to tighter specifications. Appendix F gives the specifications for the various types of conditioning. While the influence of conditioning on overall line cost rapidly becomes a minor part of line cost as the length of the line increases, even that cost can be reduced by purchasing modern modems that will operate on lines with little or no conditioning.

The third and most important feature of private lines is that they can offer cost savings if there is sufficient traffic between the two points involved. The cost justification for a private line is a rather complex process and depends on the application. First of all, private lines are in general unsuitable for applications where the end points of calls vary. These include situations where various users call a time-sharing service, or worse yet, call several time-sharing services. Private lines are usually unsuitable for applications where calls are infrequent, such as inventory control systems where each plant calls the central computer once a day for five minutes, or where the central computer calls each plant for a similar length of time. On the other hand, when data traffic is heavy or when the calls are so frequent that call set-up time would be annoying, private lines are ideal. Reservation systems, process control networks, and similar computer-to-computer communications networks are examples. The basic questions to be answered are:

1. Is the application suited to private lines?

2. How does the cost of separate telephone calls compare to the cost of a private line?

3. Does a private line offer a necessary feature such as a four-wire operation?

4. Can a back-up system be installed?

If a private line is desirable, it becomes necessary to consider the various modems that are available for private line use and the installer options available on them. Because synchronous transmission has not yet been discussed, reference to synchronous modems is deferred to Chapter 14.

The simplest modems available for private line use are the Bell System 108 series, successors to the Bell System 103F. These modems, when arranged for "originate" frequencies (108F, 108H), convert the data presented on the Transmit Data lead to tones of 1070 Hertz for a binary "0" (SPACE) and 1270 Hertz for a binary "1" (MARK). When the modem receives a tone of 2025 Hertz, it applies a SPACE signal to the Received Data lead, and when it receives a tone of 2225 Hertz, it applies a MARK signal to the Received Data lead. The 1070/1270 Hertz signals are being sent to, and the 2025/2225 Hertz signals are being received from, a similar 108 which is equipped for "answer" frequencies (108G, 108J). A 108 equipped for answer frequencies transmits a SPACE at 2025 Hertz and a MARK at 2225 Hertz. It interprets a received signal of 1070 Hertz as a SPACE and a received signal of 1270 Hertz as a MARK.

When configuring a private line with Bell System 108 modems, one of the questions to be asked is whether an RS-232-C interface (see Chapter 5) is desired or whether a 20 milliampere interface (see Chapter 3) is desired. If an RS-232-C interface is desired, a 108F (originate mode, RS-232-C) is used at one end of the line and a 108G (answer mode, RS-232-C) is used at the other end. If a 20 milliampere interface is desired, a 108H (originate mode, 20 milliampere) is used at one end of the line and a 108J (answer mode, 20 milliampere) is used at the other end.

While one of the benefits of private wire configurations is that four-wire service is available for a marginal increase in cost, it should be noted that the 108 modems can operate in full-duplex mode on two-wire facilities. They accomplish this essentially by dividing the two-wire transmission path into two channels on the basis of the frequencies used. One channel is the band of frequencies from 300–1700 Hertz, and the other from 1700–3000 Hertz. This separation is accomplished with filters as shown in Figure 4-8.

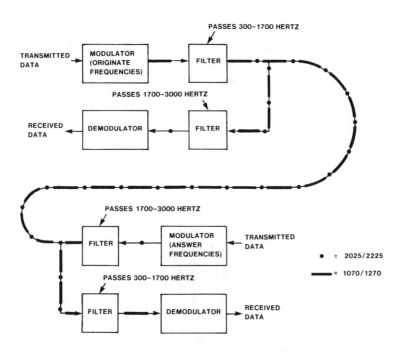

Figure 4-8. 300 Baud Full-Duplex Modem Frequency Assignment and Operation

The transmitter section of the modem that uses "originate" frequencies has a filter which allows the 300–1700 Hertz frequencies to reach the line. This filter is provided to prevent various extraneous frequencies generated by the modulation process from reaching the line. The receiver section of that same modem has a filter that allows only the 1700–3000 Hertz frequencies through. This filter prevents the receiver from "hearing" the transmitter in the same modem. The modem at the other end of the line has exactly the opposite set of filters. A filter on the transmitter allows 1700–3000 Hertz to be transmitted to the line and a filter in front of the receiver blocks these same frequencies from reaching the receiver. Note, however, that each receiver's filter does allow the frequencies from the other modem's transmitter to pass through.

The 108 modems have a relatively small number of control leads. There is a "Request to Send" lead which turns on the modem's transmitter section. The purpose of this lead varies with application. In multipoint systems, where a master station transmits to a number of slave stations, the master station would have its Request to Send lead asserted, while the slave stations, with the exception of the slave responding to the poll from the master station, would have their Request to Send leads negated.

An additional lead called "Received Line Signal Detect" or "Carrier Detect" has the following function in a 108-type modem: when asserted it indicates that the receiver section of the modem is receiving tones from the distant modem.

The 108-type modem uses the frequency spectrum available on a voice grade line to transmit data in both directions simultaneously as shown in Figure 4-9. It is also possible to use the frequency spectrum that is shown in Figure 4-10. Here a SPACE is represented by 2200 Hertz and a MARK by 1200 Hertz, and data is transmitted in only one direction at a time. If four-wire facilities are used, two frequency spectrums are available: one for data transmitted from west to east and one for data transmitted from east to west. In diagram form this would be represented as two copies of Figure 4-10.

Frequency shift keying between frequencies of 1200 and 2200 Hertz permits the transmission of data at rates of up to 1800 bits per second (bps) on

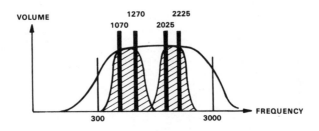

Figure 4-9. Frequency Utilization for 300 Baud Full-Duplex Modem

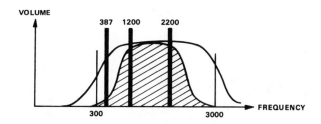

Figure 4-10. Frequency Utilization for 1200 Baud Half-Duplex Modem with Reverse Channel

conditioned private lines but only 1200 bps on dial-up connections. The Bell System 202 modems are typical examples. In dial applications, a frequency of 387 Hertz is also used as a reverse channel. This signal is keyed off and on at bit rates up to five bits per second. Further details and application information will be discussed in Chapter 9.

The modems discussed above are all equipped with an "EIA interface," which will be described in Chapter 5.

5
Interface Standards

In the early days of data communications in the United States, the associated operating companies of American Telephone and Telegraph Company were, for all practical purposes, the only providers of data communications service. Therefore, the modems developed by the engineers at Bell Laboratories and manufactured by Western Electric were the standards of the industry. To a large extent they still are. There were, however, a large number of computer and data terminal manufacturers who needed to know the electrical characteristics of the Bell modem interfaces. In addition, independent modem manufacturers offered a few high speed synchronous modems for private line use, and these manufacturers needed to know the electrical characteristics of the computer and terminal manufacturers' interfaces. To solve these problems, the Electrical Industry Association (EIA) in cooperation with the Bell System, the independent modem manufacturers, and the computer manufacturers, developed a standard for the Interface between Data Terminal Equipment and Data Communication Equipment Employing Serial Binary Interchange. This standard is called RS-232, or more specifically RS-232-C, reflecting the latest (C) revision. Copies of this standard may be purchased from the EIA Engineering Department, Electronic Industries Association, 2001 Eye Street, N.W., Washington, D.C. 20006. Newer standards, RS-422 and RS-423, have been issued which will in time supplant the RS-232-C standard, but RS-232-C is still the standard to which modem interfaces are designed.

In countries other than the United States, telephone service is generally provided by government post, telegraph, and telephone (PTT) authorities. While each of these authorities is in a position to determine interface standards for its own country, many of the modems, terminals, and computers used to provide data communications services in one country are manufactured in another. To permit the economic manufacture of these modems, terminals, and computers, and to facilitate data communications between various countries, the PTTs of the United Nations countries have, in conjunction with the Comite Consultatif International Telephonique et Telegraphique (CCITT), promulgated standards for data communications interfaces and for other aspects of telecommunications. The CCITT, a part of the International Telecommunications Union, which in turn is part of the United Nations, recognizes that varying national requirements, nationalism, and other factors preclude firm standards, so the working committees develop "recommendations" which are adopted and published by the CCITT as a whole. These recommendations cover all phases of telecommunications from operator procedures to controlling electrical interference from trolley/tram lines into telecommunications cables. The recommendations are reviewed at Plenary Assemblies held at approximately four year intervals and are then published in sets of books referred to by color. For example, the Second Plenary Assembly was held in New Delhi in 1960 and resulted in the publication of the *Red Book;* the third was held in Geneva in 1964 and resulted in the *Blue Book;* the fourth was held in Mar Del Plata, Argentina, in 1968 and resulted in the *White Book*. The fifth, sixth, and seventh were held in Geneva in 1972, 1976, and 1980 and resulted in the *Green Book,* the *Orange Book,* and the *Yellow Book.** Each of these books consists of numbered volumes covering various phases of telecommunications. The volume relating to Data Transmission is Volume VIII and contains recommendations prefixed with the letters V and X. These volumes are available from:

United Nations Bookstore
Room 32B
UN General Assembly Building
New York, New York, 10017

They can also be ordered from:

International Telecommunications Union
General Secretariat
Sales Service
Place de Nation, CH 1211
Geneva 20, Switzerland.

*The publication of CCITT books is delayed a year or more after the Plenary Assembly to which they pertain. Hence the definitions given in this book are from the *Orange Book*.

A preliminary letter of inquiry is recommended, as prepayment is required. Some of the applicable recommendations for data communications interfaces are listed below. All are contained in Volume VIII.

V.10   Electrical Characteristics for Unbalanced Double-current Interchange Circuits for General Use With Integrated Circuit Equipment in the Field of Data Communications.

V.11   Electrical Characteristics for Balanced Double-current Interchange Circuits for General Use With Integrated Circuit Equipment in the Field of Data Communications.

V.24   List of Definitions for Interchange Circuits between Data Terminal Equipment and Data Circuit Terminating Equipment.

V.25   Automatic Calling and/or Answering Equipment on the General Switched Telephone Network, Including Disabling of Echo-suppressors on Manually Established Calls.

V.28   Electrical Characteristics for Unbalanced Double-Current Interchange Circuits.

V.35   Transmission of 48 Kilobits per Second Data Using 60-to 108-kHz Group Band Circuits.

X.20   Interface Between Data Terminal Equipment (DTE) and Data-circuit Terminating Equipment (DCE) for Start-stop Transmission Services on Public Data Networks.

X.20 bis   V.21-compatible Interface Between Data Terminal Equipment (DTE) and Data-circuit Terminating Equipment (DCE) for Start-stop Transmission Services on Public Data Networks.

X.21   General Purpose Interface Between Data Terminal Equipment (DTE) and Data-circuit Terminating Equipment (DCE) for Synchronous Operation on Public Data Networks.

X.21 bis   Use on Public Data Networks of Data Terminal Equipments (DTE) Which Are Designed for Interfacing to Series V Recommendations Modems.

X.25   Interface Between Data Terminal Equipment (DTE) and Data-circuit Terminating Equipment (DCE) for Terminals Operating in the Packet Mode on Public Data Networks.

Returning to the EIA standard, it is important to note exactly what this standard contains: 1) the electrical signal characteristics, 2) the interface mechanical characteristics, 3) a functional description of the interchange circuits, and 4) a list of standard subsets of specific interchange circuits for specific groups of communications system applications.

Typical advertisements for computer/modem interfaces and terminals that say "RS-232-C compatible" really mean that the electrical and mechanical characteristics do not violate RS-232-C. There is little in the "RS-232-C compatible" statement to guarantee that the function of the interchange circuits meets RS-232-C or, more importantly, that the interchange circuits provided are sufficient to cover all systems applications. For example, a computer/modem interface that provides only level conversion for the transmitted data lead and the received data lead may have the proper electrical and mechanical characteristics to be RS-232-C compatible, but, due to the lack of control leads, it is virtually useless on switched network service. Thus, it is important when reviewing specifications for computer/modem interfaces and for terminals to understand what the various interface leads do and which are essential for various system configurations. This information is summarized in Table 5-1.

The remainder of this chapter contains a brief synopsis of EIA RS-232-C and CCITT V.24, as well as some applications notes. See "Applications Notes for RS-232-C," also available from EIA, for additional information.

The EIA specifications are keyed to the equivalent circuit for the interface leads shown in Figure 5-1. The following list is a condensation of the EIA standard RS-232-C rules for this interface circuit:

1. The open circuit voltage V_0 shall not have a magnitude greater than 25 volts.

2. The driver circuit shall be able to sustain a short circuit to any other wire in the cable without damage to itself or to the other equipment, and the short circuit current shall not exceed 0.5 ampere.

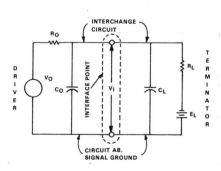

Figure 5-1. Interchange Equivalent Circuit

Table 5-1. EIA Interchange Circuit for Various Types of Communications Channels

NOTE
When Bell System Technical References refer to an "EIA RS-232-C Type D or Type E Interface," they are referring to this Chart.

	Interchange Circuit	A	B	C	D	E	F	G	H	I	J	K	L	M	Z
AA	Protective Ground	–	–	–	–	–	–	–	–	–	–	–	–	–	–
AB	Signal Ground	x	x	x	x	x	x	x	x	x	x	x	x	x	x
BA	Transmitted Data	x	x		x	x	x		x		x		x	x	o
BB	Received Data			x	x	x		x		x		x	x	x	o
CA	Request to Send		x		x		x				x		x		o
CB	Clear to Send	x	x		x	x	x		x		x		x	x	o
CC	Data Set Ready	x	x	x	x	x	x	x	x	x	x	x	x	x	o
CD	Data Terminal Ready	s	s	s	s	s	s	s	s	s	s	s	s	s	o
CE	Ring Indicator	s	s	s	s	s	s	s	s	s	s	s	s	s	o
CF	Received Line signal Detector			x	x	x		x		x	x	x			
CG	Signal Quality Detector														o
CH/CI	Data Signaling Rate Selector (DTE) (DCE)														o
DA/DS	Transmitter Signal Element Timing (DTE) (DCE)	t	t		t	t	t		t		t	t	t	t	o
DD	Receiver Signal Element Timing (DCE)		t	t	t		t		t		t	t	t		o
SBA	Secondary Transmitted Data							x		x	x	x	x	x	o
SBB	Secondary Received Data						x		x		x	x	x	x	o
SCA	Secondary Request to Send							x		x	x	x			o
SCB	Secondary Clear to Send							x		x	x	x	x	x	o
SCF	Secondary Received Line Signal Detector						x		x		x	x	x	x	o

Legend: o – To be specified by the supplier
      – – Optional
      s – Additional Interchange Circuits Required for Switched Service
      x – Basic Interchange Circuits, All Systems
      t – Additional Interchange Circuits Required for Synchronous Channel

Table 5-1.
(Continued)

Key to   A — Transmit Only
Columns: B — Transmit Only*
           C — Receive Only
           D — Duplex* Half-Duplex
           E — Duplex
           F — Primary Channel Transmit Only*/Secondary Channel Receive Only
           G — Primary Channel Receive Only/Secondary Channel Transmit Only*
           H — Primary Channel Transmit Only/Secondary Channel Receive Only
           I — Primary Channel Receive Only/Secondary Channel Transmit Only
           J — Primary Channel Transmit Only*/Half-Duplex Secondary Channel
           K — Primary Channel Receive Only/Half-Duplex Secondary Channel
           L — Duplex Primary Channel*/Duplex Secondary Channel* Half-Duplex
                Primary Channel/Half-Duplex Secondary Channel
          M — Duplex Primary Channel/Duplex Secondary Channel
           Z — Special (Circuits Specified by Supplier)

*Indicates the inclusion of Circuit CA (Request to Send) in One Way Only (Transmit) or Duplex Configuration where it might ordinarily not be expected, but where it might be used to indicate a non-transmit mode to the data communication equipment to permit it to remove a line signal or to send synchronizing or training signals as required.

3. Signals shall be considered to be in the MARK ("1") state when the voltage V_1 is more negative than -3 volts with respect to Circuit AB (Signal Ground). Signals shall be considered to be in the SPACE ("0") state when V_1 is more positive than $+3$ volts with respect to Signal Ground. The region between -3 and $+3$ volts is defined as the transition region, within which the signal state is not defined.

4. The load impedance (R_L and C_L) shall have a DC resistance R_L which is less than 7000 ohms when measured with an applied voltage of from 3 to 25 volts but more than 3000 ohms when measured with a voltage of less than 25 volts.

5. When the terminator load resistance R_L meets the requirements of Rule 4 above, and the terminator open circuit voltage (E_L) is zero, the voltage V_1 shall be between 5 volts and 15 volts in magnitude.

6. The driver shall assert a voltage between -5 and -15 volts relative to signal ground to represent a MARK signal condition. The driver shall assert a voltage between $+5$ and $+15$ volts relative to signal ground to represent a SPACE signal. Note that this rule in conjunction with Rule 3 above allows 2 volts of noise margin. This will be discussed more fully in Appendix A.

7. The driver shall change the output voltage at a rate not exceeding 30 volts per microsecond but the time required for the signal to pass

through the -3 to $+3$ transition region shall not exceed 1 millisecond or 4 percent of a bit time, whichever is smaller.

8. The shunt capacitance of the terminator (C_L) shall not exceed 2500 picofarads, including the capacitance of the cable.

9. The impedance of the driver circuit under power off conditions shall be greater than 300 ohms.

These rules are summarized in Table 5-2a, and the CCITT V.28 specifications are reproduced in Table 5-2b.

Table 5-2a.   Condensed EIA RS-232-C Electrical Specifications

Driver output logic levels with 3K to 7K load	$15\,V > V_{oh} > 5\,V$ $-5\,V > V_{ol} > -15\,V$
Driver output voltage with open circuit	$/V_0/ < 25\,V$
Driver output impedance with power off	$R_0 > 300$ ohms
Output short circuit current	$/I_0/ < 0.5\,A$
Driver slew rate	$dv/dt < 30\,V\,\mu s$
Receiver input impedance	$7\,k\,\Omega > R_{in} > 3\,k\,\Omega$
Receiver input voltage	$\pm 15\,V$ compatible with driver
Receiver output with open circuit input	MARK
Receiver output with $+3\,V$ input	SPACE
Receiver output with $-3\,V$ input	MARK
$\left.\begin{array}{l}+15 \\ +5\end{array}\right\}$	LOGIC "0"=SPACE= CONTROL ON
$\left.\begin{array}{l}+5 \\ +3\end{array}\right\}$	Noise margin
$\left.\begin{array}{l}+3 \\ -3\end{array}\right\}$	Transition region
$\left.\begin{array}{l}-3 \\ -5\end{array}\right\}$	Noise margin
$\left.\begin{array}{l}-5 \\ -15\end{array}\right\}$	LOGIC "1"=MARK= CONTROL OFF

Table 5-2b.   CCITT V.28 Electrical Characteristics for
Unbalanced Double-Current Interchange Circuits

(Geneva, 1972)

1.   **Scope**
        The electrical characteristics specified in this Recommendation apply generally to interchange circuits operating with data signaling rates below the limit of 20,000 bits per second.

2.   **Interchange equivalent circuit**
        Figure 1/V.28 shows the interchange equivalent circuit with the electrical parameters, which are defined in this section.

        This equivalent circuit is independent of whether the generator is located in the data circuit-terminating equipment and the load in the data terminal equipment or vice versa.

        The impedance associated with the generator (load) includes any cable impedance on the generator (load) side of the interchange point.

V_0 is the open-circuit generator voltage.

R_0 is the total effective d.c. resistance associated with the generator, measured at the interchange point.

C_0 is the total effective capacitance associated with the generator, measured at the interchange point.

V_I is the voltage at the interchange point with respect to signal ground or common return.

C_L is the total effective capacitance associated with the load, measured at the interchange point.

R_L is the total effective d.c. resistance associated with the load, measured at the interchange point.

E_L is the open-circuit load voltage (bias).

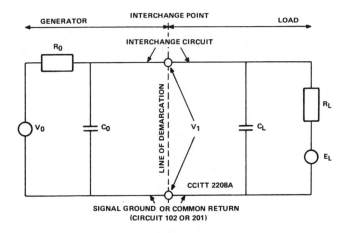

Figure 1/V 28.   Interchange Equivalent Circuit

Table 5-2b. (Continued)

3. **Load**
The test conditions for measuring the load impedance are shown in Figure 2/V.28.

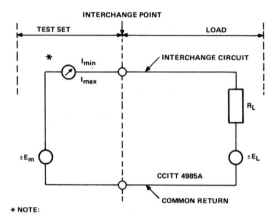

Figure 2/V 28. Equivalent Test Circuit

The impedance on the load side of an interchange circuit shall have a d.c. resistance (R_L) neither less than 3000 ohms nor more than 7000 ohms. With an applied voltage (E_m), 3 to 15 volts in magnitude, the measured input current (I) shall be within the following limits:

$$I_{min,max} \quad - \quad \left| \frac{E_m \pm E_{L\,max}}{R_{L\,max,min}} \right|$$

The open-circuit load voltage (E_L) shall not exceed two volts.

The effective shunt capacitance (C_L) of the load, measured at the interchange point, shall not exceed 2500 picofarads.

To avoid inducing voltage surges on interchange circuits the reactive component of the load impedance shall not be inductive.

NOTE
This is subject to further study.

The load on an interchange circuit shall not prejudice continuous operation with any input signals within the voltage limits specified in paragraph 4.

4. **Generator**
The generator on an interchange circuit shall withstand an open circuit and a short circuit between itself and any other interchange circuit (including generators and loads) without sustaining damage to itself or its associated equipment.

Table 5-2b. (Continued)

The open circuit generator voltage (V_0) on any interchange circuit shall not exceed 25 volts in magnitude. The impedance (V_0 and C_0) on the generator side of an interchange circuit is not specified; however, the combination of V_0 and R_0 shall be selected so that a short circuit between any two interchange circuits shall not result in any case in a current in excess of one-half ampere.

Additionally, when the load open-circuit voltage (E_L) is zero, the voltage (V_I) at the interchange point shall not be less than 5 volts and not more than 15 volts in magnitude (either positive or negative polarity), for any load resistance (R_L) in the range between 3000 ohms and 7000 ohms.

The effective shunt capacitance (C_0) at the generator side of an interchange circuit is not specified. However, the generator shall be capable of driving all of the capacitance at the generator side (C_0), plus a load capacitance (C_L) of 2500 picofarads.

NOTE
Relay or switch contacts may be used to generate signals on an interchange circuit, with appropriate measures to insure that signals so generated comply with the applicable clauses of paragraph 6.

5. **Significant levels (V_1)**
For data interchange circuits, the signal shall be considered into the binary "1" condition when the voltage (V_I) on the interchange circuit measured at the interchange point is more negative than -3 volts. The signal shall be considered in the binary "0" condition when the voltage (V_I) is more positive than $+3$ volts.

For control and timing interchange circuits, the circuit shall be considered ON when the voltage (V_I) on the interchange circuit is more positive than $+3$ volts, and shall be considered OFF when the voltage (V_I) is more negative than -3 volts. (See Figure 3/V.28)

$V_1 < -3$ VOLTS	$V_1 > +3$ VOLTS
1	0
OFF	ON

Figure 3/V 28. Correlation Table

NOTE
In certain countries, in the case of direct connection to d.c. telegraph-type circuits only, the voltage polarities in Figure 3/V.28 may be reversed.

The region between $+3$ volts and -3 volts is defined as the transition region. The signal state or circuit condition is not uniquely defined when voltage (V_I) is in the transition region. For an exception to this, see paragraph 7.

6. **Signal characteristics**
The following limitations to the characteristics of signals transmitted across the interchange point, exclusive of external interference, shall be met at the interchange point when the interchange circuit is loaded with any receiving circuit which meets the characteristics specified in paragraph 3.

Table 5-2b. (Continued)

These limitations apply to all (data, control, and timing) interchange signals unless otherwise specified.

1. All interchange signals entering into the transition region shall proceed through this region to the opposite signal state and shall not re-enter this region until the next significant change of signal condition, except as indicated in 6 below.

2. There shall be no reversal of the direction of voltage change while the signal is in the transition region, except as indicated in 6 below.

3. For control interchange circuits, the time required for the signal to pass through the transition region during a change in state shall not exceed one millisecond.

4. For data and timing interchange circuits, the time required for the signal to pass through the transition region during a change in state shall not exceed one millisecond or three percent of the nominal element period on the interchange circuit, whichever is the lesser.

5. To reduce crosstalk between interchange circuits the maximum instantaneous rate of voltage change will be limited. A provisional limit will be 30 volts per microsecond.

6. When electromechanical devices are used on interchange circuits, points 1 and 2 above do not apply to data interchange circuits.

7. **Circuit failures**
   The following interchange circuits, where implemented, shall be used to detect either a power-off condition in the equipment connected through the interface or the disconnection of the interconnecting cable:

   Circuit 105 (Request to Send)
   Circuit 107 (Data Set Ready)
   Circuit 108/1–108/2 (Connect Data Set to
        Line/Data Terminal Ready)
   Circuit 120 (Transmit Backward Channel Line Signal)
   Circuit 202 (Call Request)
   Circuit 213 (Power Indication).

   The power-off impedance of the generator side of these circuits shall not be less than 300 ohms when measured with an applied voltage (either positive or negative polarity) not greater than 2 volts in magnitude referenced to signal ground or common return.

   The load for these circuits shall interpret the power-off condition or the disconnection of the interconnecting cable as an OFF condition on these circuits.

A few years ago, each interface designer took his turn at trying to meet the electrical specifications in Table 5-2a, with varying degrees of success. Now the integrated circuit manufacturers have come to the rescue and are providing circuits which meet these specifications in terms of voltages used, rate of change of voltages, impedances, etc. However, there are certain aspects of the electrical characteristics which can still pose problems. First, in order for the driver to assert voltages of $+5$ and -5, the hardware in which these circuits are located must contain power supply voltages that are more positive than +6 and more negative than −6. The reason for this is that the drivers use transistors to control the voltages on the line being driven; these transistors are in series with the power provided to the integrated circuit and a voltage drop of about a volt occurs across the transistors. Typically, voltages of +12 and −12 are used to power the driver integrated circuits.

The second electrical problem is that of cable capacitance. The EIA standard specifies that the capacitance of the circuit being driven (the terminator) shall be less than 2500 picofarads, including the cable to it. Since 40–50 picofarads per foot is fairly common capacitance of multiconductor cable, a cable length of 50 feet is the maximum possible before the capacitance specification is violated. The most obvious consequence of violating the capacitance specification is that the amount of time needed to accomplish a transition from the MARK state to the SPACE state and vice versa will be increased from the 4 percent maximum allowed by the RS-232-C standard. Since it is also likely that the resistance of the driver and receiver circuitry is different for the MARK-SPACE transition than for the SPACE-MARK transition, there will always be a different amount of time required to charge the cable capacitance in the two transitions. The increased capacitance caused by going beyond 50 feet will compound that difference with the result that the receiver circuits will produce MARK bits that are longer than SPACE bits ("marking distortion") or SPACE bits that are longer than the MARK bits ("spacing distortion"). This type of distortion, called "bias distortion," can cause characters to be received incorrectly, especially if clock speed distortion is present or if there is noise associated with the transitions between the signal states. Examples of these effects are shown in Figure 5-2. In the speed versus distance charts shown in Appendix A, a bias distortion limit of 10 percent was arbitrarily chosen as a maximum to allow for the existence of other types of distortion. As the speed versus distance charts indicate, it is perfectly possible to use EIA interfaces over cable distances in excess of 50 feet, but it should be understood that to do so violates the standard.

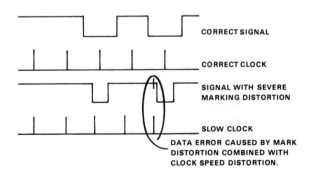

CORRECT SIGNAL

CORRECT CLOCK

SIGNAL WITH SEVERE MARKING DISTORTION

SLOW CLOCK

DATA ERROR CAUSED BY MARK DISTORTION COMBINED WITH CLOCK SPEED DISTORTION.

Figure 5-2. Effect of Clock Distortion and Bias Distortion

In addition to the capacitance problems posed by distances over 50 feet, further difficulty may be had with crosstalk, especially when synchronous interfaces which contain clock leads are used. Shielded clock leads are recommended, but discussion of synchronous interfaces will be deferred until Chapter 14.

The third and final problem of electrical properties of the EIA interface not solved by integrated circuits is that of ground reference. In the rules listed above, the voltage V_1 is always measured relative to the Signal Ground, Circuit AB. In order that V_1 not reach arbitrarily large values relative to the logic ground at the receiver, it is customary to connect Circuit AB to the logic ground of the device containing the receiver circuit. Unfortunately, since logic ground at the transmitting station and logic ground at the receiving station may differ, a ground current may flow through the Signal Ground wire. Since that wire has non-zero resistance, a voltage drop will exist across it. That voltage drop will cause the voltage applied to the interchange circuit by the driver to appear differently to the receiver than would be the case if no ground differential existed. For example, in Figure 5-3, the driver is asserting +5 volts, but the receiver sees only +3 volts.

In Figure 5-4, the driver is asserting −5 volts, but the receiver sees −7 volts. The 2 volt drop in the "ground" wire remains the same regardless of the assertion of the driver because the 2 volt differential is due to a difference between logic ground at the transmitting and receiving stations, independent of the data being transmitted. The difference between the logic grounds is probably due to differences between the electrical grounds at the transmitting and receiving stations, which in turn is due to the two stations being on different electrical feeders, etc.

Comparison of Figures 5-3 and 5-4 to the condensed set of EIA rules listed above will indicate that the data will still be interpreted correctly, despite the ground potential differences at the receiving and transmitting stations, because the potential difference is absorbed in the "noise margin" provided in

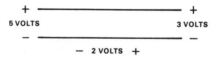

Figure 5-3. Effect of Ground Potential Differences on a +5 Volt Signal

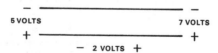

Figure 5-4. Effect of Ground Potential Differences on a −5 Volt Signal

the EIA spec. Consider, however, the same examples with a ground potential difference of 9 volts; the receiver will see − 4 volts and − 14 volts respectively in the two figures. Each of these will be interpreted as a MARK. In fact, the potential difference does not have to be that big for loss to occur. A potential difference of 3 volts is sufficient for the receiver to see +2 volts in Figure 5-3, and +2 volts is in the undefined (transition) region.

Furthermore, since ground potential differences cause receivers to change their threshold points, the effects of the bias distortion caused by cable capacitance is increased. See Appendix A, Figures A2–A7.

In summary, EIA Standard RS-232-C was intended as an interface specification for connection of computer/modem interfaces and terminals to modems over distances of 50 feet or less. It will work moderately well over greater distances, as indicated in Appendix A, and in fact will work over distances far greater than those shown. However, cable capacitance, clock speed distortion, noise, and ground potential difference make successful operation in many cases increasingly unlikely at distances beyond those shown in Appendix A.

Realizing the unsuitability of a single specification for both local connection and longer distance transmission, the Electronic Industries Association has come out with three new specifications, RS-422 (Electrical Characteristics of Balanced Voltage Digital Interface Circuits), RS-423 (Electrical Characteristics of Unbalanced Voltage Digital Interface Circuits), and RS-449 (General Purpose 37-position and 9-position Interface for Data Terminal Equipment and Data Circuit-Terminating Equipment Employing Serial Binary Data Interchange).

Figure 5-5 shows a balanced digital interface circuit appropriate to EIA RS-422. Briefly stated, the rules are: 1) the A terminal of the generator shall be negative with respect to the B terminal for a binary "1" (MARK or OFF) state, and 2) the A terminal of the generator shall be positive with respect to the B terminal for a binary "0" (SPACE or ON). There are also various rules concerning open circuit voltages, short circuit currents, power-off characteristics, output signal waveform, receiver input current/voltage relationships, input sensitivity, and input balance. The characteristics of the interconnecting cable and the grounding arrangements are presented in far greater detail than in RS-232. The most important part of the new specification is that the receiver makes its determination of what is a MARK and what is a SPACE on the basis of the relationship of the A terminal to the B, and not the relationship of the terminal to ground. RS-422 includes a speed vs. distance table which is reproduced in Appendix A.

EIA Standard RS-423 applies to unbalanced voltage interfaces. Figure 5-6 shows a generator and load arrangement appropriate to RS-423.

The rules here are: 1) the A terminal of the generator shall be negative with respect to the C terminal for a binary "1" (MARK or OFF) state, and 2) the A terminal of the generator shall be positive with respect to the C

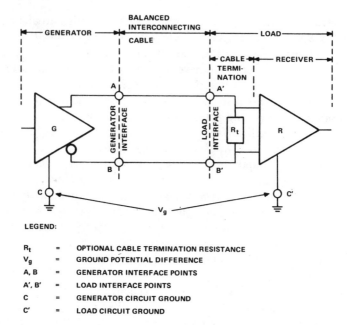

LEGEND:

R_t	=	OPTIONAL CABLE TERMINATION RESISTANCE
V_g	=	GROUND POTENTIAL DIFFERENCE
A, B	=	GENERATOR INTERFACE POINTS
A', B'	=	LOAD INTERFACE POINTS
C	=	GENERATOR CIRCUIT GROUND
C'	=	LOAD CIRCUIT GROUND

Figure 5-5.   Balanced Digital Interface Circuit

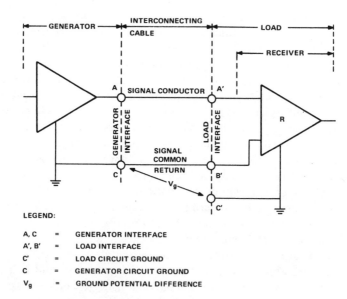

LEGEND:

A, C	=	GENERATOR INTERFACE
A', B'	=	LOAD INTERFACE
C'	=	LOAD CIRCUIT GROUND
C	=	GENERATOR CIRCUIT GROUND
V_g	=	GROUND POTENTIAL DIFFERENCE

Figure 5-6.   Unbalanced Digital Interface Circuit

terminal for a binary "0" (SPACE or ON) state. As with RS-422, there are also various rules concerning the open circuit voltages, the short circuit currents, etc. The most important aspect of this specification is that the receiver determines the signal being transmitted on the basis of the voltage of lead A relative to the signal ground lead. Only a limited amount—4 volts—of V_g (ground potential difference) can be accommodated. RS-423 also includes a speed versus distance table, which is reproduced in Appendix A.

EIA Standard RS-449 specifies the functional and mechanical characteristics of the RS-422 and RS-423 interfaces. It divides the interchange circuits into two categories, Category I (2 data, 3 timing, and 5 other circuits) and Category II (all other circuits). Below 20,000 bits per second, Category I circuits can be implemented with RS-422 or RS-423 drivers and receivers. Above 20,000 bits per second, RS-422 circuitry must be used. The Category II circuits, which are generally status and maintenance circuits, are always RS-423. RS-449 also specifies the mechanical characteristics of the connectors to be used and specifies the circuit names, functions, and pin assignments.

Since RS-449 permits the use of RS-423 drivers and receivers at speeds below 20,000 bits per second, and RS-423 is an unbalanced interface, it is possible to interoperate an RS-449 interface and an RS-232-C interface at speeds below 20,000 bits per second if certain precautions are taken. EIA Industrial Electronics Bulletin Number 12, "Application Notes on Interconnection Between Interface Circuits Using RS-449 and RS-232-C" explains these precautions in detail. The precautions involve overvoltage protection, fail-safe circuitry, load resistance, and signal waveshaping in addition to the mechanics of connecting 37-pin connectors to 25-pin connectors.

The following definitions of the functions of interface circuits are limited to those circuits required for interfacing a private line modem. In Chapter 9, this list will be expanded to include the interface leads required for controlling modems on switched network connections. Since these definitions are taken from EIA Specification RS-232-C and are reproduced here by permission of EIA, the term "data set" is used throughout, rather than the term "modem" which has been used in the rest of this book. The CCITT definitions are taken from Recommendation V.24 and are reproduced here by permission of the CCITT.

EIA RS-232-C Definitions	CCITT V.24 Definitions
Circuit AA—Protective Ground Direction: Not applicable This conductor shall be electrically bonded to the machine or the equipment frame. It may be further connected to external grounds as required by applicable regulations.	No equivalent circuit. Circuit 101, which formerly performed this function, was removed from V.24 at the Sixth Plenary Assembly, Geneva 1976.

EIA RS-232-C **Definitions**	**CCITT V.24** **Definitions**

Circuit AB—Signal Ground or Common Return (CCITT 102)
Direction: Not applicable

This conductor establishes the common ground reference potential for all interchange circuits except Circuit AA (Protective Ground). Within the data communication equipment, this circuit shall be brought to one point, and it shall be possible to connect this point to Circuit AA by means of a wire strap inside the equipment. This wire strap can be connected or removed at installation, as may be required to meet applicable regulations or to minimize the introduction of noise into electronic circuitry.

Circuit 102 — Signal Ground or Common Return

This conductor establishes the signal common return for unbalanced interchange circuits with electrical characteristics according to Recommendations V.28 and the d.c. reference potential for balanced circuits according to V.11 and V.35. Within the Data Communications Equipment, this circuit shall be brought to one point, and it shall be possible to connect this point to protective ground or earth by means of a metallic strap within the equipment. This metallic strap can be connected or removed at installation, as may be required to meet applicable regulations or to minimize the induction of noise into electronic circuitry.

Circuit BA—Transmitted Data (CCITT 103)
Direction: TO data communication equipment

Signals on this circuit are generated by the data terminal equipment and are transferred to the local transmitting signal converter for transmission of data to remote data terminal equipment.

The data terminal equipment shall hold Circuit BA (Transmitted Data) in marking condition during intervals between characters or words, and at all times when no data are being transmitted.

In all systems, the data terminal equipment shall not transmit data unless an ON condition is present on all of the following four circuits, where implemented.

1. Circuit CA (Request to Send)
2. Circuit CB (Clear to Send)
3. Circuit CC (Data Set Ready)
4. Circuit CD (Data Terminal Ready)

All data signals that are transmitted across the interface on interchange circuit BA (Transmitted Data) during the time an ON condition is maintained on all of the above four circuits, where implemented, shall be transmitted to the communication channel.

Circuit 103—Transmitted Data
Direction: To DCE

The data signals originated by the DTE, to be transmitted via the data channel to one or more remote data stations, are transferred on this circuit to the DCE.

Circuit BB—Received Data (CCITT 104)
Direction: FROM data communication equipment

Signals on this circuit are generated by the receiving signal converter in response to data

Circuit 104—Received Data
Direction: From DCE

The data signals generated by the DCE, in response to data channel line signals received

EIA RS-232-C
Definitions

signals received from remote data terminal equipment via the remote transmitting signal converter. Circuit BB (Received Data) shall be held in the binary "1" (marking) condition at all times when Circuit CF (Received Line Signal Detector) is in the OFF condition.

On a half-duplex channel, Circuit BB shall be held in the binary "1" (marking) condition when Circuit CA (Request to Send) is in the ON condition and for a brief interval following the ON to OFF transition of Circuit CA to allow for the completion of transmission (see Circuit BA—Transmitted Data) and the decay of line reflections.

Circuit CA—Request to Send (CCITT 105)
Direction: TO data communication equipment

This circuit is used to condition the local data communication equipment for data transmission and, on a half-duplex channel, to control the direction of data transmission of the local data communication equipment.

On one way only channels or duplex channels, the ON condition maintains the data communication equipment in the transmit mode. The OFF condition maintains the data communication equipment in a non-transmit mode.

On a half-duplex channel, the ON condition maintains the data communication equipment in the transmit mode and inhibits the receive mode. The OFF condition maintains the data communication equipment in the receive mode.

A transition from OFF to ON instructs the data communication equipment to enter the transmit mode. The data communication equipment responds by taking such action as may be necessary and indicates completion of such actions by turning ON Circuit CB (Clear to Send), thereby indicating to the data terminal equipment that data may be transferred across the interface point on interchange Circuit BA (Transmitted Data).

A transition from ON to OFF instructs the data communication equipment to complete the transmission of all data which was previously transferred across the interface point on interchange Circuit BA and then assume a non-transmit mode or a receive mode as appropriate. The data communication equipment responds to this instruction by turning

CCITT V.24
Definitions

from a remote data station, are transferred on this circuit to the DTE.

Circuit 105—Request to Send
Direction: To DCE

Signals on this circuit control the data channel transmit function of the DCE.

The ON condition causes the DCE to assume the data channel transmit mode.

The OFF condition causes the DCE to assume the data channel non-transmit mode, when all data transferred on Circuit 103 (Transmitted Data) have been transmitted.

Interrelationship of Circuits 103, 105, and 106

The DTE signals its intent to transmit data by turning ON Circuit 105 (Request to Send). It is then the responsibility of the DCE to enter the transmit mode, i.e., be prepared to transmit data, and also to alert the remote DCE and condition it to receive data. The means by which a DCE enters the transmit mode and alerts and conditions the remote DCE are described in the appropriate modem Recommendation.

When the transmitting DCE turns Circuit 106 (Ready for Sending) ON, the DTE is permitted to transfer data across the interface on Circuit 103 (Transmitted Data). By turning ON Circuit 106 it is implied that all data transferred across the interface prior to the time that any one of the four circuits: 105, 106, 107, 108/1–108/2 is again turned OFF, will be transferred to the telecommunication channels; however, the ON condition of Circuit 106 is not necessarily a guarantee that the remote DCE is in the receive mode. (Depending on the complexity and sophistication of

EIA RS-232-C Definitions	CCITT V.24 Definitions

Circuit CA (Cont.)

OFF Circuit CB (Clear to Send) when it is prepared to again respond to a subsequent ON condition of Circuit CA.

NOTE

A non-transmit mode does not imply that all line signals have been removed from the communication channel.

When Circuit CA is turned OFF, it shall not be turned ON again until Circuit CB has been turned OFF by the data communication equipment.

An ON condition is required on Circuit CA as well as on Circuit CB, Circuit CC (Data Set Ready) and, where implemented, Circuit CD (Data Terminal Ready) whenever the data terminal equipment transfers data across the interface on interchange Circuit BA.

It is permissible to turn Circuit CA ON at any time when Circuit CB is OFF regardless of the condition of any other interchange circuit.

Circuit 105 (Cont.)

the transmitting signal converter, there may be a delay ranging from less than a millisecond up to several seconds between the time a bit is transferred across the interface until the time a signal element representing this bit is transmitted on the telecommunication channel.)

The DTE shall not turn Circuit 105 OFF before the end of the last bit (data bit or stop element) transferred across the interface on Circuit 103. Similarly, in certain full-duplex switched network applications where Circuit 105 is not implemented (see specific DCE Recommendations), this requirement applies equally when Circuit 108/1–108/2 is turned OFF to terminate a switched network call.

Where Circuit 105 is provided, the ON and OFF conditions on Circuit 106 shall be responses to the ON and OFF conditions on Circuit 105. For the appropriate response times of Circuit 106, and for the operation of Circuit 106 when Circuit 105 is not provided, refer to the relevant Recommendation for DCE.

When Circuit 105 or Circuit 106 or both are OFF, the DTE shall maintain a binary "1" condition on Circuit 103. When Circuit 105 is turned OFF it shall not be turned ON again until Circuit 106 is turned OFF by the DCE.

Circuit CB—Clear to Send (CCITT 106—Ready for Sending)
Direction: FROM data communication equipment

Signals on this circuit are generated by the data communication equipment to indicate whether or not the data set is ready to transmit data.

The ON condition together with the ON condition on interchange circuits CA, CC and, where implemented, CD, is an indication to the data terminal equipment that signals presented on Circuit BA (Transmitted Data) will be transmitted to the communication channel.

The OFF condition is an indication to the data terminal equipment that it should not transfer data across the interface on interchange Circuit BA.

Circuit 106—Ready for Sending
Direction: From DCE

Signals on this circuit indicate whether the DCE is conditioned to transmit data on the data channel.

The ON condition indicates that the DCE is conditioned to transmit data on the data channel.

The OFF condition indicates that the DCE is not prepared to transmit data on the data channel.

EIA RS-232-C Definitions	CCITT V.24 Definitions

The ON condition of Circuit CB is a response to the occurrence of a simultaneous ON condition on Circuits CC (Data Set Ready) and Circuit CA (Request to Send), delayed as may be appropriate to the data communication equipment for establishing a data communication channel (including the removal of the MARK HOLD clamp from the Received Data interchange circuit of the remote data set) to a remote data terminal equipment.

Where Circuit CA (Request to Send) is not implemented in the data communication equipment with transmitting capability, Circuit CA shall be assumed to be in the ON condition at all times, and Circuit CB shall respond accordingly.

The Clear to Send (CB) signal means slightly different things in different modems. In a full-duplex modem equipped with the "CB-CF Common" option, it is connected directly to the carrier detection circuitry in the modem. Thus it indicates whether carrier is being received from the distant modem and is a fairly good indication that a suitable communications channel exists.

In full-duplex modems equipped with the "CB-CF Separate" option, and in half-duplex modems, Clear to Send is merely a delayed version of Request to Send. The modem interface control asserts Request to Send and a timer in the modem, upon detecting this assertion, waits up to 200 milliseconds (depending upon option arrangements) and then asserts Clear to Send back to the modem interface. In this case, Clear to Send is really "Probably Clear to Send."

In some full-duplex modems, such as the Bell System 108F and 108G, options are available to select whether Clear to Send is controlled by the carrier detection circuitry or is a delayed version of Clear to Send. Further details may be found in Appendix B.

EIA RS-232-C Definitions	CCITT V.24 Definitions
Circuit CC—Data Set Ready (CCITT 107) Direction: FROM data communication equipment.	*Circuit 107*—Data Set Ready Direction: From DCE
Signals on this circuit are used to indicate the status of the local set.	Signals on this circuit indicate whether the DCE is ready to operate.

EIA RS-232-C Definitions	CCITT V.24 Definitions

Circuit CC (Cont.)

The ON condition on this circuit is presented to indicate that:

a) the local data communication equipment is connected to a communication channel ("OFF HOOK" in switched service), and

b) the local data communication equipment is not in test (local or remote), talk (alternate voice), or dial* mode, and

c) the local data communication equipment has completed, where applicable

   1. any timing functions required by the switching system to complete call establishment, and

   2. the transmission of any discrete answer tone, the duration of which is controlled solely by the local data set.

Where the local data communication equipment does not transmit an answer tone, or where the duration of the answer tone is controlled by some action of the remote data set, the ON condition is presented as soon as all the other above conditions (a, b, and c-1) are satisfied.

This circuit shall be used only to indicate the status of the local data set. The ON condition shall not be interpreted as either an indication that a communication channel has been established to a remote data station or the status of any remote station equipment.

The OFF condition shall appear at all other times and shall be an indication that the data terminal equipment is to disregard signals appearing on any other interchange circuit with the exception of Circuit CE (Ring Indicator). The OFF condition shall not impair the oper-

Circuit 107 (Cont.)

The ON condition indicates that the signal-conversion or similar equipment is connected to the line and that the DCE is ready to exchange further control signals with the DTE to initiate the exchange of data.

The OFF condition indicates that the DCE is not ready to operate.

Operation of Circuits 107 and 108/1 and 108/2**

Signals on Circuit 107 (Data Set Ready) are to be considered as responses to signals which initiate connection to line, e.g., Circuit 108/1 (Connect Data Set to Line). However, the conditioning of a data channel, such as equalization and clamp removal, cannot be expected to occur before Circuit 107 is turned ON.

When Circuit 108/1 or 108/2 (Data Terminal Ready) is turned OFF, it shall not be turned ON again until Circuit 107 is turned OFF by the DCE.

A wiring option shall be provided within the DCE to select either Circuit 108/1 or Circuit 108/2 operation.

When the DCE is conditioned for automatic answering of calls, connection to the line occurs only in response to a combination of the calling signal and an ON condition on Circuit 108/2.

In certain special dedicated circuit (leased line) applications, Circuit 108/1 might not be implemented, in which case the condition on this circuit is assumed to be permanently ON.

Under certain test conditions, both the DTE and the DCE may exercise some of the interchange circuits. It is then to be understood that when Circuit 107 is OFF, the DTE is to

---

*The data communication equipment is considered to be in the dial mode when circuitry directly associated with the call origination function is connected to the communication channel. These functions include signaling to the central office (dialing) and monitoring the communication channel for call progress or answer back signals.

**Circuits 108/1 and 108/2 are discussed in Chapter 9.

EIA RS-232-C Definitions	CCITT V.24 Definitions

ation of Circuit CE or Circuit CD (Data Terminal Ready).

When the OFF condition occurs during the progress of a call before Circuit CD (Data Terminal Ready—see Chapter 9) is turned OFF, the data terminal equipment shall interpret this as a lost or aborted connection and take action to terminate the call. Any subsequent ON condition on Circuit CC is to be considered a new call.

When the data set is used in conjunction with Automatic Calling Equipment, the OFF to ON transition of Circuit CC shall not be interpreted as an indication that the ACE has relinquished control of the communication channel to the data set. Indication of this is given on the appropriate lead in the ACE interface (see EIA Standard RS-366).

NOTE
Attention is called to the fact that if a data call is interrupted by alternate voice communication, Circuit CC will be in the OFF condition during the time that voice communication is in progress. The transmission or reception of the signals required to condition the communication channel or data communication equipment in response to the ON condition of interchange Circuit CA (Request to Send) of the transmitting data terminal equipment will take place after Circuit CC comes ON, but prior to the ON condition on Circuit CB (Clear to Send) or Circuit CF (Received Line Signal Detector).

Circuit CF—Received Line Signal Detector (CCITT 109)
Direction: FROM data communication equipment

The ON condition on this circuit is presented when the data communication equipment is receiving a signal which meets its suitability criteria. These criteria are established by the data communication equipment manufacturer.

The OFF condition indicates that no signal is being received or that the received signal is unsuitable for demodulation.

The OFF condition of Circuit CF (Received

ignore the conditions on any interchange circuit from the DCE except those on Circuit 125 (Calling Indicator) and the timing circuits. Additionally, when Circuit 108/1 or 108/2 is OFF the DCE is to ignore the conditions on any interchange circuit from the DTE. The ON conditions on Circuits 107 and 108/1 or 108/2 are therefore prerequisite conditions for accepting as valid the signals on interchange circuits from the DCE or DTE respectively, other than Circuit 125. The OFF condition on Circuit 108/1 or 108/2 shall not disable the operation of Circuit 125.

Circuit 109—Data Channel Received Line Signal Detector
Direction: From DCE

Signals on this circuit indicate whether the received data channel line signal is within appropriate limits, as specified in the relevant Recommendation for DCE.

The ON condition indicates that the received signal is within appropriate limits.

The OFF condition indicates that the received signal is not within appropriate limits.

EIA RS-232-C Definitions	CCITT V.24 Definitions

Circuit CF (Cont.)

Line Signal Detector) shall cause Circuit BB (Received Data) to be clamped to the Binary "1" (marking) condition.

The indications on this circuit shall follow the actual onset or loss of signal by appropriate guard delays.

On half-duplex channels, Circuit CF is held in the OFF condition whenever Circuit CA (Request to Send) is in the ON condition and for a brief interval of time following the ON to OFF transition of Circuit CA (See Circuit BB.)

Received Line Signal Detector, commonly called "Carrier Detect," indicates that there is an appropriate tone being received from the distant modem. In a full-duplex arrangement, it is ON whenever the communications channel exists and the distant modem has its Request to Send lead asserted—i.e., is transmitting. In half-duplex applications, it is ON whenever carrier (tone) is on the line and the local modem's Request to Send lead is OFF; if the local modem is not transmitting the tone must be from the other modem. One exception to this rule is the Bell System 202S or 202T modem when equipped with the "Local Copy" option. In that case the Carrier Detect lead is independent of the state of the local Request to Send lead, and thus is ON whenever either the local or distant modem has its transmitter on.

The Carrier Detect lead usually has an immunity to very short losses of carrier. Losses of less than 20 ± 10 milliseconds are, as a rule, not reflected in the Carrier Detect lead.

There are a substantial number of EIA and CCITT circuits which have not been described in the preceding lists. The lists, however, are intended as a core to which other chapters will add as further applications are discussed.

In the past three chapters, various technical details of the facilities used for getting data from one place to another have been discussed. Chapter 6 will return to the simple interface discussed in Chapter 2, but will add in leads associated with the transmission facilities—in particular, modem control and status leads. The more complicated case of modem control and status for switched network use will be treated in Chapter 9. A completely different concept in modem control and status, serial signaling using CCITT Recommendations X.20 and X.21, will be discussed in Chapter 27.

6

A Single Line
Asynchronous Interface
With Control for
Private Line Modems

In Chapter 2, Figure 2-1 presented a block diagram of a single line asynchronous interface. Address selection logic was provided to gate the contents of the receiver buffer and various registers onto the computer I/O bus via "bus drivers," and to record the data from the I/O bus receivers into designated registers during write operations directed toward those registers. The interrupt control logic permitted the program running in the computer to be notified whenever a received character arrived, or whenever the transmitter was capable of transmitting another character.

Figure 6-1 is a reprint of Figure 2-1, but a Request to Send control lead has been added along with two new status leads, Clear to Send and Carrier Detect. Underlining on Figure 6-1 emphasizes the position of these leads in the block diagram.

Also shown in Figure 6-1 is a change in the leads that enter the Interrupt Control Logic. In addition to the Receiver Interrupt lead and Transmit Interrupt lead, a Data Set Interrupt lead is provided.

The register bit assignments for the single line interface shown in Figure 2-1 and the single line interface with control for private line modems shown above are compared in Figure 6-2.

As did Figure 6-1, Figure 6-2 includes underlining to emphasize the new signal leads that have been added. Bit 15 has been assigned as "Data Set Interrupt" (DS INT) and is set whenever either the Clear to Send lead or the Carrier Detect lead changes state. The program may examine the current state of those leads by reading bits 13 (CLR SND) and 12 (CAR DET) of this register. The setting of bit 15, indicating a change of state of these leads, causes an interrupt if the generation of interrupts for data set lead changes is enabled—i.e., if bit 05, Data Set Interrupt Enable (DS IE), is set.

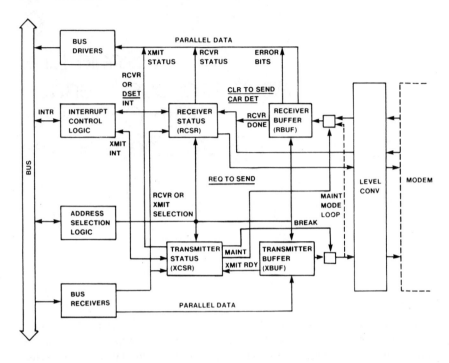

Figure 6-1. Block Diagram of a Single Line Asynchronous Interface with Control for Private Line Modems

15	14	13	12	11	10	09	08	07	06	05	04	03	02	01	00
DS INT		CLR SND	CAR DET					RCVR DONE	RCVR IE	DS IE			REQ SND		

Figure 6-2. Sample Bit Assignments for a Single Line Asynchronous Interface with Control for Private Line Modems

The program may also control the state of the Request to Send lead by setting bit 02 (REQ SND) to assert the Request to Send lead to the ON state, or by clearing bit 02 to put the Request to Send lead in the OFF state.

The simplified interface shown in Chapter 2 was connected to the following circuits:

- (AA) Protective Ground or Earth
- CCITT 102 (AB) Signal Ground
- CCITT 103 (BA) Transmitted Data
- CCITT 104 (BB) Received Data

The interface described in this chapter connects to these circuits and adds:

- CCITT 105 (CA) Request to Send
- CCITT 106 (CB) Ready for Sending (Clear to Send)
- CCITT 109 (CF) Data Channel Received Line Signal Detector (Carrier Detect)

This accounts for all of the modem control leads described in Chapter 5 with the exception of CCITT 107 (CC) Data Set Ready. No bit assignment was made for Data Set Ready because the computer manufacturer interface being used for these examples does not provide it. Bit 09 could, however, be used for this purpose and could be incorporated into the transition detecting logic so that transitions of Data Set Ready set bit 15, Data Set Interrupt. This latter connection is not a necessity, as the program could also period- ically check the status of the Data Set Ready bit which does not change fre- quently. Some telecommunications administrations, notably the German Post Office authorities, require that all modem interfaces monitor the status of this lead. In some cases, the negation of this lead is used to indicate, in switched network use, that the modem has successfully disconnected itself from the communications line when told to do so.

So far, all discussion of computer interfaces for data communications has dealt with interfaces for a single communications line. Multi-line appli- cations often use somewhat different arrangements, as will be discussed in Chapter 7.

7

Asynchronous
Multiplexers

Previous chapters have described interfaces which allow asynchronous transmission and reception of characters on a communications line attached to a computer. Characters arriving in bit serial fashion are assembled into characters, an interrupt is generated to the computer to indicate that a received character is ready and a path is set up to transfer the character into the computer. In like fashion, the interface indicates by means of an interrupt to the computer that it can transmit a character, the computer loads a character into the interface, and the interface serializes the character onto the line. A simple block diagram of such a device is shown in Figure 7-1.

Note that certain units, such as the Interrupt Facility and the Bus Interface, are not directly associated with the communications line, but rather form a path for control signals and data to reach the computer's Input/Output (I/O) Bus. Since the receiver and transmitter functions are now performed by a single LSI chip which is extremely inexpensive, the major costs are for line conditioning and cables (not shown), plus the cost of the Interrupt Facility and Bus Interface. That such a high proportion of the costs should exist in these items is especially painful since they are used only briefly: once for each character transmitted and once for each character received. A "multiplexer" permits a number of transmitter and receiver units to share the same Clocks, Interrupt Facility, and Bus Interface. A simplified diagram of a typical asynchronous multiplexer is shown in Figure 7-2.

Here, each line has its own receiver and its own transmitter, but all other components are shared. There are two new components added—scanners and a FIFO. The receiver scanner sequentially checks each receiver for a character available flag. When it sees one, it automatically reads that character,

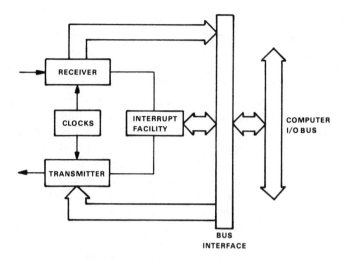

Figure 7-1. Block Diagram of a Single Line Asynchronous Interface

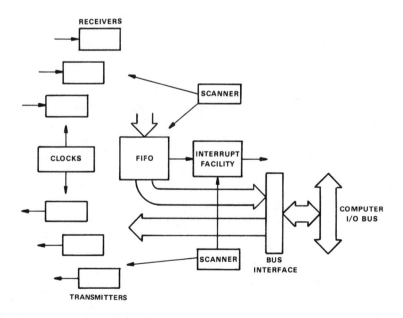

Figure 7-2. Block Diagram of a Multi-Line Asynchronous Interface (Multiplexer)

along with its line number (i.e., the scanner position) and any error flags (such as overrun or framing error) into a first-in first-out buffer (FIFO). The existence of characters in the FIFO is reported to the computer by means of the Interrupt Facility. A similar scanner checks the transmitters for flags indicating that the transmitter holding buffer is empty. Upon finding such a flag, the scanner stops and reports the flag and line number to the computer, again by using the interrupt facility. Thus, with the addition of scanners, which are essentially simple counters, the Interrupt Facility and the Bus Interface can be shared by a number of lines. The number is usually a power of two for convenience in presenting the line numbers in binary form. Four line, 8 line, 16 line, 32 line, 64 line, 128 line, and 256 line multiplexers are common. Because the Interrupt Facility, Bus Interface, and Clocks are not repeated for each line, cost is saved not only in components, but also in printed circuit board space. It is possible to build a four or eight line multiplexer on a card that previously housed just a single line interface.

The choice of multiplexer size (2, 4, 8, 16 etc. lines) is influenced by the packaging which the computer manufacturer uses and the number of lines his customers typically buy. While the cost benefits are greatest with the larger multiplexers, users that typically install a dozen lines on their computer systems will not be enthused about a 256 line multiplexer, no matter how low the cost per line.

Because the complicated equipment can be shared in a multiplexer, it is possible to include features that would not be economic in single line interfaces. Among these are full modem control for many or all of the interface leads, program selectable character formats, program selectable line speeds, character recognition, direct deposition of characters into computer memory, and the FIFO buffer.

Full modem control is treated in detail in Chapter 9. Program selectable format is the capability of conditioning the various receivers and transmitters to communicate with terminals with differing numbers of bits per character, numbers of stop bits, and parity conventions. Program selectable line speeds is the ability to change the clocking used for the various transmitters and receivers to accommodate terminals whose signaling rates differ. These features, along with character recognition and direct deposition of received characters, are discussed in greater detail in Chapters 12 and 21. The FIFO is a simple multiplexer addition, however, and will be discussed here.

A FIFO is literally a first-in first-out buffer. It resembles, in concept, a farm silo where silage is placed in the top and falls as far down the silo as possible before coming to rest on other accumulated silage. The silage is retrieved from the bottom of the silo as needed, and, as some is withdrawn, the remaining silage moves downward to take its place. In the FIFO, characters are loaded in by the receiver scanner and they propagate as far toward the output as they can, until they encounter another stored character. There is a flag to indicate to the scanner that there is room in the FIFO to store a character (typical capacity is 64 characters) and a flag which indicates that there is a character available at the output of the FIFO. This latter flag can be connected to the Interrupt Facility and is used to indicate to the computer that it can read the "bottom" of the FIFO to obtain a received character. The computer does not have to figure out which line caused the interrupt (the scanner position for the character is stored along with the character and indicates the line number), and the FIFO permits the computer to delay responding to the interrupt for a substantial time without data being lost. Note, however, that the computer must keep up with the arriving character rate on a long term basis or the FIFO will eventually fill. A less obvious feature of the FIFO is that it actually improves throughput.

When a computer responds to an interrupt it must store away certain information relative to the task which it was performing at the time, and it must then execute various instructions associated with entering the "interrupt service routine." This process must be repeated in reverse order for exiting from the interrupt service routine. The time spent to do this is essentially useless overhead, as no computation gets done. Thus if each received character generates an interrupt this overhead is incurred for each character received. If, however, an interrupt occurs whenever there are characters in the FIFO, and the interrupt service routine processes all of the characters in the FIFO before exiting the routine, chances are good that several characters will be processed on each interrupt. The overhead is therefore spread out over more characters. Best of all, as the processing load increases, and the computer subsequently becomes more tardy in responding to the interrupt, more characters accumulate in the FIFO while waiting for the computer to respond. Since this results in more characters being serviced on each interrupt service routine, the overhead per character is even more drastically reduced. The system actually becomes more efficient as the load on the computer increases!

While a FIFO is a very helpful and simple device to have on the receiver side of a multiplexer, a FIFO common to all lines cannot be added to the transmitter side. A high speed line would want to withdraw its characters quickly while a slow speed line would want to withdraw its characters slowly; thus the characters for both types of line could not be stored one behind the other in the same FIFO. A separate FIFO could be provided for each line, however. Such an arrangement would allow the overhead of transmit interrupts to be averaged over a greater number of characters. Care in design would be required to make sure that transmission could be suspended when necessary.

The primary benefits of multiplexers are: 1) much lower cost per line than single line interfaces (typically the crossover point is around six lines for simple asynchronous multiplexers vs. simple single line units), 2) availability of special features, especially those that improve throughput, 3) reduced space and power requirements, and 4) reduced electrical loading on the computer I/O bus due to fewer bus interfaces.

The drawbacks are: 1) if the manufacturer sells n-line multiplexers and you need n+1 lines, you may have to buy two n-line multiplexers, 2) the programming of a multiplexer is generally more complicated, and 3) if the multiplexer fails, lots of lines go down. Note, however, that the cost differential in large line sizes is often such that you can afford two n-line multiplexers (one as a backup) for the cost of n single line interfaces.

In Chapter 2, a very simple interface was presented. In Chapters 3, 4, and 5 some properties of data transmission facilities were discussed which lead to the more sophisticated interfaces treated in Chapter 6 and 7. It is now time to go a step further and discuss a much more complicated data transmission facility, the switched telephone network.

8

Telephone Switching Systems

In the early days of telephony, people bought telephones in pairs. Doctor Smith would have one for himself and one at the other end of the line for the pharmacy. The harness maker would have one for himself and one for the livery stable. Soon all of the doctors in town were on a common line with Doctor Smith and the pharmacy. Similar professional common interest groups had similar telephone hook-ups. After a while the various groups wanted to talk to one another and residential telephone subscribers wanted to talk to all of the various professional men and businesses. Thus was born the need for the telephone switchboard.

Early telephone instruments obtained the power for their transmission from batteries located near the telephone. A bell associated with the telephone alerted subscribers that someone was trying to reach them. When more than one person had a telphone on the same line (as was the usual case) coded ringing, such as one long ring followed by two short rings, identified which of the parties on the line was being contacted. In addition, a hand cranked magneto was installed in the telephone which permitted each subscriber to signal the others by applying ringing current to the line.

When switchboards were first utilized, a person desiring to make a call would first ring the operator who would place a plug in the jack of the caller's line to talk to him or her. After learning to whom the caller wished to speak, the operator would place another plug in the jack of that person's line and ring the line with the appropriate ringing code.

When the conversation was over, the two parties would apply ringing to the line again, signaling the operator that the connection could be taken down. Because the batteries that supplied the power were local to the telephone instruments, and because of the type of signaling used, such arrangements were called "magneto local battery" systems. While only one magneto system exists in the US today (Bryant Pond, Maine), such systems have left their mark on telephony in such terms as "drop," "ring off," and "take down the connection."

To aid operators in identifying the lines which were trying to get their attention, each line jack had a metallic flag which dropped down when the subscriber rang the line. This flag was called a "drop," and the term is still used to refer to the line to a subscriber's home, in particular the part from the pole to the house. The wire used to make that connection is even called "drop wire."

The phrase is rarely used anymore, but at one time people who were about to terminate their telephone conversation would often say: "Well, I think I'll ring off now," referring to the practice of ringing at the end of a call to signal the operator to "take down the connection." The latter term, "take down the connection," refers to switchboard construction. Subscriber lines appear as jacks on a vertical panel in front of which is a shelf containing "cord sets." These are two plugs interconnected with a cord and a little bit of circuitry to bring the operator's telephone in and out of the connection. Taking down a connection refers literally to removing the plugs from the vertical panel and restoring the cord set to its rest position.

Local battery magneto systems were followed by "common battery manual" systems. In the common battery system, all telephone instruments received their power from a common battery located on the telephone company premises near the switchboard. By placing sensitive relays in the circuit between the subscriber telephones and the battery, it became possible to determine when a telephone was "on-hook" (drawing no current) and when it was "off-hook" (drawing current). The telephone subscriber did not have to ring the operator in order to place a call; the caller simply lifted the receiver off the hook to start drawing current. The relay for his or her line would then signal the operator by means of a light over the appropriate line jack on the switchboard. In similar fashion, relays placed in the cord circuit between the two plugs used to connect callers together could determine when the two parties hung up their telephones, and alert the operator to take down the connection.

The process of determining whether or not a telephone is off-hook or on-hook is called "supervision" and is one of the most important concepts in telephony (especially when the subscribers pay to place calls). The principal contribution to the telephonic lexicon from common battery switchboards was the identity of the conductors used to make the connections at the switchboard. The plug used to make a connection to a subscriber's line jack had a "Tip" portion which was of positive potential and a "Ring" portion for the negative side of the line. The terms Tip and Ring are still used to identify the two conductors of a telephone line.

In the later 1880s, a number of efforts were made to automate the switching of telephone calls. The first truly successful system was that devised by Almon B. Strowger, an undertaker. How an undertaker came to design the world's longest lasting and most pervasive telephone switching system is a classic story. Almon Strowger was one of two undertakers in a small town in the midwestern United States, and the other undertaker's wife was the town telephone operator. When town residents suffered a death in the family, they would often ask the operator for "an undertaker," and would of course be connected to the operator's husband. Strowger saw that his prospects for business were small unless he could eliminate the operator, so he devised a simple rotary switch mechanism using a celluloid shirt collar and some common pins as a sample. He subsequently sold his idea to the Automatic Electric Company which refined and developed his idea into the famous two motion mechanical switch that is still used in more than 25 percent of the telephone switching systems in the United States and in a greater percentage of systems in various other countries. The Strowger system is called "step-by-step" by the Bell System Companies.

Subsequent switching systems have gradually centralized the control logic, moving it from each switch, where it was in the Strowger system, to a progressively smaller number of more sophisticated controllers, such as the two computer processors that run the Bell System #1 ESS. There are a number of texts, several of which are listed at the end of this chapter, that describe the Strowger and subsequent systems in great detail.

The aspects of telephone switching systems that are of primary interest to the data communications system designer are call set-up time, traffic capacity, circuit characteristics, noise, and multi-line hunt groups.

As was indicated in the brief outline of common battery manual telephone systems, a telephone which is "on-hook" is an "open circuit" and one which is "off-hook" appears as a resistance (about 50 ohms) between the Tip and Ring conductors of the telephone line. In electromechanical systems, the presence of that resistance causes current flow which is detected by a "line relay." In #1 ESS, the current flow saturates a magnetic "ferrod" which is periodically scanned by the central processor. Once the "off-hook" condition has been detected, the switching system connects the line to apparatus suitable for recording the dialed digits. When the digit recording apparatus has been connected to the subscriber's line, "dial tone" is returned to the subscriber to indicate that he may proceed to dial. It is general North American telephone practice to return dial tone within three seconds on 90 percent of all subscriber call attempts.

The selection of the number to be called is performed either by interrupting the current through the subscriber telephone in a precisely timed way (dial pulsing) or by means of tone generators within the subscriber telephone set.

The pulsing rate for telephone dials must be uniform and within the range of 8 to 11 pulses per second (10 pulses per second nominal). Each pulse consists of an interval of "break" followed by an interval of "make." The break portion must be 58 to 64 percent of the pulse interval. The pulses that represent a dialed digit are separated from the pulses that represent the next dialed digit by a period known as the "interdigital interval." The interdigital interval must be at least 600 milliseconds long in order for the switching equipment to determine where one digit (string of pulses) ends and the next digit (string of pulses) begins.

Using the above figures, an average digit of five pulses, at a 10 pulse per second rate, will be completed in 500 milliseconds (1/2 second) plus the 600 millisecond interdigital time—roughly 1.1 seconds per digit dialed.

Tone signaling from subscriber sets, also referred to as dual tone multi-frequency (DTMF) signaling, consists of two sinusoidal signals. One signal is from a high group of three frequencies and one from a low group of four frequencies; together they represent one of the 12 characters shown in Table 8-1.

The frequencies are required to be within 1.5 percent of their nominal values and 1.2 percent accuracy is preferred. The minimum duration of a two-frequency signal is 50 milliseconds and the minimum interdigital time is 45 milliseconds. The mathematics does not quite work out, but the mimimum cycle time is one digit per 100 milliseconds. Note that this is one eleventh of the time necessary to dial pulse the same information if the digit "5" is dialed.

Bell System Technical Reference PUB 47001, "Electrical Characteristics of Bell System Network Facilities at the Interface with Voiceband Ancillary and Data Equipment," can be purchased from:

Publishers' Data Center, Inc.
P.O. Box C738
Pratt Street Station
Brooklyn, New York 11205

Correspondence concerning Bell System Technical References should be directed to:

District Manager—Information Release Services
Bell System Purchased Products
American Telephone and Telegraph Company
5 Wood Hollow Road—Room 2M28
Parsippany, New Jersey 07054

The Bell System reference was used to obtain the dial pulse and DTMF signaling information listed above and contains additional specifications not only for those types of signals but also for other aspects of telephone line signals.

Table 8-1. Touch Tone ® Frequency Assignment

		1209	1336	1477
Nominal	697	1	2	3
Low Group	770	4	5	6
Frequencies	852	7	8	9
(Hz)	941	*	0	#

® Registered service mark of American Telephone and Telegraph Company.

So far we have discussed the delay in receiving dial tone and the time required to dial digits by dial pulsing or tone signaling. The remaining topic is the amount of time necessary to complete the call. In the Bell System 1969–1970 Switched Telecommunications Network Survey, measurements were taken of the time which elapsed between dialing the last digit of the telephone number and the receipt of a test tone supplied by automatic answering equipment at that number. For connections over short distances (around 200 miles or less), call completion took about 11 seconds. For moderate distances (about 200 to 700 miles), call completion took about 15 seconds, and for long distances (about 800 to 3000 miles), call completion took about 14 seconds.

The call completion timings performed in the aforementioned survey showed considerable variation. One of the major factors contributing to variation was the ringing cycle, which is typically two seconds on, four seconds off. In electromechanical switching systems, when a call is completed to a number that is not busy, the number is first made busy to protect against seizure by another arriving call. The ringing signal from one of several common ringing buses is then applied to the line. The ringing signal is split onto several different distribution buses within the telephone switching equipment, some of which are "ringing" while the others are "silent" and vice versa. This is so that the machines which generate the ringing signal will have their load spread out in time, rather than being overloaded for two seconds and loafing for the next four seconds. Which bus supplies the ringing to a particular telephone is determined by where in the equipment that line is located, and it makes no difference whether the ringing bus is ringing or silent at the time the connection is made. Thus it is quite possible that the ringing signal may not begin for as many as four seconds after the connection is made to the line. In some electronic switching systems, notably #1 ESS, the equipment which connects the ringing signal to the line has its choice of which ringing bus to use, and can be directed to use one which will cause ringing to begin immediately. As this type of switching system becomes more prevalent, connection times and the variations therein will be reduced. The effect will be greatest on short distance calls where routing effects make less of a contribution to connection time variations and where the ringing cycle is a large part of the connection time.

A question may arise as to why the delay for medium length connections exceeds that for longer distances. This is probably due to the fact that connections over medium distances frequently involve the same number of intermediate switching points and the same amount of signaling as do longer connections. Some of the intermediate switching points used for medium distance calls involve older switching machines which are slower in call completion and use slower signaling systems.

While the statistics quoted are for the Bell System in the United States, similar results with slightly longer connection times may be expected for connections in Europe. Specifically, CCITT Recommendation V.25 concerning automatic dialing units specifies that the timers that determine whether or not a call has probably failed should be variable from 10 seconds to 40 seconds. This implies that most calls are completed in less than 40 seconds.

In the future, a new common channel interoffice signaling (CCIS) system will transfer signaling information between processors that control electronic switching systems, permitting connection times in the two to three second range.

The second aspect of telephone switching systems of interest to data communication system designers is traffic capacity. While the high degree of success usually had in completing calls may lead one to believe that there is ample telephone equipment to handle all possible traffic, this is not the case. On the contrary, typical telephone systems will only accommodate the origination of calls by about 10 percent of the subscribers. If that 10 percent calls another 10 percent, 20 percent of the subscribers could be on the telephone simultaneously. In business telephone systems, especially in businesses where the telephone is used a lot, capacity is usually provided for 15 or 20 percent of the subscribers to originate calls. The arrangement of telephone equipment to serve what appears to be such a small percentage is based on economics. If the present arrangements only deny service on one or two percent of the call attempts during the busiest hour of the day, will the subscribers be willing to pay twice as much to reduce that denial to one-half percent or some similar small figure? In general, the answer is that they will not.

These economic considerations are, to a large degree, based on today's technology, where additional capacity takes up additional equipment and floor space. In time division multiplex switching systems, presently limited to relatively small line sizes, conversations are sampled and these samples are placed in "time slots" on a common electrical bus. The equipment associated with the person to whom you are talking is then synchronized so as to sample the signal on the bus at the appropriate time. In such a system, the cost of additional call handling capacity is the cost of bandwidth on the common bus. This cost does not rise as steeply as the cost of equipment in present day "space division" switching systems where each call takes up physical space. Thus in future communications systems call carrying capacity will probably be less of a design problem.

A call handling capacity of 10 percent of the subscribers originating calls was mentioned above. It must be noted that in common control systems, such as the non-Strowger electromechanical systems and most electronic systems, the number of subscribers that can be simultaneously dialing is substantially less than the number who can be simultaneously carrying on conversations on calls which they placed. This latter number is the 10 percent cited above. The number of simultaneous "dialers" that can be accommodated varies from system to system, but a figure of 60 in a 10,000 subscriber system would not be uncommon. It is therefore important that computer systems employing automatic dialers not use programs which permit more than a dozen or so to be active at once, since that computer system might otherwise have a noticeable effect upon local telephone service.

In similar fashion, large quantities of terminating traffic may be a problem. If a time-sharing service with 32 incoming lines is located in a town served with a Strowger system, there can be several problems. First, Strowger systems are, in general, unable to automatically search groups of lines ("hunt groups") of more than 10 lines, at least not without some very special switches. Second, there are typically 10 connector switches (the final switch in a call placed in Strowger) per 100 subscriber lines, so only 10 of those 32 lines will be able to receive calls unless this problem is recognized. Because of problems like these, it is important to talk with the local telephone company people as soon as possible when planning the installation of a computer system. The availability of suitable telephone service should be as carefully considered as are heat, light, floor space, and rental rates. Too often people assume that, because the telephone company has no trouble putting a telephone in a home, putting 32 lines in a time-sharing computer center should not be substantially more difficult. This is decidedly not the case.

While on the subject of hunt groups, it is important to note that the number of lines desired immediately, the number of lines required two years hence, and the number of lines required five years hence be discussed with the local telephone company. As mentioned above, Strowger systems are unable to hunt over more than 10 lines unless special equipment is added ("trunk and level hunting connectors"). Even then the initial choice of directory number is important; while 234-5600 is an attractive number to advertise, Strowger switches cannot commence hunting from numbers that end in 0. A far better number would be 234-5611. In crossbar switching systems, the 234-5600 number could be used as the beginning of a hunt group. Supplementary relays are required for continuing the hunt beyond groups of 10 numbers, but these are relatively trivial additions. Only hunt groups which traverse 1000-group boundaries, such as 234-5990 to 234-6100, pose a problem, as a special device called an "allotter" must be used. In electronic switching systems much greater hunting flexibility is possible, including the ability to search lines in non-sequential order, etc. These are the various restrictions that will influence the telephone company in choosing the serving switching system (if such a choice exists) and in choosing the listed number for the computer center.

Noise is another characteristic of switching systems that should be considered. There are many possible sources of noise in telephone systems. Some of the noise sources, such as crosstalk between conductors in cables, will exist both in private lines and in switched network connections. Other sources of noise, usually impulse type noise, are primarily introduced by the switching systems. Studies of such noise have revealed that the bursts of noise occur at a rate of about 10 times per second, a rate suspiciously close to the rate of dial pulses. In Strowger systems sliding wipers pass over contacts carrying conversations, but this is a relatively minor contribution, since these wipers are not electrically connected at the time the wiping action occurs. The real demon is the vibration of the frames upon which the switches are mounted. Once the telephone call is in progress, a dozen wiper-to-contact connections may be involved, even on a local call. As other calls are placed on switches adjacent to any of these connections, the switch that is being mechanically stepped by the calling person's dial pulses shakes, vibrating the entire mounting frame slightly. This in turn slightly shakes the other switches on that frame, causing the wiper-to-contact connections to move slightly. Since the contacts are not ultra-clean, noise is introduced.

While crossbar systems also use contacts that are exposed to dust, the mechanical motions involved in crossbar switching are much less violent and the mounting frames do not shake appreciably. Hence the noise introduced by the setting up of other calls is much less. In #1 ESS, and other computer controlled reed-switching systems (TXE-4, etc.), the speech path is switched by contacts that are sealed in airtight glass capsules where dirt and dust cannot enter. In addition, the mechanical motions involved are negligible and mechanical vibration is totally absent. Newer systems, such as #5 ESS, use TDM (Time Division Multiplex) switching in which the speech path switching is entirely electronic.

One other source of noise in switching systems is the battery supply used to power the telephone transmitters in typical voice conversations. Although there is no need for telephone instrument transmitters in most data communications, battery is still needed to establish "loop current" to the calling and called parties so that off-hook and on-hook conditions can be detected. The battery in the telephone company central office is also used to power the switching equipment, and various electrical noises from the switching equipment can be present on the battery. In many cases, telephone companies have added extra filtering to the battery supply feeding portions of the switching equipment that serve many data communication customers. Also, the battery in electronic switching systems is electrically quieter than the battery in electromechanical systems—yet another reason the electronic switching systems are preferred for data communications.

Finally, switched telephone service presents circuit characteristics to the data communication system designer which are somewhat different from those of private line service. The nationwide telephone network in the United States is organized in a hierarchy shown in Figure 8-1.

As indicated in Figure 8-1, there are five classes of telephone switching offices, one of which includes a sub-class (4X). There are 12 Class 1 or Regional Center offices in the US/Canada area. There are approximately 18,000 Class 5 or End Offices, the type to which subscriber telephones are connected. A local call from a home to the butcher shop is typically within the same office—i.e., 234-5678 to 234-7654. A call to a person in another town is handled differently. If the two towns are close enough together, or if there are a lot of calls between the two towns, there might be direct circuits from one town to the other. Such a group of circuits is called a "high usage" group. If these circuits are busy or simply do not exist, the call is "route ad-

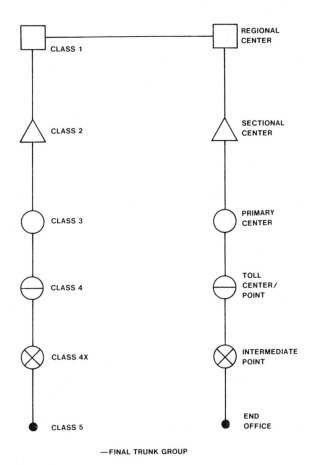

Figure 8-1. Switching System Classification and Interconnection

vanced" to the Class 4 office associated with the Class 5 office for which the call is destined.

Figure 8-2 shows a typical routing pattern within the US/Canada telephone network, with high usage groups shown as heavy dashed lines. The final choice of circuits between End Office A and End Office P involves nine links, shown as solid lines. (Two more links are possible in cases where Class 4X offices, which are optional offices eliminated from the diagram for simplicity, are involved.) Additional information about switched telephone network routing may be obtained from an AT&T book, "Notes on the Network–1980", available from:

> Western Electric
> Commercial Sales
> Guilford Center
> P.O. Box 20046
> Greensboro, North Carolina 27420

Correspondence in advance is recommended to confirm ordering arrangements and price.

In addition to a US/Canada switching plan, there is also a transmission plan. The transmission plan is designed to achieve a high degree of user satisfaction by precisely controlling loss, noise, and echo.

While noise and echo are evil, loss is not always undesirable. In fact, there is a relationship between loss and echo that is of interest to the data communications system designer. Connections between four-wire and two-wire transmission facilities (see Chapter 4) and other connections between various transmission media often produce echoes. Studies have shown that these echoes are not annoying to telephone users unless they are loud or occur after a substantial delay. To control the adverse effects of echoes, telephone companies intentionally introduce loss into telephone connections. Two plans are used for doing this. One is called the "Via Net Loss" plan, abbreviated VNL, and is used for analog circuits. The other plan is called the "Switched Digital Network" plan, abbreviated SDN, and is used for digital circuits. The VNL plan allocates various amounts of loss to various links in the switching hierarchy shown in Figure 8-1, while the SDN plan uses a fixed amount of loss inserted at the digital to analog conversion process. Because the delays and noise associated with digital switching are much less than those associated with analog systems, the use of a compromise value is acceptable. As the switched telephone network becomes more and more digital, the use of the SDN plan will predominate. Further details on both the VNL and SDN system are contained in "Notes on the Network."

On very long connections (over 1850 miles), echoes returning after a long delay are a problem. To solve this problem, echo suppressors are installed. Echo suppressors are devices that detect which party is talking louder and

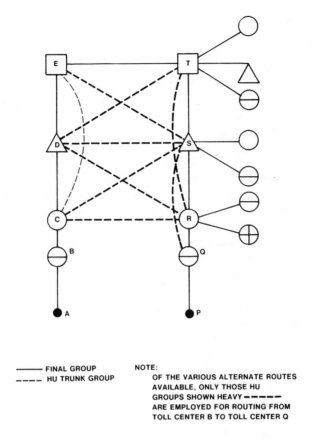

——— FINAL GROUP
———— HU TRUNK GROUP

NOTE:
OF THE VARIOUS ALTERNATE ROUTES
AVAILABLE, ONLY THOSE HU
GROUPS SHOWN HEAVY ———
ARE EMPLOYED FOR ROUTING FROM
TOLL CENTER B TO TOLL CENTER Q

Figure 8-2. Typical Routing Pattern

allow transmission only from the speaker to the other party; thus the echoes, which are traveling in the opposite direction, are not heard. The effect of echo suppressors is not usually noticeable unless an earth satellite is in the connection, or a volume level or echo suppressor sensitivity problem causes noise on one side of the communication channel. In the former case the delays involved make the echo suppressor action noticeable; in the latter, the noise triggers the echo suppressor, cutting up the conversation of the distant party. For full-duplex data transmission, the echo suppressors must be disabled. While this keeps them from functioning, filters within the modems keep the echoes from interfering with the transmission. To disable the echo suppressors a single frequency tone with a level 0 to 5 db below the maximum specified data signal level within the band 2010–2240 Hz, is applied for at least 400 milliseconds. No other tone or signal should be applied during this period. The echo suppressor remains disabled if the data signal (or other energy of similar magnitude) is applied within 100 milliseconds after the disabling tone is removed from the line. Any interruptions in the subsequent signal over 100 milliseconds in duration will permit the echo suppressor to again become enabled. The 2225 Hertz tone applied to the line by a typical low speed asynchronous modem answering a call meets the specifications for echo suppressor disabling.

Returning to the figures concerning the hierarchical nature of the telephone system, it should be noted that subsequent calls may take different routes, due to changing traffic conditions. Also, American Telephone and Telegraph, in conjunction with its operating companies, uses a technique called "networking management" to maximize utilization of its facilities. Since when it is nine a.m. in New York City and Miami it is only six a.m. in San Francisco, additional call capacity between New York and Miami at that hour of the day may be obtained by routing calls to San Francisco and back. The routes used have low transmission loss since they are at the top of the hierarchy shown in Figure 8-2. Furthermore, they are available for use because no one is calling between San Francisco and any East Coast points at that time. During general periods of high traffic this type of routing is not normally done; while a few people would be happy to get their calls through, the facilities used to get those calls through could have been used to place several shorter distance calls.

Routing is important to the data communication system designer since the circuit delay between two simultaneously placed calls, or between two calls placed at different times of day, may vary. In the first case, the variation is due to changed routing caused by momentary traffic fluctuations; in the second it is due to network management.

Now that the data transmission facility has been discussed, it is time to deal with the modems and modem controls that work with it.

References

1. Hobbs, Marvin, *Modern Communications Switching Systems*, Tab Books, Blue Ridge Summit, Pennsylvania (1974).
2. Rubin, Murray, and Haller, C.E., *Communications Switching Systems*, Krieger Publishing, Huntington, New York (1974).
3. Syski, Robert, *Introduction to Congestion Theory in Telephone Switching Systems*, Oliver & Boyd, London (1960).
4. Talley, David, *Basic Telephone Switching Systems*, Hayden Books, Rochelle Park, New Jersey (1979).
5. Talley, David, *Basic Electronic Switching for Telephone Systems*, Hayden Books, Rochelle Park, New Jersey (1975).

9

Modem Control
For Switched Network Use

The modem interface leads that were defined in Chapter 6 are shown again in Table 9-1.

Briefly reviewed, Circuit 102 provides a ground connection for electrical reference. The data which the computer wishes the modem to transmit over the communications channel is applied to the Transmitted Data lead. The data being received over the communications channel is delivered by the modem to the computer over the Received Data lead. The Request to Send lead is provided to turn the modem transmitter on and off for half-duplex applications. The readiness of the modem to accept data for transmitting over the communications channel is reflected by the Clear to Send lead. The Data Set Ready lead indicates that the modem is powered and not in voice or test mode. Finally, reception of signals from the distant modem is indicated by the Data Channel Received Line Signal Detector (Carrier Detect). With

**Table 9-1. Interface Leads for Low-Speed Asynchronous
Full-Duplex Private Line Modem**

Designation		
EIA	CCITT	Name
AA		Protective Ground
AB	102	Signal Ground
BA	103	Transmitted Data
BB	104	Received Data
CA	105	Request to Send
CB	106	Clear to Send
CC	107	Data Set Ready
CF	109	Data Channel Received Line Signal Detector

the exception of this last named signal, each of the signal names is quite simple and very descriptive of the function of that lead. Even the phrase "Received Line Signal Detector" is self-explanatory; it basically means: "I hear something that sounds like a modem talking to me."

While the above signals are sufficient to permit the control of asynchronous modems on private lines, the use of modems on the switched telephone network requires some additional leads, notably Data Terminal Ready and Ring Indicator. The definitions for these leads are given below.

EIA RS-232-C
Definitions

CCITT V.24
Definitions

Circuit CD—Data Terminal Ready (CCITT 108/2)
Direction: TO data communication equipment

Signals on this circuit are used to control switching of the data communication equipment to the communication channel. The ON condition prepares the data communication equipment to be connected to the communication channel and maintains the connection established by external means (e.g., manual call origination, manual answering, or automatic call origination).

When the station is equipped for automatic answering of received calls and is in the automatic answering mode, connection to the line occurs only in response to a combination of a ringing signal and the ON condition of Circuit CD (Data Terminal Ready): however, the data terminal equipment is normally permitted to present the ON condition on Circuit CD whenever it is ready to transmit or receive data, except as indicated below.

The OFF condition causes the data communication equipment to be removed from the communication channel following the completion of any "in process" transmission.* See Circuit BA (Transmitted Data). The OFF condition shall not disable the operation of Circuit CE (Ring Indicator).

Circuit 108/2—Data Terminal Ready
Direction: To DCE

Signals on this circuit control switching of the signal-conversion or similar equipment to or from the line.

The ON condition, indicating that the DTE is ready to operate, prepares the DCE to connect the signal-conversion or similar equipment to the line and maintains this connection after it has been established by supplementary means.

The DTE is permitted to present the ON condition on Circuit 108/2 whenever it is ready to transmit or receive data.

The OFF condition causes the DCE to remove the signal-conversion or similar equipment from the line, when the transmission to line of all data previously transferred on Circuit 103 and/or Circuit 118 has been completed.

---

*An important note to this definition is that the relationship of the OFF condition of Data Terminal Ready to the completion of transmitted data transfer is not an automatic function of the modem. The modem is merely a level conversion device and does not interpret the meaning of the bit stream passing through. Thus the modem does not know when transmission is over. The program which has control of the Data Terminal Ready lead must decide when to bring it to the OFF state. The use of double-buffered transmitters such as those found in the UART requires that two character times elapse between the time the UART transmitter is loaded with the final character and the time that the final character has been shifted out onto the line. Some modems require that even more additional time be allowed before the modem control program brings Data Terminal Ready to the OFF state.

EIA RS-232-C Definitions	CCITT V.24 Definitions
In switched network applications, when circuit CD is turned OFF, it shall not be turned ON again until Circuit CC (Data Set Ready) is turned OFF by the data communication equipment.	
Circuit CE—Ring Indicator (CCITT 125—Calling Indicator) Direction: FROM data communication equipment	*Circuit 125*—Calling Indicator Direction: From DCE
The ON condition of this circuit indicates that a ringing signal is being received on the communication channel.	Signals on this circuit indicate whether a calling signal is being received by the DCE. The ON condition indicates that a calling signal is being received.
The ON condition shall appear approximately coincident with the ON segment of the ringing cycle (during rings) on the communication channel. The OFF condition shall be maintained during the OFF segment of the ringing cycle (between "rings") and at all other times when ringing is not being received. The operation of this circuit shall not be disabled by the OFF condition on Circuit CD (Data Terminal Ready).	The OFF condition indicates that no calling signal is being received, and this condition may also appear during interruptions of a pulse-modulated calling signal.

The interaction of all of these leads can best be appreciated by comparison to the receipt of a typical telephone call at home. When the telephone rings (Circuit CE (125)—Ring Indicator), you hear the ring. If you wish to answer the telephone, you pick up the handset so as to go into the "off-hook" state, a step similar to asserting Circuit CD (108/2)—Data Terminal Ready. You say "hello" and await a response, a process similar to monitoring Circuit CF (109)—Data Channel Received Line Signal Detector/Carrier Detect. If you do not hear anything, you hang up (negate Data Terminal Ready). If you do hear someone, you converse and hang up later when you are done. An automatically answered call from one low speed full-duplex asynchronous modem (Bell System 103) to another functions exactly this way.

These three leads, Ring Indicator, Data Terminal Ready, and Data Channel Received Line Signal Detect, are the absolute minimum required for switched network operation of modems. In some countries Data Set Ready is also required.

As indicated above, Data Terminal Ready may be left on, allowing incoming calls to be answered. This suggests the possibility of leaving Data Terminal Ready on at all times. While this would work for answering the call, a problem arises when the call is to be terminated. Some types of switching equipment provide a line polarity reversal to the called party when the calling party hangs up at the end of a call. This causes the called modem to disconnect from the line. This cannot be relied upon, however, so conservative design procedure and European post and telegraph authority regulations call for program control of the Data Terminal Ready lead so that it may be negated at the end of the call. Furthermore, some modems use a circuit which works differently from Data Terminal Ready. This circuit is CCITT Circuit 108/1, Connect Data Set to Line.

EIA RS-232-C Definitions	CCITT V.24 Definitions
No EIA equivalent to this circuit.	*Circuit 108/1*—Connect Data Set to Line Direction: To DCE
	Signals on this circuit control switching of the signal-conversion equipment to and from the line. The ON condition causes the data communication equipment to connect the signal-conversion or similar equipment to the line. The OFF condition causes the data communication equipment to remove the signal-conversion or similar equipment from the line, when the transmission to the line of all data previously transferred on Circuit 103 and/or Circuit 118 has been completed. (This interlock of the data transmitted on Circuit 103 is a program function, not a modem function.)

This lead is essentially the same as the Data Terminal Ready lead (108/2) previously described, except that no interlocking with the Ring/Calling Indicator circuit is involved. Thus, when this type of circuit is used, assertion of the lead in advance of call reception is not permitted. This would be equivalent to a person taking his or her phone off-hook and leaving it that way. Instead, the program which controls the computer/modem interface must wait to receive a Calling Indicator signal and then may assert Connect Data Set to Line. North American practice is to use the Data Terminal Ready lead (Circuit 108/2), while European practice varies.

In summary, computer interface hardware for modem control for switched network use must allow the program to control the state of the Data Terminal Ready lead. Computer software may choose to assert Data Terminal Ready and wait for Ring Indicator, or it may wait for Ring Indicator and then assert Data Terminal Ready. The latter approach is more universal, as it also works in those cases where Connect Data Set to Line is used instead of Data Terminal Ready.

The Ring/Calling Indicator lead is important for three reasons. First, it is necessary in the case where Circuit 108/1—Connect Data Set to Line—is used, in order that the program know when to assert 108/1. Second, if either Data Terminal Ready or Connect Data Set to Line is used, Ring/Calling Indicator is needed to define when to start looking for Received Line Signal Detect to differentiate between a voice call and a data call. Third, Ring/Calling Indicator is needed to safeguard user files in time-sharing systems by enabling the computer system software to determine the difference between a temporary interruption in transmission and a new call.

The first of the above reasons for Ring/Calling Indicator has already been explored in detail. The second requires some elaboration, which will explain in the process one of the uses for Data Channel Received Signal Detector in switched network modems. One of the problems which faces a data communication system attached to the switched network is that of misdirected voice telephone calls. Assume that a person making an ordinary voice telephone call accidently reaches a modem. Ring/Calling Indicator is asserted to the modem interface and the computer program directs the assertion of Data Terminal Ready from the interface to the modem. The modem answers the call. At this time, appropriately written computer software starts a software timer to check for the assertion of carrier from the calling modem. Since in this case the caller is a person, not a modem, there will be no carrier forthcoming. No Data Channel Received Line Signal Detector assertion will occur and the software timer will expire. Another method is for the program to send a "who are you" message and await a reply. In either case, the important feature of the Ring/Calling Indicator lead is to alert the computer program that it should enter this routine.

The third reason for the use of the Ring/Calling Indicator is related to the possibility of momentary losses of carrier during data transmission. When the carrier returns after such a loss, a question could arise as to whether the caller is still the same one that was there before the carrier outage. If it is, the system program may allow the caller to resume work on the files which he or she was manipulating. If the identity of the caller has changed, this is plainly not permissible. The Ring/Calling Indicator solves this dilemma by announcing new calls. This description of the function of Ring/Calling Indicator may seem at odds with previous statements that manipulation of the Data Terminal Ready lead is required in order to terminate an existing call. Strictly speaking it is, but the objective here is to mention what could happen; with some types of switching systems it is possible for a call to disappear momentarily. The most conservative programming practice would be to automatically close out a user's job and drop Data Terminal Ready on any line suffering a carrier loss (negation of Data Channel Received Line Signal Detect) for more than 500 milliseconds. Certainly the arrival of a new call (assertion of Ring/Calling Indicator) on a line which the software believes already has a job in progress is a sure sign that that job should be terminated.

The preceding discussions have not mentioned the use of Circuit CC (107), Data Set Ready. This lead is used to indicate that the modem is in data mode (rather than in test mode) and is connected to the communications channel. Assertion of this lead does not necessarily mean that a connection has been completely established, i.e. that handshaking with a distant modem has taken place. In applications where Data Terminal Ready is left asserted in anticipation of call arrival, a program could monitor Data Set Ready instead of monitoring Ring/Calling Indicator. This circuit is used in Europe and is specified in CCITT Recommendation V.21: "200 Baud Modem Standardized for Use in the General Switched Telephone Network." It is used there both to announce the commencement of call billing and to confirm that the negation of Connect Data Set to Line has indeed been successful in disconnecting the modem from the line.

The interface leads required for switched network operation of a low speed (200 or 300 baud) modem on the switched network are summarized in Table 9-2.

When it becomes desirable to transmit and receive data at speeds over 300 baud on the switched network, the task of the data communication system designer becomes more complex. One solution is to use 1200 baud full-duplex switched network modems that utilize a high frequency channel and a low frequency channel as do low speed asynchronous modems, but substitute complex modulation schemes for the simple frequency shift keying system described in Chapters 4 and 10. These have the benefit of using the same interface just described for low speed asynchronous use, minimizing or eliminating the need for interface or programming changes. Vadic, UDS, Bell System, and several other companies offer such modems.

Table 9-2. Interface Leads for Low-Speed Asynchronous Full-Duplex Switched Network Modem

Designation		
EIA	CCITT	Name
AA		Protective Ground
AB	102	Signal Ground
BA	103	Transmitted Data
BB	104	Received Data
[CA]	[105]*	
CB	106	Clear to Send†
CC	107	Data Set Ready‡
CD	108/1	Connect Data Set to Line, or
	108/2	Data Terminal Ready
CF	109	Data Channel Received Line Signal Detector †
CE	125	Ring/Calling Indicator

*Request to Send is not used in full-duplex switched network modems such as the 200 baud or 300 baud types discussed here.

†In low speed asynchronous modem interfaces, provision of either Clear to Send or Data Channel Received Line Signal Detect is sufficient unless PTT regulations dictate otherwise.

‡For a minimum-feature modem interface, Data Set Ready is not necessary unless PTT regulations indicate otherwise.

For those who do not wish to use the 1200 baud full-duplex modems or who cannot because of availability or PTT regulations, speeds above 300 baud will require the use of half-duplex operation. Modems which operate at 600 baud half-duplex and/or 1200 baud half-duplex are common and use simple frequency shift keying transmission schemes similar to those previously described. However, they use the full bandwidth available in the switched telephone connection, rather than separating it into two chunks by means of filters. Filters are still used on the transmitters, but these are to eliminate the unwanted byproducts of the modulation process.

Speeds of 600 and 1200 baud were used relatively early in data communications with the advent of the high speed paper tape sender. Companies would batch together data or other messages and transmit to other plants, saving money on the telephone call cost by means of the increased line transmission speed. One of the features of high speed paper tape transmission systems was error correction. The characters transmitted were grouped in blocks of 128 characters and each block was followed by a block check character which was computed from the ones and zeros of the preceding characters. This was called an LRC block check character; the LRC method of block checking is described in greater detail in Chapter 13. The receiving station would read the data received over the communication line and perform the same calculation on the characters as was being done simultaneously at the transmitting station. When the transmitting station sent the block check, the receiving station would check that against the result which it had calculated. If the block check did not agree, it would ask for retransmission. All of the aforementioned calculating and checking was done in the "data terminal equipment," not in the modem ("data communication equipment"). The modem became involved with the request for retransmission.

One way to request retransmission is to have the transmitting station relinquish control over the communications channel at the end of each message, and then have the receiving station seize the channel and send back a retransmission request. This is rather elaborate and time consuming.

A better method is to use a low speed channel from the receiving station to the transmitting station to indicate that data blocks are being received satisfactorily. The speed requirements of this channel can be determined as follows. At a 1200 bit per second rate, assuming 10 bits per character, 120 characters per second are being sent. Hence a block of 128 characters is completed only once every second and the OK/not-OK signal needs to be sent only once every second.

The Bell System 202 modems perform this function by providing a single frequency tone (387 Hertz) which can be keyed on and off by the receiving station to indicate whether or not the block check is acceptable. Since this information is being supplied in a direction that is backward to the main data channel, this signaling facility is called the "reverse channel," "backward channel," or "supervisory channel."

An early Bell System 202-series modem, the 202C, controlled the supervisory channel via Circuit SA, Supervisory Transmitted Data, on pin 11, and reported the status of the received supervisory signal via Circuit SB, Supervisory Received Data, on pin 12. This utilization of signal names and pins conflicted with the EIA RS-232-C definition, which is as follows.

Circuit SBA—Secondary Transmitted Data (CCITT 118)—Lead 14
Direction: To data communication equipment

This circuit is equivalent to Circuit BA (Transmitted Data) except that it is used to transmit data via the secondary channel. Signals on this circuit are generated by the data terminal equipment and are connected to the local secondary channel transmitting signal converter for transmission of data to remote terminal equipment. The data terminal equipment shall hold Circuit SBA (Secondary Transmitted Data) in marking condition during intervals between characters or words and at all times when no data are being transmitted. In all systems, the data terminal equipment shall not transmit on the secondary channel unless an ON condition is present on all of the following four circuits, where implemented:

1. Circuit SCA–Secondary Request to Send
2. Circuit SCB–Secondary Clear to Send
3. Circuit CC–Data Set Ready
4. Circuit CD–Data Terminal Ready

All data signals that are transmitted across the interface on interchange Circuit SBA during the time when the above conditions are satisfied shall be transmitted to the communication channel. When the secondary channel is usable only for circuit assurance or to interrupt the flow of data in the primary channel (less than 10 baud capability), Circuit SBA (Secondary Transmitted Data) is normally not provided, and the channel carrier is turned ON or OFF by means of Circuit SCA (Secondary Request to Send)—Lead 19. Carrier OFF is interpreted as an "interrupt" condition.

NOTE
Despite this distinction, this book will refer to the "Secondary Transmitted Data" lead, regardless of speed. The only exception will be in Appendix B, Modem Options, where the 202S and 202T modems are discussed.

Circuit SBB—Secondary Received Data (CCITT 119)—Lead 16
Direction: From data communication equipment

This circuit is equivalent to Circuit BB (Received Data) except that it is used to receive data on the secondary channel. When the secondary channel is usable only for circuit assurance or to interrupt the flow of data in the primary channel, interchange Circuit SCF (Secondary Received Line Signal Detector)—Lead 12 is usually provided in place of Circuit SBB. In this case, the ON condition shall indicate circuit assurance or a non-interrupt condition. The OFF condition shall indicate circuit failure (no assurance) or the interrupt condition.

NOTE
Despite this distinction, this book will refer to "Secondary Received Data" regardless of speed. The only exception will be in Appendix B, Modem Options, where the 202S and 202T are discussed.

CCITT Recommendation V.24 defines these circuits as follows.

Circuit 118—Transmitted Backward Channel Data
Direction: To data communication equipment

This circuit is equivalent to Circuit 103 (Transmitted Data) except that it is used to transmit data via the backward channel.

Circuit 119—Received Backward Channel Data
Direction: From data communication equipment

This circuit is equivalent to Circuit 104 (Received Data) except that it is used for data received on the backward channel.

The newest versions of 202, the Bell System 202S and 202T, control the supervisory channel via Secondary Request to Send (SCA) on pins 11 and 19, while reporting the status of the received supervisory signal via Secondary Received Line Signal Detector (SCF) on pin 12. Thus these modems follow the EIA specification, while retaining compatibility with interfaces designed for the 202C by providing Secondary Request to Send on both pins 11 and 19.

The important concepts of the reverse channel are summarized in Figure 9-1.

Note that a computer interface must have four leads for data transfer to handle such a modem: Transmitted Data, Received Data, Secondary Transmitted Data, and Secondary Received Data. In the case of the Bell System 202C, D, E, S, T, or similar modem utilizing a reverse/backward channel of only five baud capability, the reverse channel data may be transmitted and received by simple program toggling of a bit for transmission and program sampling of a bit for reception. The UART type of receiver/transmitter such as that described in Chapter 2 is not required. However, the backward channel is not always only five baud.

CCITT Recommendation V.23 describes a 600/1200 baud modem for switched network use that utilizes a 75 baud backward channel. A backward channel of that capability permits use of the backward channel not only for circuit assurance (i.e., indication that the receiving station is still there) and requests for retransmission such as previously described, but also for actual keyboard input. This is especially so if some buffering is provided to smooth out the rapidity with which a typist can type certain tri-grams such as t-h-e. There are two disadvantages to such a use. First, a full 75 baud signaling rate requires using a UART on the Backward Channel Transmit and Backward Channel Receive leads rather than depending upon program bit sampling. If

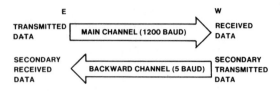

Figure 9-1a. East-to-West Transmission

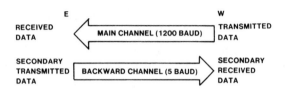

Figure 9-1b. West-to-East Transmission

the main channel is always in the same direction (i.e., computer to terminal), a single "split speed" UART could be used in each interface to implement Figure 9-1a *or* Figure 9-1b. However, if the direction of the main channel will be changing, two UARTs are required because there would be four interface leads needed to implement both Figure 9-1a *and* Figure 9-1b. Second, a problem with all half-duplex systems including this type is that the data cannot be looped around from the transmitter to the receiver of the same modem to check the circuitry—i.e., one cannot create the configuration shown in Figure 9-2.

Loopback 1 permits one to ascertain that the data is leaving the data terminal equipment correctly. Loopback 1A checks that the data is arriving at the data circuit-terminating equipment (modem) correctly. Loopback 2 permits one to test that the data is being received and demodulated correctly by the distant modem. These tests and various intermediate loopbacks, which may be possible depending upon the specific hardware used, permit the easy location of faults. These loopbacks are not possible (except at a 75 baud speed) in the modem just described, since the main channel will accom-

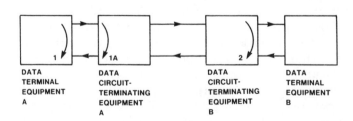

Figure 9-2. Maintenance Loopbacks

modate 1200 baud in only one direction at a time. For a detailed treatment of maintenance loopbacks, including an expanded version of Figure 9-2, refer to CCITT Recommendation V.54.

Before the advent of 1200 baud full-duplex modems for switched telephone network use, efforts were made to build modems with a 1200 baud main channel and a 150 baud backward channel. While these worked quite well technically, the need to have a UART with "split speed" in each interface (one baud rate for the main channel receive/transmit and one baud rate for the backward channel receive/transmit), the problems of loop-around testing, and the lack of an industry wide standard inhibited widespread adoption of those modems. The creation of the 1200 baud full-duplex switched network modem has probably doomed the 1200/150 modem forever.

The future of the 1200/75 modem is brighter than that of the 1200/150 modem, because the 1200/75 modem is supported by an international standard and is available from the PTT's in some countries at very favorable rental rates.

So far, only the control leads for switched network modems have been discussed. To more fully appreciate the function of the control leads, it might be useful to explore the internal operation of switched network modems; that is the subject of the next chapter.

10
Asynchronous Modems for Switched Network Use

An idealized presentation of the typical frequency response of a switched network telephone connection is shown in Figure 10-1.

The presence of a signaling tone at 2600 Hertz makes use of this frequency undesirable, as a single tone of this frequency will cause the telephone call to be disconnected. This and the relative unpredictability of the frequency response characteristics in the 2600–3000 Hertz area have caused modem designers to use tones between 300 and 2400 Hertz.

As shown in Figure 10-2, 300 baud, asynchronous modems (often referred to as "103-type") provide full-duplex operation over two-wire telephone circuits by use of frequency division multiplexing (FDM).

With FDM, two data channels are obtained by operating in separate frequency bands, one for each direction of transmission. In the case of 103-type modems, these frequency bands are centered at 1170 Hz and 2125 Hz. The close proximity of the transmit and receive spectra of both modems is illustrated in Figure 10-3 to emphasize the importance of channel separation filter quality.

Two types of modems are required for operation on separate frequency bands: originate mode modems (transmit on 1070/1270) and answer mode modems (transmit on 2025/2225). This nomenclature has come into use because Bell 103A modems are automatically switched into the originate mode when a call is originated, and into answer mode when a call is answered. For private line applications, as discussed in Chapter 4, the network configuration is known and the operating mode of each modem must be specified in advance.

For applications such as time-sharing systems where terminals always call the computer, economies can be gained by having the modem at the terminal

86

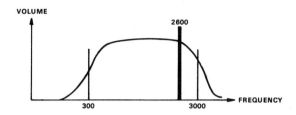

Figure 10-1. **Location of Signaling Tone in Switched Network Frequency Response**

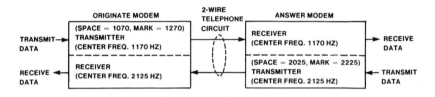

Figure 10-2. **U.S. Low-Speed Asynchronous Full-Duplex Modem Frequency Assignments**

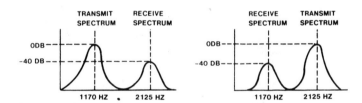

Figure 10-3. **U.S. Low-Speed Asynchronous Full-Duplex Modem Frequency Spectra**

be an originate-only variety and the modem at the computer be an answer-only variety. Originate-only and answer-only modems are simpler because they do not have to be able to change their transmitters, receivers, and filter arrangements from transmit 1070/1270 and receive 2025/2225 to transmit 2025/2225 and receive 1070/1270.

An interesting problem arises in the case of a "booked call" in which a telephone operator is asked to establish a call and then to call the originating party when she has the called party available. If this is done with modems, the operator is calling both modems and they both go into the answer mode. In countries where this is a problem, a "booked call" button is provided which insures that the originating modem stays in originate mode despite the fact that it receives a call from the operator.

Figures 10-4 and 10-5 are repeats of Figures 10-2 and 10-3, but with the frequency assignments of CCITT Recommendation V.21: "200 Baud

Modem Standardized for Use in the General Switched Telephone Network." Note that not only are the frequency assignments different, but also that the higher frequencies of each pair represent the SPACE state rather than the MARK.

There are a variety of implementations for a low speed asynchronous modem of the "103-type," one of which is shown in block diagram form in Figure 10-6.

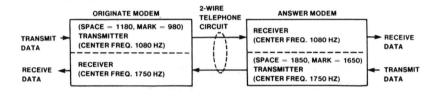

Figure 10-4. **CCITT Low-Speed Asynchronous Full-Duplex Modem Frequency Assignments**

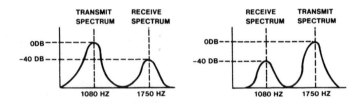

Figure 10-5. **CCITT Low-Speed Asynchronous Full-Duplex Modem Frequency Spectra**

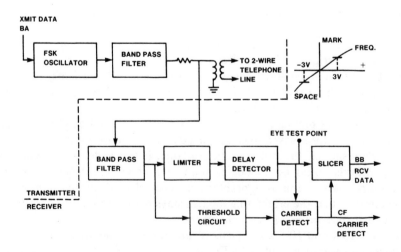

Figure 10-6. **Block Diagram of Low-Speed Asynchronous Modem**

Transmit Data (EIA:BA/CCITT:103) is applied to the Frequency Shift Keying (FSK) oscillator which responds by shifting its frequency in accordance with the MARK/SPACE data. The output of the oscillator is applied to a bandpass filter which restricts the sidebands of the oscillator output. (The process of shifting back and forth between 1070 and 1270 (or 2025 and 2225) produces additional frequencies which should not be applied to the telephone line.) The bandpass filter output is coupled to the telephone line by a line matching transformer.

At the receiver, the signal from the telephone line comes in through the line matching transformer and is applied to a bandpass filter. This filter attenuates out-of-band noise and the adjacent transmit signal by only passing frequencies of approximately 1800-2400 Hz (originate modem) or 900-1500 Hz (answer modem). The filter output is applied to a limiter which eliminates amplitude variations of the signal. The limiter functions over a large enough volume range for its output not to vary in volume, but only in frequency. The output of the limiter is connected to the delay detector which compares the signal to a delayed version and produces an output voltage proportional to frequency.

As shown in Figure 10-6, the output of the delay detector is referred to as the eye test point. If random data is sent, an eye pattern can be observed at this point. Figure 10-7 shows both an eye pattern for a line receiving error-free data and an eye pattern for a line upon which data errors are occurring. The pattern is called an eye pattern because of its resemblance to a human eye. Note that in the good eye pattern, transitions from the top of the eye to the bottom are smooth and cross a center line drawn from left to right cleanly and without wavering. This center line is implemented by a circuit called a "slicer" into which the eye pattern is fed. The slicer converts the analog signal that comes out of the delay detector back to MARK/SPACE digital data for the Received Data lead (BB/104). Note that the slicer output (BB/104) is under control of the Carrier Detect (CF/109) signal. For the

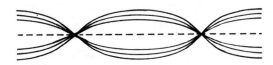

Figure 10-7a.   Good Eye Pattern

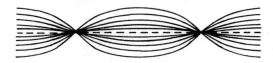

Figure 10-7b.   Bad Eye Pattern

slicer to operate normally, Carrier Detect must be on. Whenever CF/109 goes off, the slicer output is forced to a MARK, preventing erroneous data from appearing on the Received Data lead. This operation will now be explained in somewhat more detail.

As shown in Figure 10-6, signals for carrier detect operation are picked off two separate points in the receive data channel. The first point feeds a threshold circuit which turns CF off whenever the receive signal drops below a certain threshold such as −45 dbm. The second point monitors the delay detector output to determine whether the incoming signal is valid data or noise. Since the frequency spectra of valid, randomly-keyed data and noise are quite similar, the carrier detect circuit must average for a relatively long time to properly distinguish between the two signals. Waveforms that illustrate the operation of the carrier detect circuit are shown in Figure 10-8. Note that CF/109 stays on for a signal loss of less than 30 ms.* When a signal loss of greater than 30 ms occurs, CF/109 goes off after 30 ms and BB/104 is forced to a MARK condition; 150 ms* after the signal reappears, CF turns back on and valid data is again present at BB/104. Note that BB/104 is invalid whenever the line signal is lost, but CF/109 is still on.

Figure 10-9 shows how 103-type modems use up the frequency response available in a typical switched network call. Figure 10-10 shows how a 1200 baud modem, such as the Bell System 202, uses that same frequency response.

Like the 103-type modem, the 202-type modem transmits data by means of frequency shift keying, using a tone of 2200 Hz to represent a SPACE and a tone of 1200 Hz to represent a MARK. As indicated in Figure 10-10, the frequency spectrum produced by such keying uses most of the available frequency response of the telephone connection and transmission is therefore possible only in one direction at a time. Some information transmission is possible in the reverse direction by means of the receiving modem trans-

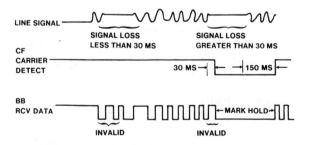

Figure 10-8. Carrier Detect Operation During Dropouts

*These numbers are from a particular company's version of 300 baud asynchronous modem.

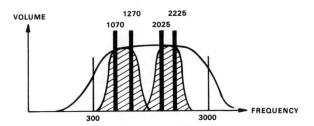

Figure 10-9. Frequency Utilization for 300 Baud Full-Duplex Modem

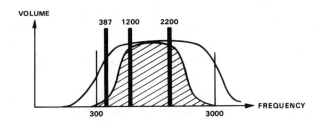

Figure 10-10. Frequency Utilization for 1200 Baud Half-Duplex Modem with Reverse Channel

mitting a 387 Hz tone back to the transmitting modem. This tone, when present, indicates that the circuit between the two modems is still there. It can also be used for the receiving station to inform the transmitting station that the previous message contained errors and to request retransmission of that message.

The international version of the 202-type modem is the "600/1200 Baud Modem Standardized for Use in the General Switched Telephone Network," as described in CCITT Recommendation V.23. The modulation rates and frequencies for the main data transmission channels are:

	MARK	*SPACE*
Mode 1 (up to 600 baud)	1300 Hz	1700 Hz
Mode 2 (up to 1200 baud)	1300 Hz	2100 Hz

Note that, as with the 103-type modem, the international version uses closer frequency spacing than its North American counterpart.

The CCITT V.23 modem also differs from its North American counterpart in that the reverse channel has a 75 baud capability and uses real FSK rather than ON/OFF keying. On the reverse channel, 390 Hz represents a

MARK and 450 Hz represents a SPACE. The interface is arranged such that if no interface lead is provided, the reverse channel sends a MARK.

The 202-type modem has some characteristics which may be of interest to programmers. Some versions of the 202-type modem leave the receiver circuitry on while transmission is taking place. Since the frequencies used by the transmitter are identical to those used by the receiver, the receiver sees the line signal being produced by the transmitter, demodulates it, and produces a copy of the Transmitted Data for delivery to the Received Data lead. This feature is called "local copy." In addition, the Carrier Detector lead is asserted whenever either the local modem is transmitting or the distant modem is transmitting.

In the late 1970's the cost of electronics became low enough for it to be economically feasible to use some of the more advanced modulation techniques, such as phase modulation (normally used in synchronous modems), for asynchronous modems. The result has been a 1200 baud modem that operates in full-duplex mode on switched telephone network connections. The frequency spectra used are similar to those for a 103-type modem, as shown in Figure 10-9. Two industry standards have emerged for this type of modem, the original Vadic design and the Bell System 212 design. The designs are incompatible, but it is possible to buy a "triple modem" that can be switched between 103-compatibility, 212-compatibility, and Vadic 3400-compatibility modes. The Vadic 3400 and Bell System 212 eliminate the problems of reverse channel operation and provide program compatibility with 103-type modems. Extension of the 212/VA3400 principles to reach 2400 baud full-duplex operation on the switched network has been accomplished by at least one major modem manufacturer.

11

Automatic
Calling Units

Previous chapters have dealt with data communications between two computers connected by private lines and have discussed data communications over the switched telephone network with the calls being answered automatically by the computer. In addition to these arrangements, it is also possible to have systems where the computer automatically originates the calls. One of the applications is inventory control systems where the computer calls various warehouses or retail stores, usually after business hours, and reaches a terminal which has various inventory or sales information stored in it. If the terminal is ready to transmit the data, it automatically answers the call and allows the central computer to read the data. Needless to say, the terminal must be designed so that a random person calling the number will not elicit transmission of the data. A second application is the automatic establishment of a "dial back-up" circuit when a private line fails. In this application, the software in a computer system detects that a private line between it and another computer or a terminal has failed. Automatic calling is used to dial up a port on the other computer and re-establish communications, although often at a reduced signaling rate.

In the United States, the most common automatic dialing units are the Bell System (Western Electric) 801A Automatic Calling Unit (dial pulse) and 801C Automatic Calling Unit (Touch Tone®). Independent equipment manufacturers and various Post and Telegraph authorities throughout the world have similar units available. The applicable CCITT Recommendation is V.25, and the applicable EIA Specification is RS-366.

®Registered service mark of American Telephone and Telegraph Company.

The computer and its associated interface to the automatic calling unit are responsible for:

1. Insuring that the data communications equipment (i.e., the calling unit and the line) is available for operation.

2. Providing the telephone number to be dialed.

3. Deciding to abandon the call if it is unsuccessfully completed.

4. Supervising the call to determine when to take down the connection. (In general the supervision task is handed over to the modem when the call has been established.)

Two leads are provided to perform the first task. One of these indicates that the automatic calling unit has its power on and is called "PoWer Indicator" (PWI) on the 801s and Circuit 213 in CCITT Recommendation V.25. The second circuit indicates whether or not the communications line is presently in use, either by a person using the associated telephone set (if there is one) or by a previously established data call. This lead is called "Data Line Occupied" (DLO) or Circuit 203.

To actually seize the communications line to place a call, the "Call Request" lead is provided (CRQ or CCITT Circuit 202).

Thus, to obtain dial tone, the computer/interface checks to see that PWI/213 is ON and that DLO/203 is OFF, and then asserts CRQ/202. Data Terminal Ready (CCITT Circuit 108/2) may also be asserted by the interface to the modem at this time.

NOTE

Good "defensive programming" practice and the provisions of Recommendation V.25 suggest that leads CRQ/202, DLO/203, DSC/204, ACR/205 and PND/210 also be OFF before CRQ/202 is asserted.

The communications line is now placed in the "off-hook" condition by the automatic calling unit, and the telephone switching equipment returns dial tone to the automatic calling unit. In the Bell System 801A and some similar units, the detection of dial tone requires a special alteration to the telephone line called "Ground Start." As explained in Chapter 8, telephone systems generally detect the "off-hook" condition as essentially a short between Tip and Ring. The "Line Relay" is sufficiently sensitive, however, that a ground applied to the Ring (negative) side of the line energizes one winding of the Line Relay and is sufficient to cause the Line Relay to operate. This in turn causes the proper events to occur so that dial tone is applied to the line. The important feature of a line wired for Ground Start is that the contacts of the Cut-off Relay, which are interposed between the Line Relay and the subscriber telephone, have been insulated in such a fashion that the Tip side (ground) of the line is floating rather than being ground through a coil. This arrangement is shown in Figure 11-1. Only when the linefinder or similar device has found the line, and the line has been connected through to a first selector (step-by-step) or originating register (crossbar/ESS), does the Cutoff Relay operate and transfer the subscriber's line to the battery feed coil of the first selector or originating register. The battery feed coil of the first selector or originating register provides resistance battery on the Ring and resistance ground on the Tip. Thus a detector circuit in the 801A can determine when the first selector/originating register is applied to the line by looking for the time when the Tip changes from floating to resistance ground. Since first selectors or originating registers supply dial tone, looking for that resistance ground is equivalent to looking for dial tone. The 801C uses a tone detection circuit that responds to the 350 Hz/440 Hz precise tones that represent dial tone in Bell Systems switching offices where Touch Tone® service is provided.

There are two important points in all this: 1) the 801A and some similar units require Ground Start lines, and 2) such units cannot detect dial tones beyond the first one. What this means is that in systems (PBX) where dial tone is obtained, "9" is dialed for an outside (city) trunk, and a wait for city trunk dial tone is involved, this second wait must usually be timed by system software, and after a reasonable interval the receipt of dial tone must be assumed. Some dial pulse automatic calling units use tone detectors with rather broad opinions about what constitutes dial tone to avoid the use of Ground Start lines. Certain unused codes on the dialed digit leads are assigned to indicate that the calling unit should wait for dial tone, thus obviat-

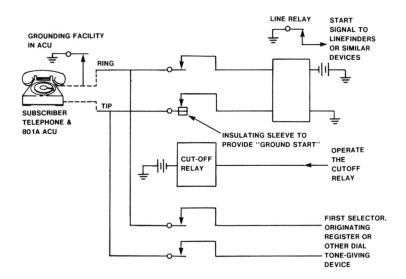

Figure 11-1. "Ground-Start" Line

ing the need for software timing. Automatic dialers built to CCITT Recommendation V.25 provide a delay when the Separation (SEP) code (1101) is applied to the digit leads.

Once the automatic calling unit has seized the line and recognized dial tone, it is time for the interface to undertake the second task: providing the telephone number to be dialed. A lead called "Present Next Digit" (PND, CCITT Circuit 210) is provided from the automatic calling unit to the computer/interface which, when asserted, indicates that the automatic calling unit is ready to be told a digit to dial. The digit-to-be-dialed information is presented from the interface to the calling unit over four digit leads referred to as NB1, NB2, NB4, and NB8 (CCITT V.25 Circuits 206, 207, 208, and 209 respectively). Table 11-1 applies.

The transfer of information on the digit leads is done in parallel, just as described in Chapter 1. The "clock" or "strobe" signal is provided by an additional lead from the interface to the calling unit, called "Digit Present" (DPR, CCITT Circuit 211). With most calling units it is permissible for the interface to present the digit information and the assertion of the DPR/211 lead simultaneously, but in all cases DPR must not be asserted unless the proper information is present on the digit leads. The automatic calling unit indicates that it has accepted the digit for dialing by negating the Present Next Digit (PND/210) lead. The digit lead information and the DPR/211 signal must not be changed until this negation occurs.

The automatic calling unit re-asserts PND/210 when it has completed dialing that digit. The interface may then present new information on the digit leads (which may actually be changed as soon as PND negates) and may assert DPR/211 to indicate that the new digit should be dialed.

The process of presenting digit information proceeds until the last digit has been dialed. The interface then places the EON (End Of Number) code on the digit leads and asserts Digit Present if Recommendation V.25 applies.

Table 11-1. Automatic Calling Unit Digit Lead Coding

Digit	209 NB8	208 NB4	207 NB2	206 NB1	CCITT Designations 801 Designations
1	Off	Off	Off	On	
2	Off	Off	On	Off	
3	Off	Off	On	On	
4	Off	On	Off	Off	
5	Off	On	Off	On	
6	Off	On	On	Off	
7	Off	On	On	On	
8	On	Off	Off	Off	
9	On	Off	Off	On	
0	On	Off	On	Off	
EON	On	On	Off	Off	End Of Number
SEP	On	On	Off	On	SEParation

If modems in the United States such as the Bell System 103 series or equivalent are involved, the Bell System 801A and 801C calling units provide an option called "Detect Answer" which obviates the need for an EON code.

Having dialed the number, the automatic calling unit and its associated interface are now ready for the third task: abandoning the call if it is unsuccessfully completed.

There are three possible ways this can be done. The CCITT Recommendation V.25 method is for the "abandon call timer" to begin operating when the calling unit has negated Present Next Digit in response to receiving the End of Number (EON) code on the digit leads. If the call is answered by a data terminal, a tone is received by the calling unit and the abandon call timer is turned off. If the call is not answered, or is answered by something or someone other than a data terminal, the timer continues running. After 10–40 seconds (selectable) the calling unit asserts Abandon Call (ACR on 801s, CCITT 205) which directs the interface to disconnect the call; it does so by dropping Call Request (CRQ/202). If the call is successfully answered by a data terminal, the calling unit asserts the signal Distant Station Connected (Circuit 204) and the control of the telephone line is passed to the modem. The modem continues to hold the connection intact under the control of the Data Terminal Ready lead (CCITT Circuit 108/2) which must be asserted by the interface by this time. The Call Request lead may then be dropped without disconnecting the call. The modem interface, in conjunction with the computer software, then controls the assertion of Data Terminal Ready and disconnects the call when appropriate.

NOTE
The foregoing is a summary of CCITT Recommendation V.25 and the reader is directed to that document or EIA RS-366 for further details.

When using Bell System 801A and 801C automatic calling units to place calls to modems such as the Bell System 103J, the sequence of events is the same as that described for Recommendation V.25, except that the Distant Station Connected circuit is called Data Set Status (DSS), and EON codes are not used (see next paragraph for an exception). The customer should order the "Detect Answer" option and the "Terminate Call After DSS Goes On, Via Data Set" option. This latter option is particularly important when using multiplexed interfaces that give a computer the ability to set up calls on several lines using a common auto dialer interface which moves from line to line. When the common logic is moved on to the next line, the Call Request lead is dropped; if the "Terminate Call After DSS Goes On, Via CRQ" option has been ordered, the dropping of CRQ disconnects the call. With the "Via Data Set" option, the continuity of the call is controlled by Data Terminal Ready, not CRQ, so the dropping of CRQ after call establishment is inconsequential.

Table 11-2. Special Character Sequences Used on Interface Circuits of a Non-Bell Automatic Calling Unit

Character	ASCII Code	Function
STX (Control B)	002	Condition the automatic calling unit for reception of numeric input.
Digits	060-071	String of numbers representing the telephone number to be dialed. If the initial digit is used within a PBX to access an "outside line," use of a "pause" character (see below) is necessary.
=	075	Pause—this character is equivalent to the SEParation code defined in V.25. It allows time to obtain a second dial tone.
SI (Control O)	017	Buffer Limit (Vadic VA831)
ETX (Control C)	003	End of numeric input. Dialing can begin in Vadic VA831 (dialing occurs simultaneously with input in the Digital DF03-AC).
SOH (Control A)	001	Abort the call attempt (for use before the automatic calling unit returns Response A—Data Set Status).
<	074	Transfer telephone line to modem after the telephone number has been dialed without waiting for an answer tone. This is equivalent to the use, in an 801, of the "End of Number" option rather than the "Detect Answer" option.

The automatic calling unit responds with the following possible responses:

A	101	Data Set Status—the telephone line has been transferred to the modem.
B	102	Abandon Call and Retry—the call attempt did not succeed.
D	104	Framing Error (VA 831 only)
E	105	Parity Error (VA 831 only)
		The above two errors indicate that the serial data transferred to the VA831 had the types of errors indicated.
F	106	Overrun (VA 831 only)
		A number consisting of too many digits was loaded between the STX and SI characters.
G	107	Data Line Occupied—a fault condition.

Note: Signals are appropriate to a Vadic VA831 RS232/801 adapter and Digital Equipment Corporation DF03-AC dialer.

If calls are being placed from a Bell System 801A or 801C to a modem that does not answer with a tone in the 2000–2400 Hz range, the End of Number operating mode must be used and the following options must be ordered:

1. End of Number Operation (instead of Detect Answer)
2. Do Not Stop ACR When DSS Goes On (instead of Stop ACR).

In an operation of this type, the modem is connected to the line immediately when the EON code is strobed into the calling unit on the digit leads. Thus, Data Set Status, which in the 801 really means that the modem has control of the line, is immediately asserted. The abandon call and retry timer is allowed to expire and the assertion of the ACR/205 lead is used to notify the computer program that it should send a "who are you?" or some other kind of inquiry on the communications line to see if a call has been successfully established.

In addition to the Bell System 801A and 801C, automatic calling units are available which do not use the RS-366/V.25 parallel interface described above. Rather, these automatic calling units use special character sequences on the Transmit Data and Receive Data interface circuits to control the dialing function and report on call status. Table 11-2 gives an example of dialing using such a calling unit, utilizing signals appropriate to the Vadic VA831 RS232/801 adaptor and the Digital Equipment DF03-AC dialer.

Automatic calling on public data networks is accomplished via the CCITT Recommendation X.20 and X.21 interfaces described in Chapter 27.

12

Asynchronous Multiplexers With Modem Control

It was noted in Chapter 7 that computer systems which have a number of asynchronous communication lines connected to them can generally profit from the introduction of multiplexers. This is so both because a large number of communication lines can share a single bus interface and because other features that all of the lines could use can be added economically. The features most commonly added are programmable formats and speeds, direct memory transfers, and modem control. Some of these features, notably modem control, are also found in single line interfaces, but they are more commonly found in multiplexers.

Programmable formats and speeds enable a multiplexer to answer a switched network telephone call and then adjust itself, perhaps with program assistance, to the operating characteristics of the terminal on the other end of the telephone call. Appendix E lists some of the possible formats for asynchronous data transmission.

To accommodate these various formats and speeds, an asynchronous multiplexer can have a Line Parameter Register arranged as shown in Figure 12-1. This register is loaded after the program has loaded a line selection register to indicate the line number to which this information applies.

The setting of bit 14 permits this multiplexer to operate with half-duplex communications media where transmitted data appears on the Received

15	14	13	12	11	10	09	08	07	06	05	04	03	02	01	00
	HD	TRANSMIT SPEED				RECEIVER SPEED				OP	PE		SB	CHAR LEN	

Figure 12-1.   Line Parameter Register

Table 12-1. Speed Selection Table

		Bit			Bits Per Second
Transmitter	13	12	11	10	
Receiver	09	08	07	06	
	0	0	0	0	0
	0	0	0	1	50
	0	0	1	0	75
	0	0	1	1	110
	0	1	0	0	134.5
	0	1	0	1	150
	0	1	1	0	200
	0	1	1	1	300
	1	0	0	0	600
	1	0	0	1	1200
	1	0	1	0	1800
	1	0	1	1	2400
	1	1	0	0	4800
	1	1	0	1	9600

Data lead. This could occur when no modem is being used or when the half-duplex modem being used does not contain a feature that will clamp the received data lead during assertion of Request to Send. The Half-Duplex (HD) bit, when set, blinds the receiver while the transmitter is sending characters.

The transmitter speed is controlled by bits 10–13 and the receiver speed may be independently set in bits 06–09. Both of the four-bit speed selection groups use speeds from Table 12-1.

The speeds shown in Table 12-1 have the following significance:

Zero: Enables the program to shut off reception on a line. Not particularly useful for transmission.

50, 75:   Used in some low speed applications, especially with Baudot (five-bit) code.

110:           Used in Teletype Corporation's Model 33 and Model 35 teleprinters.

134.5:   Used for IBM Model 2741 and Model 1050 terminals.

150:           Used for modern teleprinters with electronic rather than mechanical transmitter/receiver units. This speed is falling into disuse because of the availability of higher speed terminals and modems.

200: Top speed of British Post Office Datel 200 service and similar European switched telephone network offerings.

300: Top speed of Bell System 103J modem and newer European switched telephone network offerings. This speed is very common in terminals, but is falling into disuse due to the availability of higher speed terminals and modems.

600: Slower speed used in 600/1200 bit per second asynchronous modems built according to CCITT Recommendation V.23. Principally used in Europe.

1200: Top speed of Bell System 212 and similar full-duplex modems on switched network service. Higher speed used in 600/1200 bit per second asynchronous modems built according to CCITT Recommendation V.23. This speed is very common in both CRT and printing terminals and is rapidly replacing lower speeds.

1800: Top speed of Bell System 202 and similar half/full-duplex asynchronous modems on private line service. Not a common terminal speed.

2400, 4800, 9600: Commonly used speeds for CRT terminals when used close enough to the computer for line drivers rather than modems to suffice.

The unused codes of 1110 and 1111 can be used for special clocks if desired.

Bit 04, when set, indicates that the line will be operated with the transmitter affixing a parity bit to each character transmitted and the receiver checking each received character for proper parity. Whether odd or even parity will be used is determined by the state of bit 05, Odd Parity (OP).

Bit 02 determines whether a single STOP unit follows the data bits (bit 02 clear) or whether two STOP units are used (1.5 STOP units in the case of five bit codes). Finally, bits 01 and 00 determine the length of the characters transmitted and received, according to Table 12-2.

The character lengths in Table 12-2 do not include the parity bit.

A second feature made possible by the common equipment sharing permitted by multiplexer design is direct memory transfers. This feature permits a program to specify to the multiplexer that a message, beginning at a

Table 12-2. Character Lengths

| Bit | | Character |
01	00	Length
0	0	5 bits
0	1	6 bits
1	0	7 bits
1	1	8 bits

particular address in memory and of a specified length, is to be sent on a selected line. The multiplexer, upon receiving these details, directly transfers the characters from the memory location to the communication line, as the transmitter for that line becomes available. It will not take any of the program's time until the job is completed; the multiplexer then notifies the program, by means of an interrupt, that the task has been completed.

The hardware required is a scratchpad memory that will hold the "current address" for each line and the "byte count" for each line. The current address is the memory address at which the next character to be sent is located. The current address is initially loaded by the computer program to specify the location of the first character of the message. Once the multiplexer begins the transmission, it obtains the character stored at that location, loads it into the transmitter unit of the appropriate line, and then increments the current address value so that it will obtain the next character from the next location. The byte count is a count of the number of characters to be transmitted (assuming that characters have been stored one character per eight bit byte). Like the current address, the value stored in the byte count memory is adjusted each time a character is sent. In some designs, the program loads the byte counter register with the two's complement of the number of characters to be sent and the register is incremented each time a character is sent. Transmission is stopped when the byte count has been up-counted to zero. This method only requires counters that increment, an important goal in early designs. In newer designs the program loads this register with the number of characters to be sent and the register is decremented each time a character is sent. Again, transmission is stopped when the byte count reaches zero.

To provide direct memory access transmission, two additional registers would be required, in addition to the Line Parameter Register previously discussed. These are shown in Figures 12-2 and 12-3.

These two registers must be replicated for each line. Thus, before loading them, a program must first select the line number whose current address and byte count registers it wishes to access. This permits the hardware to store the information in a random access memory and to use the line numbers as addresses to select the desired information.

To complete the direct memory access logic, the appropriate circuitry to control the computer bus during the data transfers from memory is required.

CURRENT ADDRESS REGISTER

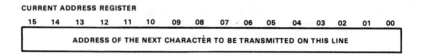

Figure 12-2. Current Address Register

BYTE COUNT REGISTER

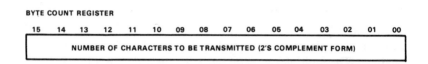

Figure 12-3. Byte Count Register

Obviously, a similar set of registers can be provided to accommodate a similar process on the receiver side. Many computer operating systems use special characters, however, which immediately connect the terminal operator to a higher level program, and cease the execution of his current program, or which stop the output of characters to his terminal. These special characters must be recognized immediately when they are typed. In addition, some operating systems echo back each character to the terminal as it is typed to confirm to the terminal operator that the computer received the information he or she thinks it did. When these types of operating systems are used, it is often of little advantage to use direct memory transfers in the receiver section of a multiplexer. Rather, it is preferable to have a multiplexer smart enough to do character recognition, or to leave the receiver section of the multiplexer a simple interrupt operated silo (FIFO) system such as that described in Chapter 7. Chapter 21 explores character recognition interfaces in some detail.

The third feature most commonly added to multiplexers is modem control. While single line interfaces are also built with modem control, the equipment sharing done in multiplexers permits the construction of some rather interesting implementations of modem control.

As indicated in Chapter 9, any modem control must include control of Data Terminal Ready (CCITT 108/2) or Connect Data Set to Line (CCITT 108/1). This lead must be asserted to maintain a call connection in switched network service, but must be negated in order to drop that connection at the conclusion of data transmission. The Ring Indicator lead (CCITT 125) must also be monitored so that a computer program will know when a new call has been established and will treat the new caller accordingly. A Clear to Send lead (CCITT 106) must be provided so that the transmitter will know when it is safe to begin transmission, and a Carrier Detect lead (Data Channel Received Line Signal Detector—CCITT 109) must be provided to advise the receiver logic of the likely validity of the data on the Received Data lead (CCITT 103). If half-duplex modems or multi-point line operation are envisioned, a Request to Send lead (CCITT 105) will be needed to turn the transmitter section of the modem off and on.

Modem controls which intend to support the operation of low speed reverse channels in modems such as the Bell 202 must provide an interface for Supervisory Transmitted Data/Secondary Request to Send and Supervisory Received Data/Secondary Received Line Signal Detector. Finally, since the program may wish to ignore modem leads for lines subject to extreme noise conditions or connected to faulty modems, an enable bit to permit the program to ignore them is a useful feature.

The control leads mentioned above can all be arranged in a Line Status Register, one of which would be provided for each line in the multiplexer. The program can condition some line selection bits (not shown) to determine which line it wishes to monitor/change before addressing the Line Status Register; the information for that selected line could then be gated to and from a single Line Status Register address serving all of the multiplexer lines.

A possible bit arrangement for a Line Status Register is shown in Figure 12-4. The abbreviations used are RING for Ring, CD for Carrier Detect, CTS for Clear to Send, SRD for Secondary Received Data, STD for Secondary Transmitted Data, RTS for Request to Send, DTR for Data Terminal Ready, and ENB for Enable. The bits marked with an asterisk (*) are read-only as they represent status FROM the modem rather than control of leads going into the modem. The function of the Enable bit not only includes the presentation of the line status information in the Line Status Register, but also controls the presentation of this information to the transition detection system, which is described below.

One of the simplest ways to detect transitions on any signal lead is to build the circuit shown in Figure 12-5. The symbol shown is for an exclusive-OR gate, whose output Y is related to the inputs A and B as shown in the table accompanying Figure 12-5.

In this circuit, the present state of the lead is compared by the exclusive-OR gate with the state of the lead some time ago. "Some time" is determined by the value of the delay line—50 nanoseconds is a common value. When the present and the past are different (i.e., there has been a transition), the output of the exclusive-OR gate is asserted. After the delay time has expired, lead "B" changes to the new value; since the signals at points "A" and "B" are then identical, the output of the exclusive-OR gate is no

LINE STATUS REGISTER

15	14	13	12	11	10	09	08	07	06	05	04	03	02	01	00
								RING *	CD *	CTS *	SRD *	STD	RTS	DTR	ENB

Figure 12-4. Line Status Register

longer asserted. The output of the exclusive-OR gate is thus asserted for a length of time equal to the length of the delay line associated with point B. This output is typically used to set a bit in a register to indicate that a transition has occurred. Lead A is usually wired to another register to give the program information about the present status of the lead. The Line Status Register shown in Figure 12-4 is an example of such a register.

A transition detector such as that shown in Figure 12-5 works well, but if one wishes to monitor Ring, Carrier Detect, Clear to Send, and Secondary Received Data in a 16 line multiplexer, it will require 64 copies of the Figure 12-5 circuit, an arrangement which consumes both space and money.

Because the frequency of the transitions of modem control leads is very slow relative to computer processing speeds, the circuit shown in Figure 12-6

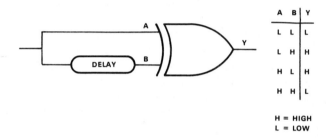

A	B	Y
L	L	L
L	H	H
H	L	H
H	H	L

H = HIGH
L = LOW

Figure 12-5.   Transition Detector

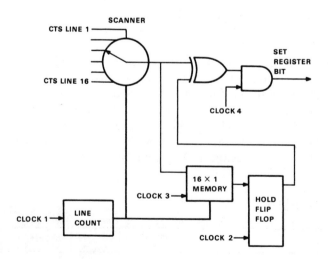

Figure 12-6.   Multiple Line Transition Detector

can be used to detect transitions of the Clear to Send lead (for example) on 16 lines.

The circuitry in Figure 12-6 works as follows: at Clock 1 time, the Line Counter is incremented causing the scanner to sample the state of the Clear to Send (CTS) lead for a new line. At the same time, the previous state of the CTS lead for that line is read out from a memory containing 16 addressable entries, each one bit wide—i.e., storage of the previous CTS lead state for each of the 16 lines. At Clock 2 time, the previous state of CTS as read from the memory is recorded in the Hold Flip-Flop and the exclusive-OR gate compares that previous state with the present state obtained from scanner. The truth table for the exclusive-OR gate is the same as that shown in Figure 12-5, and if the present state differs from the past state, the output of the exclusive-OR gate is asserted. This assertion is sampled at Clock 4 time and used to set a bit in a register as well as to stop the clocking system so that a computer program can read the setting of the line counter to determine which line has a transition of its Clear to Send (CTS) lead. At Clock 3 time (which would occur between Clock 2 time and Clock 4 time) the new state of CTS is recorded in the appropriate memory location.

This circuit may appear to have a great many more elements than the Figure 12-5 circuit, and indeed it does—but not 16 times as many. Furthermore, the same line counter can be used to run additional scanners that look at Ring, Carrier Detect, and Secondary Received Data. Since the Flip-Flop, 16 × 1 Memory, and exclusive-OR gate are normally packaged with four such units in one integrated circuit, the amount of logic needed to implement four versions of Figure 12-6 is far less than the amount needed to implement 64 versions of Figure 12-5. As with all apparent panaceas, there are some drawbacks. In particular, the computer must restart the scanner after processing information concerning the transition of a lead, and a hardware system must be devised which will, on power-up, clear the 16 × 1 memories. A modem control using the transition detection system shown in Figure 12-6 could present the transition information in a Control Status Register similar to that shown in Figure 12-7. This register is in addition to the Line Status Register shown in Figure 12-4.

The RING, CD, CTS, and SRD bits get set whenever there is a transition on the Ring lead, Carrier Detect lead, Clear To Send lead, or Secondary Received Data lead respectively. The Clear Scan (CLR SCN) bit resets the line counter shown in Figure 12-6 to 0000 after stepping through the memory lo-

CONTROL STATUS REGISTER

15	14	13	12	11	10	09	08	07	06	05	04	03	02	01	00
RING	CD	CTS	SRD	CLR SCN	CLR MUX	MNT	STP	DNE	IE	SCAN EN	BSY	LINE NUMBER			

Figure 12-7. **Control and Status Register**

cations and clearing them. The Clear Multiplexer (CLR MUX) bit clears Request to Send, Data Terminal Ready, Secondary Transmit, and Line Enable for all lines.

The Maintenance (MNT) Bit sets RING, CD, CTS, and SRD to the ON state at the scanners. Starting from a state where the "past state" memory is clear, the ON states of these leads will appear as OFF-ON transitions suitable for use in checking the transition detection logic.

The SCAN EN bit at position 05 enables the operation of the transition detection scanner. The bit is normally used in a maintenance mode, where it is cleared to stop the action of the scanner's automatic advance. The scanner is then advanced a step at a time, as directed by the maintenance program manipulating the Step (STP) bit.

The Done (DNE) bit and the Interrupt Enable (IE) bits have the same function as in the interfaces previously discussed. When an event worthy of note occurs, such as detection of a transition, the scanner stops and Done is set. An interrupt is generated, providing the program has previously indicated a willingness to be interrupted. Such an indication of willingness to be interrupted is accomplished by setting the Interrupt Enable bit. When the program clears Done, scanning resumes.

Bit 04, the Busy (BSY) bit, indicates that the scanner is operating. This bit is particularly useful when the program has set Clear Scan and is awaiting the completion of the scanner resetting to 0000 and clearing the "past state" memory. When Busy clears, this operation has been completed. In the particular interface used as an example, this bit is also used, after clearing Scan Enable, to make sure that the scanner has really stopped before changing the Line Number bits.

The Line Number bits are used for two purposes. The modem control uses them when a transition has been detected to tell the program on which line the transition was detected. The program uses them to tell the modem control which line it wishes to read or to change the Line Status Register. To keep these two uses from conflicting, the program must clear Scan Enable, check Busy to see that scanning has stopped, check Done to see that no transitions were found at scan stopping time, and then condition the Line Number bits to select the desired Line Status Register. There are some other guidelines concerning the particular interface being used as an example, but they will not be discussed here, since they are not necessarily characteristic of this type of modem control. This interface is being described only as an example; the description is not intended as a programming guide.

In the discussion of the various registers, mention has been made of the use of "secondary registers," for both the data handling and modem control portions of multiplexers. These are read after first loading a register which selects the secondary register that is going to be read. Why is this done rather than having all registers made directly accessible to the program? The principal reason is the widespread use of semiconductor memories where a large number of bits are stored in an ordered array in a single integrated circuit. The ordered array is addressed by address selection leads that are decoded inside the IC. The most convenient and economical way to use such a memory is to tie the address selection leads to a register which the program loads with the address in the ordered array to or from which it wishes to transfer data. The addressed location is then a "secondary register."

Not only are secondary registers a packaging convenience, they also reduce the computer address space required for various peripherals. Very few computer systems can afford to assign addresses for several multiplexers containing 16 current addresses and 16 byte counts discussed earlier. A scheme that employs secondary registers requires only two addresses in the computer's peripheral address space (plus a line selection section of another register).

The drawback to the use of secondary registers is that the programming becomes more complicated. Interrupt service routines must in general save the contents of the register which is being used to address secondary registers. This is because the service routine is apt to change it in the process of servicing interrupts; it will have to restore it before going back to the main program, so that the main program will be "pointing" to the same register(s) as it was before it was interrupted.

13
Error
Detection

In all electrical information transmission systems, due consideration must be given to the effects of noise. Noise is any unwanted signal and may originate from sources as spectacular as lightning strikes or as mundane as dirty contacts on telephone switching equipment.

The most important characteristic of noise in telecommunications systems is the relatively long duration of the disturbances. A noise burst of .01 second duration is not uncommon and sounds like a simple click during a voice conversation. If the .01 second noise burst occurs during a 4800 bit per second data transmission, the "simple click" is the death knell for 48 data bits. Thus, when noise causes bits to be received in error, it generally causes a great number of bits to be affected. The periods of high error rate are generally separated by relatively long intervals of low noise, low error rate data reception. Thus the error rate averaged over an hour is typically one error bit in 100,000 bits received.

The "bursty" nature of errors in telecommunications systems is very important in considering error detection.

To determine whether the bits in a character have been properly received, it would be quite simple to append an additional bit to each character and to have that bit be a one or a zero according to the rule that "all transmitted characters shall have an odd number of ones." Thus, for example, the character 01001100 would be expanded to 001001100 and the character 01101100 would be expanded to 101101100. The added, underlined bit is called the "parity" bit and using it to make the number of ones odd is called "odd parity." (Plainly, one could make the number of ones even and call it "even parity.") In a parity system, the transmitter unit calculates the state of the parity bit and appends it to the character during transmission. The receiving unit calculates the state of the parity bit and compares the calculated value to the value actually received. If they disagree, the receiver knows that a bit has been received in error.

Let us assume that the transmitter sends 101101100. Parity is odd; everything is OK. Let us assume that the second and third bits (counting from the right) are received erroneously. The received character is then 101101010. The parity is still odd and things appear OK despite the double error. The lesson to be learned is that parity on each character can detect only errors that affect a single bit (or three, or five, etc.). Errors that affect two (or four, or six, etc.) bits will not be detected. This problem exists regardless of whether "odd parity" or "even parity" is used.

Consider transmission of the six characters in Figure 13-1. Each bit (except the left-most) in the Check Character has been computed such that it and the bits immediately above it in Characters 1 through 5 total an odd number of ones. For example, the right-most bit in the Check Character is a zero because three of the right-most bits in the characters above it are ones; hence there is an odd number of ones.

In all characters, including the Check Character, the left-most bit is a parity bit, as described above.

Let us assume that the transmitter sends 101101100 (Character 1). Parity is odd; everything is OK. Let us assume that the second and third bits (counting from the right) are received erroneously. The received character is then 101101010. The parity is still odd and things appear OK despite the double error. This time, however, there is a Check Character being sent. The error just described increases the number of ones in the second column from three to four (an even number) and decreases the number of ones in the third column (counting from the right) from four to three (excluding the check character).

When the Check Character sent by the transmitter is compared in the receiver to that which the receiver has calculated from summing the ones in the various "columns" of the received characters, the second and third bit positions will be incorrect. The computed Check Character will require the second bit from the right to be a "1" to increase the number of ones in that column from four to five, and will require the third bit to be a "0" as the receiver has received only three one bits in that column. Thus the calculated Check Character and the transmitted Check Character will disagree in the second and third bit positions, which are indeed where the errors occurred.

101101100	CHARACTER 1
110101111	CHARACTER 2
001110101	CHARACTER 3
111100010	CHARACTER 4
100010111	CHARACTER 5
010111100	CHECK CHARACTER

Figure 13-1. Sample Transmission

Lest one embrace this scheme as foolproof, consider the case where Character 1 and Character 3 are received with errors in the second and third bit positions. Now there will be two more ones in the second column and two fewer ones in the third column. The number of ones in each column is now such that the receiver's calculated block Check Character and that sent by the transmitter will be the same.

Thus in the same way that a parity check within the character was defeated by a double error in the character, parity on the columns (referred to as a Longitudinal Redundancy Check or LRC) is defeated if a double error occurs in a column. There are numerous possibilities for double bit errors in characters to occur simultaneously with double bit errors in columns in such a fashion that neither the character parity (referred to as Vertical Redundancy Check or VRC) nor the column parity (LRC) will indicate that the errors have occurred. This is an especially important problem since errors in communications transmission systems tend to occur in bursts, as noted above.

The detection systems most effective at detecting errors in communications systems with a minimal amount of hardware (but more than VRC/LRC systems) are the Cyclic Redundancy Checks (CRC).

CRC calculations are customarily done in a multi-section shift register which feeds into an exclusive-OR gate whose output feeds back to other exclusive-OR gates located in between the sections of the shift register. An exclusive-OR gate is a gate where the output is a 0 if the inputs are both 0 or are both 1. If the inputs differ, the output of the exclusive-OR gate is a one. Figure 13-2 shows a typical arrangement.

The placement and quantity of the exclusive-OR gates vary for CRC-12, CRC-16, and CRC-CCITT, which are the most common Cyclic Redundancy Checks. The block check register example shown in Figure 13-2 is the implementation of CRC-CCITT. Note that the terms MSB and LSB used in the figure refer to the most significant and least significant bits of the *register*; the LSB end of the register is sent first, but corresponds to the X^{15} term of the CRC.

When the logic shown in Figure 13-2 is used in a transmitter circuit, it is initialized to all zeros. As each bit is presented to the communications line it is also applied to the point marked "A" in Figure 13-2 and a shifting pulse is

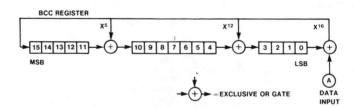

Figure 13-2. Block Check Register Implemented with Shift Registers and Exclusive-OR Gates

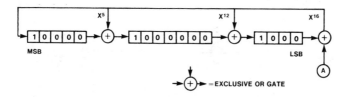

Figure 13-3. Propagation of a "1" Bit into Block Check Register

applied to the shift register. Figure 13-3 shows the contents of the shift register assuming that the first bit transmitted was a 1. Note what a dramatic effect just this single bit has and how that effect is spread throughout the register.

As the "1" bits shown in Figure 13-3 get shifted on through the segments of the shift register during the transmission of subsequent bits, they will eventually reach some of the exclusive-OR gates between the segments of the shift register. Here they will affect the state of the "feedback bits" coming from the exclusive-OR gate on the far righthand side of the diagram.

The general effect to be recognized is that the effect of any bit is reflected in the various bits of the shift register for a considerable time after that bit is transmitted.

In a CRC equipped system, a logical arrangement identical to that used in the transmitter (Figure 13-3) is also used in the receiver. Again the register is initialized to zero and data *from* the communications line is applied to point A while the shift register contents are shifted once for each bit received. At the conclusion of the message, the transmitting station sends the contents of the transmitter CRC shift register to the receiving station. The X^{15} term, marked "LSB", is sent first. The receiving station applies the incoming bit stream to point A of its CRC logic, just as it did with the preceding data bits. Properties of exclusive-OR gates shown in Figure 13-4 are reviewed below.

As the first bit of the received CRC character is applied to point A of the receiver CRC logic, the exclusive-OR gate obeys rule 1 in Figure 13-4 and produces a 0 if the first bit of the calculated CRC matches the first bit of the CRC being received. All of the other exclusive-OR gates in the Figure 13-3 style of CRC logic will obey rule 2 in Figure 13-4 and will become essentially "transparent"; a 0 will be shifted into the left end of the shift register. As long as the calculated CRC contained in the receiver CRC shift register continues to match the CRC being received from the transmitting station, the output of the right-most exclusive-OR gate will continue to be zero, and the other exclusive-OR gates will continue to be "transparent." When all of the CRC bits have been shifted, the CRC shift register bits will all be zeros. This will be true regardless of the placement of the exclusive-OR gates and hence true for all types of CRC. An exception is that SDLC and HDLC start with a pre-set value in the shift register and end with a special non-zero result.

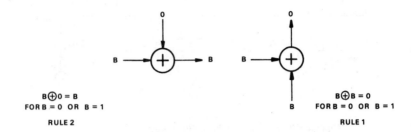

Figure 13-4. Logical Rules for Exclusive-OR Gates

The most important property of CRCs is that, due to the feedback arrangements, the exact state of the shift register is dependent on a great deal of past history. Hence it is highly unlikely that a burst of errors could produce a CRC calculation that was the same as that for the data as originally transmitted before the errors occurred.

CRC requires no bit per character like parity does, but there are two check characters at the end of each block of characters, since the CRC shift register is two character lengths long. These two characters are referred to as the Block Check Characters, abbreviated "BCC." So that the reader may correlate this simplified presentation with various trade journal articles which discuss CRC polynomials in mathematical terms, a mathematical presentation* follows.

A cyclic code message consists of a specific number of data bits and a BCC. Let n equal the total number of bits in the message and k equal the number of data bits; then n − k equals the number of bits in the BCC.

The code message is derived from two polynomials which are algebraic representations of two binary words, the generator polynomial $P(X)$ and the message polynomial $G(X)$. The generator polynomial is the type of code used (CRC-12, CRC-16, and CRC-CCITT); the message polynomial is the string of serial data bits. The polynomials are usually represented algebraically by a string of terms in powers of X such as $X^n \ldots + X^3 + X^2 + X + X^0$ (or 1). In binary form, a 1 is placed in each position that contains a term; absence of a term is indicated by a 0. The convention followed in the following presentation is to place the X^0 bit at the right. For example, if a polynomial is given as $X^4 + X + 1$, its binary representation is 10011 (3rd and 2nd degree terms are not present).

Given a message polynomial $G(X)$ and a generator polynomial $P(X)$, the objective is to construct a code message polynomial $F(X)$ that is evenly divisible by $P(X)$. It is accomplished as follows:

1. Multiply the message $G(X)$ by X^{n-k} where n − k is the number of bits in the BCC.

*From Reference 2, the Digital Equipment Corporation KG11 Manual.

2. Divide the resulting product X^{n-k} [G(X)] by the generator polynomial P(X).

3. Disregard the quotient and add the remainder C(X) to the product to yield the code message polynomial F(X), which is represented as X^{n-k} [G(X)] + C(X).

The division is performed in binary without carries or borrows. In this case, the remainder is always one bit less than the divisor. The remainder is the BCC and the divisor is the generator polynomial; therefore, the bit length of the BCC is always one less than the number of bits in the generator polynomial. A simple example is explained below.

1. Given:

   Message polynomial $G(X) = 110011$ $(X^5 + X^4 + X + X^0)$
   Generator polynomial $P(X) = 11001$ $(X^4 + X^3 + 1)$
   G(X) contains 6 data bits
   P(X) contains 5 bits and will yield a BCC with 4 bits; therefore, $n - k = 4$.

2. Multiplying the message G(X) by X^{n-k} gives:

   $$X^{n-k}[G(X)] = X^4(X^5 + X^4 + X + X^0) = X^9 + X^8 + X^5 + X^4$$

   The binary equivalent of this product contains 10 bits and is 1100110000.

3. This product is divided by P(X).

   $$
   \begin{array}{r}
   100001 \quad \longleftarrow \text{quotient} \\
   P(X) \rightarrow 1001 \overline{\smash{)}\,1100110000} \quad \longleftarrow X^{n-k}[G(X)] \\
   11001 \\
   \overline{10000} \\
   11001 \\
   \overline{1001} \quad \longleftarrow \text{remainder} = C(X) = BCC
   \end{array}
   $$

4. The remainder C(X) is added to $X^{n-k}[G(X)]$ to give F(X) = 1100111001.

The code message polynomial is transmitted. The receiving station divides it by the same generator polynomial. If there is no error, the division will produce no remainder and it is assumed that the message is correct. A remainder indicates an error. The division is shown below.

$$
\begin{array}{r}
100001 \\
P(X)\rightarrow 11001\ \overline{\left)1100111001\right.} \leftarrow F(X) \\
\underline{11001} \\
11001 \\
\underline{11001} \\
00000 \leftarrow \text{no remainder}
\end{array}
$$

A more practical example of generating a BCC by long division is shown in Figure 13-5. Generation of a BCC for the same message by use of a shift register will be shown in Figure 13-8.

In typical data communication hardware, the BCC is computed and ac-

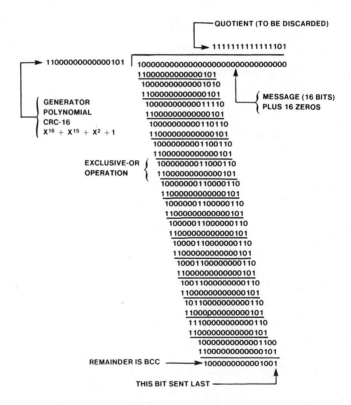

Figure 13-5. BCC Computation Using Long Division Method with CRC-16 as Generator

cumulated in a shift register. The configuration of the register is based on the CRC code to be implemented. The number of stages in the register is equal to the degree of the generating polynomial; the number of exclusive-OR elements is also a function of the polynomial. In the subsequent examples, a unique register configuration is shown for each CRC code (CRC-12, CRC-16, and CRC-CCITT).

1. *CRC-12*

   CRC-12 is applied to synchronous systems that use 6-bit characters. The BCC accumulation is 12 bits. The generator polynomial is $X^{12} + X^{11} + X^3 + X^2 + X + 1$ with prime factors of $(X + 1)$ and $(X^{11} + X^2 + 1)$. It provides error detection of bursts up to 12 bits in length.

   Figure 13-6 shows a block diagram configuration of a BCC register for use with CRC-12. A step-by-step shift pattern is shown as the data is serially applied to the register. Initially, the register contains all 0s. A 12-bit data word (a 1 followed by eleven 0s) is the input to the register. Prior to the first shift, the first data bit (LSB), which is a 1, is exclusive-ORed with the 0 from the LSB of the register. The result on the serial quotient line is a 1 which is sent via the feedback paths to the following places: bit 11 and the exclusive-ORs between bits 11 and 10, bits 10 and 9, bits 9 and 8, and bits 1 and 0. When the feedback settles down, the first shift takes place and produces the register states in the line labeled 1 under the SHIFT NO. column. The shift also presents the next data bit to the input. The process repeats until all 12 data bits are encoded. The BCC is the contents of the register after shift number 12. The most important fact to remember is that the exclusive-OR of the LSB of the BCC register and the input data bit set up the feedback path prior to the shifting operation. The result of this operation is shown under the column labeled FEEDBACK BEFORE SHIFT. When the shift takes place, the results of the exclusive-OR operations are shifted into the register.

The subsequent examples, which show the BCC accumulation for CRC-CCITT and CRC-16, can be analyzed the same way; the register length, data word length, and feedback paths are different but the process is the same.

2. *CRC-CCITT*

   CRC-CCITT is the standard used to compute a BCC for European systems. When operating with eight bit characters, the BCC accumulation is 16 bits. The generator polynomial is $X^{16} + X^{12} + X^5$

ERROR DETECTION

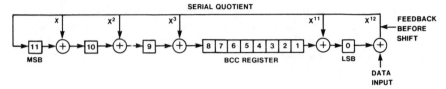

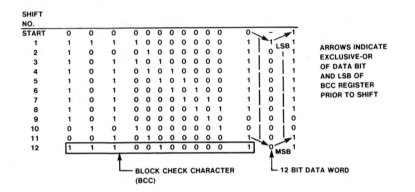

NOTES

☐ = BCC REGISTER STAGE
⊕ = EXCLUSIVE-OR
CRC-12 POLYNOMIAL = $X^{12} + X^{11} + X^3 + X^2 + X + 1$
LSB = LEAST SIGNIFICANT BIT OF REGISTER (SENT FIRST)
MSB = MOST SIGNIFICANT BIT OF REGISTER (SENT LAST)

Figure 13-6.   BCC Accumulation Using CRC-12, Transmit Sequence

+ 1. It provides error detection of bursts up to 16 bits in length. Additionally, more than 99% of error bursts greater than 12 bits can be detected.

Figure 3-7 shows a BCC accumulation using a 16-bit data word (a 1 followed by fifteen 0s).

3. *CRC-16*
    CRC-16 is applied to synchronous systems that use eight-bit characters. The BCC accumulation is 16 bits. The generator polynomial is $X^{16} + X^{15} + X^2 + 1$. It provides error detection of bursts up to 16 bits in length. Additionally, more than 99% of error bursts greater than 16 bits can be detected.

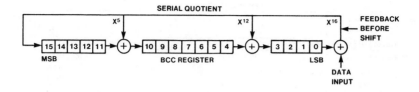

SHIFT NO.																				
START	0 0 0 0 0	0 0 0 0 0 0	0 0 0 0	–	1	
1	1 0 0 0 0	1 0 0 0 0 0	1 0 0 0	1 LSB 0	ARROWS INDICATE
2	0 1 0 0 0	0 1 0 0 0 0	0 1 0 0	0 0	EXCLUSIVE-OR
3	0 0 1 0 0	0 0 1 0 0 0	0 0 1 0	0 0	OF DATA BIT
4	0 0 0 1 0	0 0 0 1 0 0	0 0 0 1	0 1	AND LSB OF
5	1 0 0 0 1	1 0 0 0 1 0 0	1 0 0 0	0 0	BCC REGISTER
6	0 1 0 0 0	1 1 0 0 0 1 0	0 1 0 0	0 0	PRIOR TO SHIFT
7	0 0 1 0 0	0 1 1 0 0 0 1	0 0 1 0	0 0	
8	0 0 0 1 0	0 0 1 1 0 0 0	1 0 0 1	0 1	
9	1 0 0 0 1	1 0 0 1 1 0 0	1 1 0 0	0 0	
10	0 1 0 0 0	1 1 0 0 1 1 0	0 1 1 0	0 0	
11	0 0 1 0 0	0 1 1 0 0 1 1	0 0 1 1	0 1	
12	1 0 0 1 0	1 0 1 1 0 0 1	0 0 0 1	0 1	
13	1 1 0 0 1	1 1 0 1 1 0 0	0 0 0 0	0 0	
14	0 1 1 0 0	1 1 1 0 1 1 0	0 0 0 0	0 0	
15	0 0 1 1 0	0 1 1 1 0 1 1	0 0 0 0	0 0	
16	0 0 0 1 1	0 0 1 1 1 0 1	1 0 0 0	0 MSB 0	

BLOCK CHECK CHARACTER (BCC) ——— 16 BIT DATA WORD

NOTES:

☐ = BCC REGISTER STAGE
⊕ = EXCLUSIVE-OR
CRC–CCITT POLYNOMIAL = $X^{16} + X^{12} + X^5 + 1$
LSB = LEAST SIGNIFICANT BIT OF REGISTER (SENT FIRST)
MSB = MOST SIGNIFICANT BIT OF REGISTER (SENT LAST)

Figure 13-7. BCC Accumulation Using CRC-CCITT, Transmit Sequence

Figure 13-8 shows a BCC accumulation using a 16-bit data word (a 1 followed by fifteen 0s).

The three CRC examples (Figures 13-6, 13-7, and 13-8) show BCC accumulations that are to be used in a transmission sequence. Figure 13-9 shows the BCC accumulation performed on a message that has been received along with a BCC. The message and the computed BCC have been taken from Figure 13-8, i.e., a BCC accumulation using CRC-16. In Figure 13-9, the accumulation process is the same as that shown in Figure 13-8 through shift number 16. Starting with shift number 17, the BCC is sent to the data input, LSB first. A correct transmitted BCC results in all 0's in the BCC register at the end of the computation. In effect, this is a comparison of the trans-

ERROR DETECTION

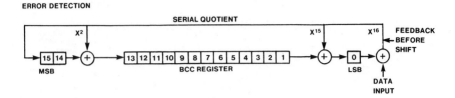

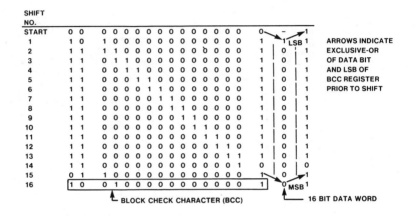

Figure 13-8. BCC Accumulation Using CRC-16, Transmit Sequence

mitted BCC with the one computed at the receiving station. A correct comparison yields a 0 remainder, or all 0s in the BCC register.

In addition to the shift register implementations of Cyclic Redundancy Checks that are shown in the preceding discussions, it is relatively simple to implement CRC calculation using a parallel arrangement of exclusive-OR gates and two registers. The CRC accumulated to date is stored in Register 1. The character just received is stored in Register 2. A network of exclusive-OR gates combines the contents of Registers 1 and 2 and the result is recorded back into Register 1.

Software algorithms (mainly table driven) have also been developed to do CRC calculation.

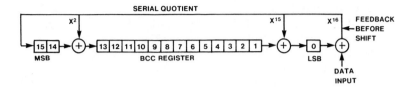

SHIFT NO.	15	14	13	12	11	10	9	8	7	6	5	4	3	2	1				
START	0	0	0	0	0	0	0	0	0	0	0	0	0	0	0	0	−		1
1	1	0	1	0	0	0	0	0	0	0	0	0	0	0	0	1	1 LSB		1
2	1	1	1	1	0	0	0	0	0	0	0	0	0	0	0	1	0		1
3	1	1	0	1	1	0	0	0	0	0	0	0	0	0	0	1	0		1
4	1	1	0	0	1	1	0	0	0	0	0	0	0	0	0	1	0		1
•	•	•		SAME AS CRC-16 TRANSMIT											•	•	•		•
•	•	•		SEQUENCE											•	•	•	DATA	•
13	1	1	0	0	0	0	0	0	0	0	0	0	0	1	1	1	0		1
14	1	1	0	0	0	0	0	0	0	0	0	0	0	0	1	0	0		0
15	0	1	1	0	0	0	0	0	0	0	0	0	0	0	0	1	0		1
16	1	0	0	1	0	0	0	0	0	0	0	0	0	0	0	1	0 MSB		1
17	0	1	0	0	1	0	0	0	0	0	0	0	0	0	0	0	1 LSB		0
18	0	0	1	0	0	1	0	0	0	0	0	0	0	0	0	0	0		0
19	0	0	0	1	0	0	1	0	0	0	0	0	0	0	0	0	0		0
20	0	0	0	0	1	0	0	1	0	0	0	0	0	0	0	0	0		0
21	0	0	0	0	0	1	0	0	1	0	0	0	0	0	0	0	0		0
22	0	0	0	0	0	0	1	0	0	1	0	0	0	0	0	0	0		0
23	0	0	0	0	0	0	0	1	0	0	1	0	0	0	0	0	0		0
24	0	0	0	0	0	0	0	0	1	0	0	1	0	0	0	0	0 BCC		0
25	0	0	0	0	0	0	0	0	0	1	0	0	1	0	0	0	0		0
26	0	0	0	0	0	0	0	0	0	0	1	0	0	1	0	0	0		0
27	0	0	0	0	0	0	0	0	0	0	0	1	0	0	1	0	0		0
28	0	0	0	0	0	0	0	0	0	0	0	0	1	0	0	1	0		0
29	0	0	0	0	0	0	0	0	0	0	0	0	0	1	0	0	1		0
30	0	0	0	0	0	0	0	0	0	0	0	0	0	0	1	0	0		0
31	0	0	0	0	0	0	0	0	0	0	0	0	0	0	0	1	0		0
32	0	0	0	0	0	0	0	0	0	0	0	0	0	0	0	0	1 MSB		0

ARROWS INDICATE EXCLUSIVE-OR OF DATA BIT AND LSB OF BCC REGISTER PRIOR TO SHIFT

BCC REGISTER ALL 0s — RECEIVED MESSAGE ASSUMED TO BE CORRECT

16 BIT DATA WORD AND BCC REGISTER

NOTES

☐ = BCC Register Stage
⊕ = Exclusive-OR
CRC-16 Polynomial = $X^{16} + X^{15} + X^2 + 1$
LSB = LEAST SIGNIFICANT BIT OF REGISTER (SENT FIRST)
MSB = MOST SIGNIFICANT BIT OF REGISTER (SENT LAST)

Figure 13-9. BCC Accumulation Using CRC-16, Receive Sequence

References

1. Boudreau, P. and Steen, R., "Cyclic Redundancy Checking by Program," *AFIPS Proceedings,* Vol. 39, 1971.
2. *KG11 Manual*, Digital Equipment Corporation.

3. Higginson, P. and Kirstein, P., "On the Computation of Cyclic Redundancy Checks by Program," *The Computer Journal* (British), Vol. 16, No. 1, Feb. 1973.
4. Marton, A. and Frambs, T., "A Cyclic Redundancy Checking (CRC) Algorithm," *Honeywell Computer Journal*, Vol. 5, No. 3, 1971.
5. Peterson, W. and Brown, D., "Cyclic Codes for Error Detection," *Proceedings of the IRE,* January 1961.
6. Peterson, W., *Error Correcting Codes,* MIT Press, Cambridge, Mass., 1961.
7. Wecker, S. "A Table-Lookup Algorithm for Software Computation of Cyclic Redundancy Check (CRC)," Digital Equipment Corporation memorandum, 1974.

Note: References 1, 3, 4, 5, and 6 are reference citations obtained from the Wecker memorandum, Reference 7.

14

Synchronous
Communication

In Chapter 1, the format for a typical character being transmitted in an asynchronous transmission system was discussed. It is repeated in Figure 14-1.

Although modern asynchronous receivers do not require a STOP interval for mechanism coasting purposes, they do require a STOP interval to guarantee that each character will begin with a 1-to-0 transition, even if the preceding character was entirely zeros. The requirement for a 1-to-0 transition to indicate the beginning of each character causes an eight bit data character to require 10 bit times to transmit. Twenty percent of the line time is being used strictly for timing purposes.

Synchronous communication requires either a separate clock lead from the transmission point to the reception point, in addition to the data lead, or a modem that includes the clock information in the modulation process that encodes the data. In typical synchronous modems phase shift keying is used. The clock is recovered from the sidebands of the received signal and is brought out of the modem on a separate lead that indicates to the data communications hardware (typically a computer interface) the appropriate instant to sample the data on the "Received Data" lead. The inclusion of the clock with the data stream or "beside" the data stream keeps the transmitter and receiver in synchronism—hence the term "synchronous communication."

Since START and STOP bits are not required in synchronous communication, all bits are used to transmit data; this eliminates the 20 percent waste characteristic of asynchronous communication. However, the character "framing" information provided by the START and STOP bits is absent, so another method of determining which groups of bits constitute a character must be provided.

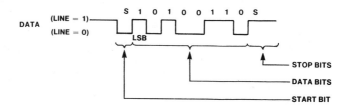

Figure 14-1. Asynchronous Data Character Format

Figure 14-2 shows the character format for synchronous transmission. Bits 1–8 might be one character and bits 9–13 part of another character, or bit 1 may be part of one character, bits 2–9 part of a second character, and bits 10–13 part of a third character, etc. The delimiting or framing of each actual character is accomplished by defining a synchronization character, commonly called "sync." The sync character is usually chosen such that its bit arrangement is significantly different from that of any of the regular characters being transmitted, and such that it has an irregular pattern (i.e., not 01010101). Thus, when a sync character is preceded and followed by regular characters, there is no likely successive pattern of bits that equals the bit pattern of the sync character except those eight bits that actually are the sync character. The sync character used in the 1968 ASCII is 10010110 (226 octal).

Typical synchronous receiver units are placed in a "sync search" mode by either hardware or software whenever a transmission begins, or whenever a data dropout has occurred and the hardware or software determines that resynchronization is necessary. In the sync search procedure, the hardware shifts a bit into the receiver shift register, compares the contents of the receiver shift register with the sync character (stored in another register), and, if no match occurs, repeats the process. If a match occurs, the receiver begins shifting in bits and raising a "character available" flag every eight bits. For even greater certainty that synchronization is occurring properly, most communications systems require that the receiver identify two successive sync characters before raising "character available" flags every eight bits.

It is fairly likely that the first sync character transmitted will be mangled in some fashion by the time it arrives on the Received Data lead of the receiving modem. Transients on the telephone line, start-up problems in the receiving modem, and a variety of other effects will contribute to the likelihood of damage to the first sync character. Therefore it is absolutely necessary in systems where the receiver reaches synchronization on receipt of one sync that at least two be sent, and in systems where the receiver "syncs up" on two syncs that at least three be sent.

Systems which require that the receiver recognize two successive sync characters to achieve synchronization are less prone to go into synchronization prematurely (i.e., less likely to be fooled by a bit pattern that looks

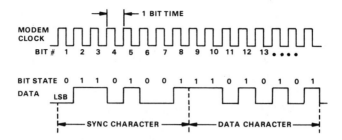

Figure 14-2. Synchronous Data Character Format

like sync but which is a combination of other characters). The requirement that two sync characters be recognized poses some interesting problems. Assume that the string of three sync characters shown in Figure 14-3 is received.

Slashes (/) have been inserted for the reader's convenience, and the first two bits received have been replaced with Xs to indicate that they were received in error. This example is exactly the case described above: the first character has been damaged, but the transmitter has sent three syncs and thus there are still two left for the receiver to recognize. Now assume reception of the characters in Figure 14-4.

In this example, the second character contains an erroneous bit. There are no two syncs in a row, thus the receiver cannot synchronize. This particular problem could be solved by sending four syncs, as illustrated in Figure 14-5.

Now, despite the erroneous bit in the second character, there are two good sync characters following, and the receiver can achieve synchronization. In this case, ability of the receiver to synchronize on the remaining two syncs will depend on how the receiver logic recovers from the erroneous second

Figure 14-3. Receipt of Three Sync Characters with Error in First Character

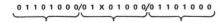

Figure 14-4. Receipt of Three Sync Characters with Error in Second Character

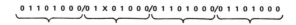

Figure 14-5. Receipt of Four Sync Characters with Error in Second Character

character. If the receiver, upon receiving each bit, does a comparison against a 16 bit register which contains two sync characters, the receiver will be able to resynchronize using the final two sync characters in this example. If the receiver, upon receiving each bit, does a comparison against an eight bit register which contains a sync character, and then sets a flag that it has "seen a sync," the receiver must shift in eight more bits and then choose between the following alternatives. If this set of eight bits is also a sync, set the "synchronization achieved" flag. If this set of eight bits is not a sync, clear the "seen a sync" flag and start all over again looking at a bit at a time. If this decision process takes too long, the third sync character will be on its way into the receiver, and a decision to resume bit-at-a-time sampling will occur too late for the first bit of the third sync character to be included in this sampling process. Thus, the receiver will not see two more complete sync characters and will not resynchronize. To cover this situation and to cover the possibility of two bits (last bit of second sync and first bit of third sync) being erroneous, conservative programming practice calls for the transmission of five sync characters. Of course, there is no rule which says one cannot transmit 20 sync characters at the beginning of each message, but to do so for a 100 character message would result in a 20 percent waste of line time, which would be just as inefficient as asynchronous transmission.

In addition to its different method for delineating characters, synchronous transmission also differs from asynchronous transmission in the type of error correction, line speeds, and modems commonly used.

Because bits arrive at a steady, predictable rate in synchronous systems, modems that use phase modulation and other techniques dependent upon constant data flow can be utilized. These modems are substantially more expensive than the simple frequency shift keying modems discussed previously, but the line speeds achieved are also substantially higher. Whereas 1200 or 1800 bits per second is the top operating speed for frequency shift keyed asynchronous modems operating on voice grade telephone lines, speeds of 4800 and 9600 bits per second are achieved with phase modulated and phase/amplitude modulated synchronous modems.

First, however, a brief review of modulation processes is in order. Most people are familiar with the two types of modulation used for commercial radio broadcast: amplitude modulation (AM) and frequency modulation (FM). In both of these modulation processes, a signal of characteristics appropriate for propagation over large distances is used, and that signal is altered at the transmitting station so as to convey information to someone receiving the signal. The signal used is called the "carrier" and the process of altering it is called "modulation." Obtaining the information back again at the receiving station is done by a process called "demodulation." By way of review, it is the combination of the words *mo*dulation and *dem*odulation that brings us the word "modem."

If one were to measure the output of a radio station during a moment when the announcer was not saying anything, and observe that output with a device which could plot voltage as a function of time (an oscilloscope), one would see only the carrier, as shown in Figure 14-6. If the announcer then began to speak, the appearance of the signal would depend on whether the radio station was an AM (amplitude modulated) station or an FM (frequency modulated) station. If it were an AM station, the oscilloscope would show a signal similar to that in Figure 14-7. If it were an FM station, Figure 14-8 would apply.

In the case of the AM station, the information has been applied to the carrier by altering its amplitude. In the FM case, the information has been applied to the carrier by altering its frequency. The asynchronous modems which were discussed in Chapter 4 performed frequency shift keying to apply information to the carrier and were thus a simplified case of FM. There are, however, methods other than AM and FM that can be used to alter the carrier to convey information. Phase modulation is the most widely used of these other methods.

The concept of "phase" may best be understood by comparison to the moon, an object widely known to have phase. Figure 14-9 shows one and a quarter cycles of the moon. The waveform shown under the faces of the

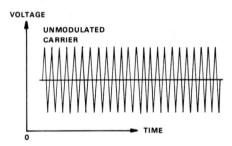

Figure 14-6. Unmodulated Carrier

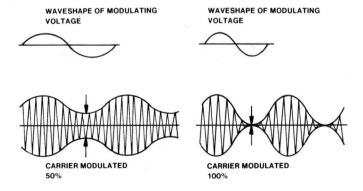

Figure 14-7. Amplitude Modulation

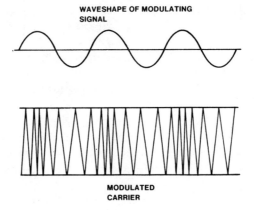

Figure 14-8.   Frequency Modulation

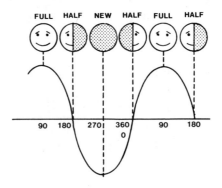

Figure 14-9.   Phases of Moon

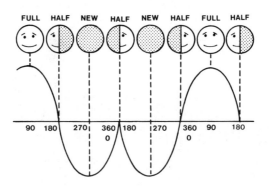

Figure 14-10.   Phase Modulation Example

moon could just as well represent the carrier signal discussed in previous paragraphs. Figure 14-10 illustrates the concept of phase modulation.

The waveform shown in both Figures 14-9 and 14-10 is one that is commonly generated by electronic equipment. It is called a sine wave because its magnitude varies in exactly the same fashion as the geometric function sine. Thus it is possible to label the horizontal axis of Figure 14-9 with the 90, 180, 270, 360/0, 90, and 180 degree markings to indicate that a sine waveform is being used. Furthermore, it is possible to represent the same information shown in Figure 14-9 in a phase diagram such as Figure 14-11. In addition to the moon phases (or signal phases) shown, any intermediate phase can be represented by a pointer such as the one drawn for a 45 degree phase angle.

Using the phase angle representation system, it is possible to represent the phase change shown in Figure 14-10 as a phase angle change of 180 degrees (see Figure 14-12).

Phase angle changes are what convey information in phase modulation. Assume a signaling arrangement where phase angle changes of 45°, 135°, 225°, and 315° are used to represent the data being transmitted. Since there

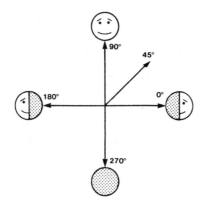

Figure 14-11.   Phase Angle Representation of Phase of Moon

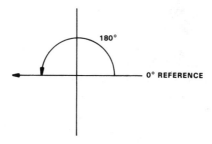

Figure 14-12.   Phase Angle Representation of the Phase Change Shown in Figure 14-10

are four different phase angle changes possible, bit combinations of 11, 10, 00, and 01 can be transmitted. In the 201C modem, these two bit combinations are referred to as "dibits" and are transmitted at a rate of 1200 dibits per second, or 2400 bits per second. Thus every 1/1200th of a second, the carrier being produced by a 201C is changed in phase 45°, 135°, 225°, or 315° depending on whether an 11, 10, 00, or 01 dibit is to be transmitted. The phase changes listed are measured relative to the phase at the beginning of the previous dibit, rather than from the end of one dibit to the beginning of the next. This distinction becomes important in those cases where there is not an integral number of carrier cycles per dibit. Note that the "baud rate" is 1200 baud, despite the 2400 bit per second data transmission rate.

Data is recovered in the 201C by using "product modulators" despite their being used in the demodulator. A product modulator multiplies two input signals. The mathematics is as follows, assuming an input signal of $\cos \omega t$ and another signal of $\cos(\omega t + \theta)$. (Cosines are used in this example, but a similar presentation can be done with sines.)

$$\cos x \cos y = 1/2 \, [\cos(x+y) + \cos(x-y)]$$

$$\cos(\omega t + \theta) \cos \omega t = 1/2 \cos(2\omega t + \theta) + 1/2 \cos \theta$$

This result is expressed schematically in Figure 14-13. The signal shown as $\cos \omega t$ is the carrier at the end of the previous dibit and the signal shown as $\cos(\omega t + \theta)$ is the carrier at the end of the present dibit.

Thus, phase angle θ is the 45°, 135°, 225°, or 315° change of phase that represents receipt of dibit 11, 10, 00, or 01. The first term in the output of the product modulator is proportional to $2\omega t$ and is called a "double frequency term." It is not useful in this application and may be removed by passing the signal through a filter which allows only low frequencies to get through. The second term does not contain a time (t) term at all and is called the "d.c. term." This term produces a positive output voltage when θ is either 45° or 315°. To determine which of the two is the value of θ, a second product modulator is used whose inputs are $\cos \omega t$ and $\cos(\omega t + \theta - 90°)$. If the output of this second product modulator is also positive, the angle θ must have been 45°, as 45° minus 90° is 315°, which is also positive. If the output of the second modulator is negative, θ must have been 315°. The same circuitry can also detect whether θ has a value of 135° or 225°, since both of those values will produce a negative d.c. term, while only the 225° value for θ will remain negative despite a minus 90° shift.

By extension of these same principles, it is possible to transmit bits three at a time (tribits), using eight different phase angles. Together with an increase in the line signaling rate from 1200 baud to 1600 baud, this results in a bit rate of 4800 bits per second. As was the case with frequency shift keying, the modulation procedure has limits. First, the receiver cannot discern the difference between different signaling indications if they occur too rapidly or are too similar. In addition, phase shift keying eventually is limited by

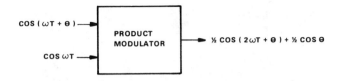

COS (ωT + θ) ——

PRODUCT MODULATOR

COS ωT ——

→ ½ COS (2ωT + θ) + ½ COS θ

Figure 14-13. Product Modulator

the performance of carrier transmission systems. These systems do not transmit the actual carrier used to perform the modulation; they just transmit the results of the modulation process. For example, a telephone conversation of 300 to 3000 Hertz would be transmitted as 200,300 Hertz to 203,000 Hertz, but the 200,000 Hertz signal itself would not be transmitted.

To perform demodulation at the receiving station, carrier must be reinserted. The reinserted carrier may vary slightly relative to the carrier used in the modulation process at the transmitting station. The difference between the carrier used for modulation and the carrier used for demodulation shows up as a phase change in the signal being transmitted through the carrier system. In voice communications a change of phase is not noticeable. With phase shift keyed modems, however, the phase change introduced by the carrier system may affect the ability of the receiving modem to perceive the phase changes from the transmitting modem that contain the data transmission information. The Switched Telecommunications Network Connection Survey (Bell System Technical Reference PUB 41007) indicates that the magnitude of the phase shifts introduced by carrier systems is rather small. This effect, however, is one of the reasons that modems designed to achieve 9600 bit per second transmission speeds use amplitude modulation in addition to phase modulation, rather than simply doubling the number of phase angles used in 4800 bit per second transmission. The 9600 bit per second modems use 12 phase angles, four of which have two amplitude values. The line signaling speed is 2400 baud. Figure 14-14 shows the phase angles used.

The modems discussed in this chapter are sensitive not only to phase changes but also to noise. They are not necessarily more sensitive to noise than slower speed modems, but the operating speeds in synchronous communications are high enough that line disturbances lasting only a few milliseconds are sufficient to invalidate substantial quantities of data. Hence, simple character parity error detection systems are insufficient and either a combination of LRC/VRC or a Cyclic Redundancy Check must be used.

There is one more point about synchronous vs. asynchronous transmission that should be noted. It is not always true that asynchronous is slow and synchronous is fast. There are terminals that operate over short distances at an asynchronous rate of 38,400 bits per second. There are also a substantial number of terminals in use that operate at 1200 bits per second synchronous.

Synchronous modems typically have the following interface leads, the functions of which were described in Chapters 5 and 9.

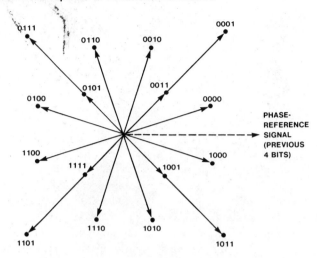

Figure 14-14. Phase Angles for 9600 Bit-per-Second Transmission

	Reference Designation		Function
EIA		**CCITT**	
AA			Protective Ground
AB		102	Signal Ground or Common Return
BA		103	Transmitted Data
BB		104	Received Data
CA		105	Request to Send
CB		106	Clear to Send
CC		107	Data Set Ready
CD		108/2	Data Terminal Ready
CE		125	Ring Indicator
CF		109	Received Line Signal Detector

In addition, interface leads are provided that are unique to synchronous modems (except as noted).

CG		110	Signal Quality Detector
CH		111	Data Signal Rate Selector (DTE Source)*
CI		112	Data Signal Rate Selector (DCE Source)*
DA		113	Transmitter Signal Element Timing (DTE Source)
DB		114	Transmitter Signal Element Timing (DCE Source)
DD		115	Receiver Signal Element Timing (DCE Source)

*The signal rate selection circuits are also used in some asynchronous modems, particularly in Europe.

The definitions of the additional modem leads are given below:

EIA RS-232-C Definitions	CCITT V.24 Definitions

Circuit CG—Signal Quality Detector (CCITT 110)
Direction: From data communication equipment

Signals on this circuit are used to indicate whether or not there is a high probability of an error in the received data.

An ON condition is maintained whenever there is no reason to believe that an error has occurred.

An OFF condition indicates that there is a high probability of an error. It may, in some instances, be used to call automatically for the retransmission of the previously transmitted data signal.

Preferably the response of this circuit shall be such as to permit identification of individual questionable signal elements on Circuit BB (Received Data).

Circuit CH—Data Signal Rate Selector (DTE Source) (CCITT 111)
Direction: To data communication equipment

Signals on this circuit are used to select between the two data signaling rates in the case of dual rate synchronous data sets or the two ranges of data signaling rates in the case of dual range non-synchronous data sets.

An ON condition shall select the higher data signaling rate or range of rates.

The rate of timing signals, if included in the interface, shall be controlled by this circuit as may be appropriate.

Circuit CI—Data Signal Rate Selector (DCE Source) (CCITT 112)
Direction: From data communication equipment

Signals on this circuit are used to select between the two data signaling rates in the case of dual rate synchronous data sets or the two ranges of data signaling rates in the case of dual range non-synchronous data sets.

An ON condition shall select the higher data signaling rate or range of rates.

Circuit 110—Data Signal Quality Detector
Direction: From DCE

Signals on this circuit indicate whether there is a reasonable probability of an error in the data received on the data channel. The signal quality indicated conforms to the relevant DCE Recommendation.

The ON condition indicates that there is no reason to believe that an error has occurred.

The OFF condition indicates that there is a reasonable probability of an error.

Circuit 111—Data Signaling Rate Selector (DTE Source)
Direction: To DCE

Signals on this circuit are used to select one of the two data signaling rates of a dual rate synchronous DCE, or to select one of the two ranges of data signaling rates of a dual range asynchronous DCE.

The ON condition selects the higher rate or range of rates.

The OFF condition selects the lower rate or range of rates.

Circuit 112—Data Signaling Rate Selector (DCE Source)
Direction: From DCE

Signals on this circuit are used to select one of the two data signaling rates or ranges of rates in the DTE to coincide with the data signaling rate or range of rates in use in a dual rate synchronous or dual range asynchronous DCE.

The ON condition selects the higher rate or range of rates.

EIA RS-232-C Definitions	CCITT V.24 Definitions
Circuit CI (Cont.)	*Circuit 112 (Cont.)*

The rate of timing signals, if included in the interface, shall be controlled by this circuit as may be appropriate.

The OFF condition selects the lower rate or range of rates.

Circuit DA—Transmitter Signal Element Timing (DTE Source) (CCITT 113)
Direction: To data communication equipment

Circuit 113—Transmitter Signal Element Timing (DTE Source)
Direction: To DCE

Signals on this circuit are used to provide the transmitting signal converter with signal element timing information.

Signals on this circuit provide the DCE with signal element timing information.

The ON to OFF transition shall nominally indicate the center of each signal element on Circuit BA (Transmitted Data). When Circuit DA is implemented in the DTE, the DTE shall normally provide timing information on this circuit whenever the DTE is in a POWER ON condition. It is permissible for the DTE to withhold timing information on this circuit for short periods provided Circuit CA (Request to Send) is in the OFF condition. (For example, the temporary withholding of timing information may be necessary in performing maintenance tests within the DTE.)

The condition on this circuit shall be ON and OFF for nominally equal periods of time, and the transition from ON to OFF condition shall nominally indicate the center of each signal element on Circuit 103 (Transmitted Data).

Circuit DB—Transmitter Signal Element Timing (DCE Source) (CCITT 114)
Direction: From data communication equipment

Circuit 114—Transmitter Signal Element Timing (DCE Source)
Direction: From DCE

Signals on this circuit are used to provide the data terminal equipment with signal element timing information. The data terminal equipment shall provide a data signal on Circuit BA (Transmitted Data) in which the transitions between signal elements nominally occur at the time of the transitions from OFF to ON condition of the signal on Circuit DB. When Circuit DB is implemented in the DCE, the DCE shall normally provide timing information on this circuit whenever the DCE is in a POWER ON condition. It is permissible for the DCE to withhold timing information on this circuit for short periods provided Circuit CC (Data Set Ready) is in the OFF condition. (For example, the withholding of timing information may be necessary in performing maintenance tests within the DCE.)

Signals on this circuit provide the DTE with signal element timing information.

The condition on this circuit shall be ON and OFF for nominally equal periods of time. The DTE shall present a data signal on Circuit 103 (Transmitted Data) in which the transitions between signal elements nominally occur at the time of the transitions from OFF to ON condition of Circuit 114.

EIA RS-232-C Definitions	CCITT V.24 Definitions

Circuit DD—Receiver Signal Element Timing (DCE Source) (CCITT 115)
Direction: From data communication equipment

Signals on this circuit are used to provide the data terminal equipment with received signal element timing information. The transition from ON to OFF condition shall nominally indicate the center of each signal element on Circuit BB (Received Data). Timing information on Circuit DD shall be provided at all times when Circuit CF (Received Line Signal Detector) is in the ON condition. It may, but need not, be present following the ON to OFF transition of Circuit CF.

Circuit 115—Receiver Signal Element Timing (DCE Source)
Direction: From DCE

Signals on this circuit provide the DTE with signal element timing information.

The condition of this circuit shall be ON and OFF for nominally equal periods of time, and a transition from ON to OFF condition shall nominally indicate the center of each signal element on Circuit 104 (Received Data).

15

A Single Line
Synchronous Interface

As with asynchronous communication interfaces, many of the required functions in synchronous communication interfaces are now performed by LSI chips. Unlike the asynchronous case, however, no single computer manufacturer led the way, nor did the migration of personnel from a single integrated circuit company spread a standard component pinning across the industry. Instead, some manufacturers produced a chip that was a synchronous/asynchronous transmitter and a second that was a synchronous/asynchronous receiver. Others combined a synchronous transmitter and receiver in a single chip. Now, progress in LSI technology has produced single chips that serve several lines.

Regardless of the number of lines served by a chip, there are usually eight leads that deliver the received characters to the computer and eight leads upon which the computer can place characters for transmission onto the communications line. There are additional leads which indicate that a received character is available for reading by the computer and which indicate that the transmitter is available for the computer to load with a character for transmission. Other leads provide overrun and underrun error indications.

As in the asynchronous case, an overrun error occurs when the characters are not read out of the receiver register as fast as they are received–this results in a character's arriving and the receiver having no place to store it. Underrun occurs when a transmitter can transmit characters faster than they are being loaded into the transmitter–this results in the transmitter's having nothing to send. This latter condition is not fatal in asynchronous communication, as the stop interval is merely made longer. Hence, asynchronous receivers do not report an error under these circumstances. Underrun can be fatal in synchronous communication, however, and the conditions under

136

which this is true are explained in the chapters describing the various protocols. Since underrun conditions at a transmitting station can cause messages to be negatively acknowledged by the receiving station, it is important that an underrun error indication be provided.

Like the UART, synchronous interface chips include leads that determine the number of bits per character, and whether or not parity operation is enabled. If parity is used, the chips include leads that determine whether that parity is odd or even.

Figure 15-1 shows a block diagram of a single line synchronous interface. The "bus" is the computer input/output bus, including the address selection lines which permit the computer to select individual registers within peripheral devices for the purpose of reading or writing those registers. When a register is to be read, the address selection logic gates the contents of the receiver buffer, the receiver status register, or the transmitter status register onto the leads labeled "parallel data" at the top of the figure. This enables the "bus drivers" to place the data that has been read onto the computer I/O bus data lines. When a register is to be written, data on the computer I/O bus data lines is received by the "bus receivers" and presented to the receiver status register, the transmitter status register, and the transmitter buf-

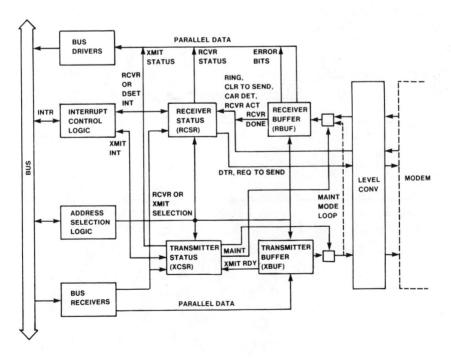

Figure 15-1. Block Diagram for Single Line Synchronous Interface

fer registers, via the "parallel data" leads at the bottom of the figure. The address selection logic strobes the data from the parallel data leads into the selected register.

The bit assignments for these registers are shown in Figure 15-2.

The one remaining block to be explained is labeled "level converters." As was mentioned in conjunction with a similar figure in Chapter 2, data communication is seldom done at transistor-transistor logic levels (TTL) once a signal lead is outside the box containing the computer and/or computer communications interface. Thus, single line synchronous interfaces typically contain level converter circuits which convert the TTL logic levels to EIA RS-232-C voltage levels. Since the RS-232-C specification is only applicable up to 20,000 bits per second, data rates above this must use some other type of interface. Some of the high speed interfaces that could be used are RS-422, RS-423, and the combined single-ended/differential interface specified in CCITT Recommendation V.35.

In Chapter 2, a single line asynchronous interface was presented (Figure 2-1) which had the bit assignments shown in Figure 15-2.

With the exception of the bit designated in parentheses, which will be commented on below, a single line synchronous interface can use, as a starting point, the exact same bits as the asynchronous interface. The meanings of the bit assignments are the same as those explained in Chapter 2. Receiver Done (RCVR DONE) indicates that a character has been received and, if Receiver Interrupt Enable (RCVR IE) is also a "1" at the time this occurs,

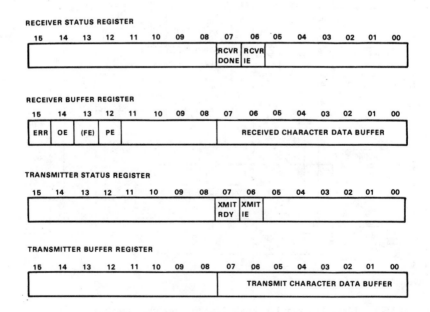

Figure 15-2. Sample Bit Assignments for Single Line Synchronous Interface

the setting of RCVR DONE will cause an interrupt to the computer. The character that has been received is presented in the Receiver Buffer Register along with any error flags that may have accompanied it. Transmitter Ready (XMIT RDY) indicates that the transmitter is ready to be loaded with a character for transmission, and the computer may load such a character by writing it into the Transmitter Buffer Register. Like the Receiver Done Flag, the Transmitter Ready Flag will generate an interrupt if the program has previously indicated the desirability of this by setting the interrupt enable bit (XMIT IE).

One of the bits shown in Figure 15-2 has its designation enclosed in parentheses. This bit, Framing Error (FE), is associated only with asynchronous communication, and will be dropped from further discussions and figures. It should be noted, however, for the sake of completeness, that Framing Error is also used when asynchronous format characters (i.e., those delineated with START and STOP bits) are sent with a clocking connection between the transmitter and receiver. This method of sending asynchronous format data by synchronous means is called "isochronous" transmission.

Because a great deal of asynchronous communication takes place between a computer and a local teleprinter terminal, typically the "console teleprinter," computer manufacturers all offer simple single line asynchronous interfaces similar to that described in Chapter 2, even though some are an integral part of the processor itself. The market for synchronous communication hardware, however, includes a much larger percentage of applications where modems are required. Thus, most single line synchronous interfaces include some type of modem control facility. This requires that the bit assignments of Figure 15-2 be expanded to those shown in Figure 15-3. It should be noted that only the Receiver Status Register and the Transmitter Status Register have had bits added. The Receiver Buffer Register and Transmitter Buffer Register have not been changed.

In the same way that bit 15 of the Receiver Buffer Register is set whenever any receiver error condition is reported (OE or PE), bit 15 of the Receiver Status Register sets whenever there is a change in modem (data set) status. This bit is called the Data Set Change Interrupt (DS INT) bit and, if set, will generate an interrupt—provided that bit 05, the Data Set Change Interrupt Enable (DS IE), is also set. The modem leads which are monitored for changes are Ring, Clear to Send, Carrier Detect, and Data Set Ready. The status of these leads is reflected at any given moment by the status of bits 14, 13, 12, and 09 respectively. The functions of these leads are described in detail in Chapter 9, but are reviewed briefly here. Ring indicates that the modem is being signaled by the telephone switching equipment that a call is being made to the line. Clear to Send is an indication to the computer interface that data applied to the Transmitted Data lead of the modem by the transmitter section of the interface will probably succeed in reaching the receiving station. Carrier Detect, also called Received Line Signal Detector, is an indication that modem carrier is being received from the distant

look for sync pulse

RECEIVER STATUS REGISTER

15	14	13	12	11	10	09	08	07	06	05	04	03	02	01	00
DS INT	RING	CLR SND	CAR DET	RCVR ACT		DS RDY	ST SY	RCVR DONE	RCVR IE	DS IE	SCH SYN		REQ SND	DTR	

RECEIVER BUFFER REGISTER

15	14	13	12	11	10	09	08	07	06	05	04	03	02	01	00
ERR	OE		PE					RECEIVED CHARACTER DATA BUFFER							

TRANSMITTER STATUS REGISTER

15	14	13	12	11	10	09	08	07	06	05	04	03	02	01	00
DNA	MAINTENANCE SYSTEM					XMIT ACT		XMIT RDY	XMIT IE	DNA IE	SEND	HALF DPLX			

TRANSMITTER BUFFER REGISTER

15	14	13	12	11	10	09	08	07	06	05	04	03	02	01	00
								TRANSMIT CHARACTER DATA BUFFER							

Figure 15-3. Expanded Bit Assignments for a Synchronous Interface

modem. Data Set Ready indicates that the modem has its power on, is not in voice mode or test mode, and is ready to transfer data.

The Receiver Status word also provides the capability for the computer program to control two of the leads that go to the modem: Request to Send and Data Terminal Ready. This is accomplished by bits 02 and 01 respectively. Request to Send is used to turn on the modem's transmitter section to initiate the transmission of data from this modem to the distant modem. In addition to turning on its transmitter, the modem responds by asserting Clear to Send (bit 13) in response to the assertion of Request to Send. The delay between Request to Send and Clear to Send can be selected (in the modem) to be zero to 250 milliseconds or greater. By this time, the modem should have propagated its signal (carrier) to the distant modem. The Data Terminal Ready lead is used to answer calls to this modem and to maintain calls that have been originated or answered by this modem. When the computer program negates Data Terminal Ready by clearing this bit, the interface drops the assertion of DTR toward the modem and the modem drops the telephone line connection. (This applies to switched telephone service only—it is not used in private line applications.)

There are two remaining bits in the Receiver Status Register whose function has not been explained. These bits are not associated with modem operation, but rather have to do with the peculiarities of synchronous transmission. Bit 08 is Strip Sync (ST SY). Since the receiver has the ability to recognize which received characters are sync characters (this is necessary to achieve synchronization), and since sync characters received in addition to those used to synchronize are of little use, it would be convenient to be able to ignore the unnecessary sync characters. Consider a case where five sync characters are transmitted, and where the reception of two syncs places the receiver in synchronism. If the line has relatively little noise, the first two syncs received will place the receiver in synchronization. What happens to the next three sync characters? Barring any special features, these three characters arrive, generate interrupts, and are serviced by the interrupt service routine portion of the computer program. Chances are that the program is arranged to throw those characters away once they are recognized as syncs, as they are unnecessary for any purpose but synchronization. The computer program could be saved from wasting its time with these extra sync characters if the synchronous interface were to throw away any sync characters received between synchronization and the receipt of the first non-sync character. This is the purpose of the Strip Sync bit and the associated logic. It is not a good idea to throw away sync characters that appear in the midst of messages, as they might be part of a "transparent text stream." This will be explained more fully in Chapters 16 and 17.

The other unexplained bit is bit 04, Search Sync (SCH SYN). When set, this bit forces the receiver logic to go out of synchronization and to resume the search for sync characters. It does this by shifting in a bit at a time and comparing the most recently received eight bits against the sync character stored within the receiver. The Search Sync bit is set by the computer program whenever it believes, based on high error rates or lack of messages, that the receiver is out of synchronism. When the receiver again recognizes the appropriate number of sync characters, the receiver logic clears Search Sync.

As mentioned in conjunction with the Underrun lead from the synchronous transmitter chip, the inability of a computer program to feed characters to a transmitter at a sufficient rate will cause the transmitter to send an idling character, such as sync. This extra character can cause the receiving station to acknowledge the message negatively, depending upon the protocol being used and the circumstances at the time the extra character is sent. While it might be stated that it does not matter whether a few extra errors are thus introduced since the telephone line will be causing a fair number of errors anyway, it is often necessary to determine exactly what is causing the negative acknowledgements in a malfunctioning communication system. For this reason, the existence of an underrun lead is important. This lead is brought to bit 15 of the Transmitter Status Register, where it is called Data Not Available (DNA). The setting of this bit generates an interrupt if the program indicates that this is desirable, which it can do by leaving Data Not Available Interrupt Enable (DNA IE—bit 05) set.

Five of the bits in the Transmitter Status Register are devoted to the maintenance system. Figure 15-4 is a block diagram of the maintenance sys-

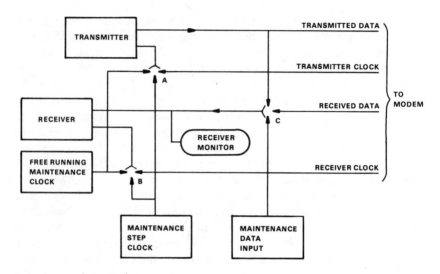

Figure 15-4. **Maintenance System for a Synchronous Interface**

tem. The points marked "A," "B," and "C" can be envisioned as three-way switches where the line going into the transmitter or receiver receives its input from one of the selected lines shown with arrowheads. The five bits devoted to maintenance in the Transmitter Status Register control the "switches" at points A and B to permit the transmitter and receiver to obtain their clocking from: 1) the modem, 2) a free-running maintenance clock, or 3) a clock that can be stepped at an arbitrary rate by loading bits into the "maintenance step clock." These various clocking schemes are used with various data path arrangements, which are controlled by the setting of switch C. Switch C is, like A and B, controlled by the maintenance bits in the Transmitter Status Register.

The system shown in Figure 15-4 functions in the following manner. Switches B and C are set so that clocking to the receiver comes from the maintenance step clock, and data for the receiver is applied to the maintenance data input. The data is applied a bit at a time and shifted in a bit at a time by manipulating the maintenance step clock. Typically two sync characters and some test characters are clocked into the receiver this way. The Receiver Status Register and Receiver Buffer Register are then checked to see if the characters have arrived correctly. The point shown as "Receiver Monitor" allows the diagnostic program to confirm that the data is entering the receiver correctly. If this test fails, it is known that there is a problem in the receiver system. If this test is passed, Switch A is arranged (if not already so arranged) so that the maintenance step clock provides clocking to both the transmitter and the receiver. Switch C is arranged so that the transmitted data is delivered to the receiver. Two sync characters and some test characters are loaded into the transmitter and clocked by the maintenance clock into the receiver. The receiver monitor (a bit in a register) may be periodically read to see whether the data is arriving at the input to the receiver. By examining the Transmitter Status Register for the Transmitter Ready Flag and examining both the Receiver Status Register and the Receiver Buffer Register, the diagnostic can, with the assistance of the Receiver Monitor bit, determine whether data is correctly passing from the transmitter to the receiver. If it is not, the diagnostic can determine the most likely point of failure. If this test is passed successfully it may be tried again–this time with the clocking coming from a free-running maintenance test clock running at 4800 or 9600 bits per second. This not only checks the ability of the synchronous transmitter/receiver system to run at typical operating speeds, but can also be used, in systems where a number of these interfaces are employed, to check system performance without requiring connection to modems.

One other test that can be performed without modems is to continue with switches A and B set so that clocking comes from the free-running maintenance clock, but to change switch C so that the received data comes from the modem. A technician then places a loop-around connector at the end of the cable so that the transmitted data goes out to the end of the cable and then returns on the Received Data lead. This checks all of the data paths within the synchronous interface and the cabling. Finally, a modem is connected and further tests may be performed.

Many modems manufactured today include loop-around features which permit the transmitted data to pass into the modem, be converted to the voltage levels used within the modem (but not be converted to tones), and then be converted back to interface voltages and sent back to the receiver over the lead shown in Figure 15-4 as "Received Data." Use of such a loop-around and remote loop-around provisions at a distant modem are extremely useful in pointing out exactly where the trouble lies. When communications interfaces, modems, and communications facilities are all provided by different vendors, such loop-around capability reduces "finger-pointing."

Two new bits not directly associated with modem control or synchronization have been added to the Transmitter Status Register: Transmitter Active and Send. The Transmitter Active bit is provided to indicate to the program when it is safe to drop the Request to Send lead in the modem control. Transmitter Active is set whenever the transmitter unit is serializing data onto the communications line and for one half bit time thereafter. When the bit clears, the transmitter is idling MARK onto the line, and Request to Send for most modems can be dropped. The Send bit is used to enable the transmitter logic.

Bit 03 of the Transmitter Status Register is for operation with half-duplex modems. When set, this bit blinds the receiver logic whenever the transmitter is in use. In this way, if the modem is of the type which produces a copy of the transmitted data on the Received Data lead, that data will not disturb the receiver logic. Figure 15-5 illustrates the function of this lead.

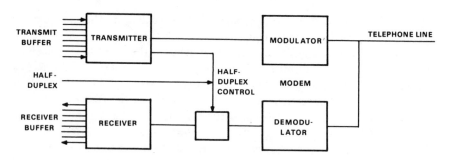

Figure 15-5. Half-Duplex Lead Logic

The modulator and demodulator sections of the modem are both connected to the telephone line, and since the frequencies and modulation methods used by the modulator are exactly the same as those used by the demodulator, the demodulator sees everything that the modulator transmits and delivers it to the receiver logic. The Half-Duplex Control lead solves this problem of extraneous data entering the receiver logic by blinding the receiver logic while the transmitter is operating.

Many modems solve this problem by interlocking the demodulator with the Request to Send lead and thus not running the demodulator while the modulator is on. When a synchronous interface is being used with this type of modem, there is no need for the half-duplex bit, although its use would not do any harm.

So far, all discussion of a single line synchronous interface has emphasized its similarity to the single line asynchronous interface described in Chapters 2 and 6. There is, however, additional information that must be loaded into registers in a synchronous interface. Most important is the specification of sync character. In addition, character length and parity are especially important in a synchronous interface. These line parameters–sync, character length, and parity–can be stored in an additional register, the Parameter Status Register. Figure 15-6 is a possible format for such a register.

Bits 10 and 11 are used to select whether character length is 5, 6, 7, or 8 bits per character. When bit 09 is set, parity operation is enabled: all characters sent have a parity bit added and all characters received are expected to have a parity bit. The parity bit makes each character one bit longer than the length specified in bits 10 and 11.

When the Parity Enable bit is set, the sense of the parity (odd or even) is controlled by bit 08. When bit 08 is set, even parity is generated by the transmitter and checked for by the receiver. The program does not have to supply a parity bit to the transmitter; this is performed by the transmitter logic. When bit 08 is cleared, odd parity is generated and checked.

Bits 00-07 of the Parameter Status Register may be loaded by the program to specify the sync character. The sync character is used by the re-

PARAMETER STATUS REGISTER

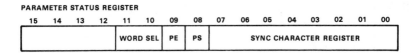

Figure 15-6. Parameter Status Register

ceiver logic to detect received sync characters and thereby to achieve synchronization. The sync character is also used by the transmitter as an idling character when it has not been provided with anything else to send.

While on the subject of idling characters, it should be noted that a moderate amount of care is required when shutting down a transmission on a synchronous line. If the transmission facility is full-duplex, the transmitter can be allowed to idle sync characters between messages. This has the benefit of keeping the receiving station in synchronization between messages. The program at the receiving station has to have some expedient means of disposing of the syncs received, however. Idling sync characters can create a problem: that line noise can, in rare cases, cause the receiver to think a new message had started. For half-duplex lines, the transmission must be shut down and the line "turned around." Shutdown is normally accomplished by the transmission of EOT (end of transmission) followed by two PAD characters (all 1s). The PAD characters insure that, when the Request to Send lead is negated and the modem turns off its transmitter, the transmitter in its last gasps will not be sending data which could be mistakenly interpreted at the receiving station.

When the receiving station recognizes the EOT, it checks to see if it has information to send; if so, it asserts its Request to Send lead, which starts a timer in the modem. After the timer has expired (up to one quarter second later), the modem returns a Clear to Send signal, and the transmitter begins transmission of sync characters. What has previously been called the receiving station is now the transmitting station. The major time delay in this line turn-around process is caused by the echo suppressors (see Chapter 8). When it is known that no echo suppressors exist in the communication facility, the Request to Send/Clear to Send delay in the modem can be selected to be a much smaller value, increasing the line utilization by allowing faster turnarounds.

16
Protocols

In Chapter 14 it was noted that synchronous communications systems use a special character called "sync" to define which groups of eight bits constitute characters. In Chapter 13 a method of error detection was described in which two "check characters" are added to the end of each message. These are examples of two of the important functions of protocols in communication systems, framing and error control.

A protocol is basically a set of rules for operating a communication system. The rules are designed to solve operating problems in the following areas:

1. Framing—the determination of which eight bit groups constitute characters, and most important, what groups of characters constitute messages.

2. Error Control—the detection of errors by means of the Longitudinal, Vertical, or Cyclic Redundancy Checks described in Chapter 13; the acceptance of correct messages; and the request for retransmission of faulty messages.

3. Sequence Control—the numbering of messages to eliminate duplicate messages, avoid losing messages, and properly identify messages that are retransmitted by the error control system.

4. Transparency—the transmittal of information (such as instrumentation data) that contains bit patterns which resemble the control characters used to implement functions 1, 2, and 3 above, without the receiving station identifying those bit patterns as control characters.

5. Line control—the determination, in the case of a half-duplex or multipoint line, of which station is going to transmit and which station(s) will receive.

6. Special Cases—solving the problem of what a transmitter sends when it has no data to send.

7. Timeout Control—solving the problem of what to do if message flow suddenly ceases entirely.

8. Startup Control—the process of getting transmissions started in a communication system that has been idle.

It is beyond the scope of this book to describe how each of the protocols commonly in use solves the problems in each of the above areas, but the chapters which follow will highlight some of the methods used.

Protocols may be divided into three categories according to the message framing techniques used. These are character oriented, byte count oriented, and bit oriented. A character oriented protocol uses special characters, such as STX to indicate the beginning of a message, and ETB to indicate the end of a block of text (i.e., the imminent arrival of the block check characters). The classic character oriented protocol is IBM's Binary Synchronous Protocol, known as BISYNC.

Byte count oriented protocols use a header which includes a beginning special character followed by a count that indicates how many characters follow in the data portion of the message and some control information such as which messages have been received correctly to date. The data portion which comes next is the specified length and is followed by block check characters. Digital Equipment Corporation's Digital Data Communication Message Protocol (DDCMP) is an example of this type of protocol.

Finally, it is possible to create a protocol that delineates which bits constitute messages by separating those messages with a special flag character such as 01111110. This type of protocol specifies that there shall never be six "1" bits in a row except for the transmission of a flag. Thus, when the receiving station receives a flag character, it knows that the previous 16 bits were the block check characters and that the bits between those 16 and the previous flag constitute the message. This type of protocol is called a "bit-stuffing" or bit oriented protocol. Examples include IBM Synchronous Data Link Control (SDLC), American National Standards Institute ADCCP, International Standards Organization HDLC, and CCITT Recommendation X.25.

Protocols of each of the three major types will be discussed in greater detail in the following chapters.

17

BISYNC and
Character Oriented Protocols

One of the most widely used protocols in the industry is IBM's Binary Synchronous Communications Protocol, known as BISYNC. It has been in use since 1968 for transmission between IBM computers and batch and video display terminals. BISYNC is a character-oriented protocol—it uses special characters to delineate the various fields of a message and to control the necessary protocol functions.

The overall format of a BISYNC message is shown in Figure 17-1. The header is optional, but if one is used it begins with SOH (Start of Header) and ends with STX (Start of Text). SOH and STX are special characters and the bit combinations to form these characters may be found in character sets for ASCII, EBCDIC, and Six Bit Transcode, the three codes most commonly used with BISYNC. The contents of the header are defined by the user, except that polling and addressing for multipoint lines are not done by the header but rather by means of a separate control message. The text portion of the message is variable in length and may contain transparent data, i.e., bits which are to be treated as data (e.g., data from a measuring instrument) and not as characters. This feature requires that the character recognition logic of the receiver be turned off so that a data pattern resembling either ETX (End of Text) or one of the other special characters will not confuse the receiver logic. To turn off the character recognition at the receiver, the transparent data is delimited by DLE (Data Link Escape) STX and DLE ETX (or DLE ETB). Regardless of whether the text field ends with ETX, ETB, DLE ETX, or DLE ETB, these special characters indicate the end of the text field and the beginning of the trailer section which contains only the block check character(s).

BISYNC employs a rigorous set of rules for establishing, maintaining, and

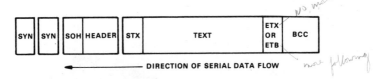

Figure 17-1. BISYNC Message Format

terminating a communications sequence. A typical exchange between a terminal station and a computer on a point-to-point private line is illustrated in Figure 17-2.

As mentioned above, BISYNC supports ASCII, EBCDIC, or Six Bit Transcode for coding the information. Certain bit patterns in each set have been set aside for the required control characters: SOH, STX, ETB, ITB, ETX, EOT, NAK, DLE, and ENQ. Some controls are two-character sequences–ACK0, ACK1, WACK, RVI, and TTD. All of these control character abbreviations are defined below.

SOH—Start of Header

STX—Start of Text

ETB—End of Transmission Block
ETB indicates the end of a block of characters that started with SOH or STX and indicates that the block check is coming next. ETB requires a response from the receiving station indicating its status: ACK0, ACK1, NAK, WACK, or RVI.

ITB—End of Intermediate Transmission Block
(This is called IUS in EBCDIC and US in ASCII)
ITB is used to separate the message into sections for error detection purposes without causing a reversal of transmission direction. The transmission of ITB indicates that the block check is coming next. While the block check is checked at this point and reset to zero, the receiving station does not reply to the transmitting station until a final block, ending in ETB or ETX, is received. Except for the first intermediate block, or a boundary between a heading block and a text block, the intermediate blocks need not begin with STX. One further exception is the use of intermediate blocks in transparent data transfer—these must all start with DLE STX.

ETX—End of Text
Terminates a block of characters transmitted as an entity and which started with SOH or STX. Its function is the same as ETB except that it also means that there are no more data blocks to be sent.

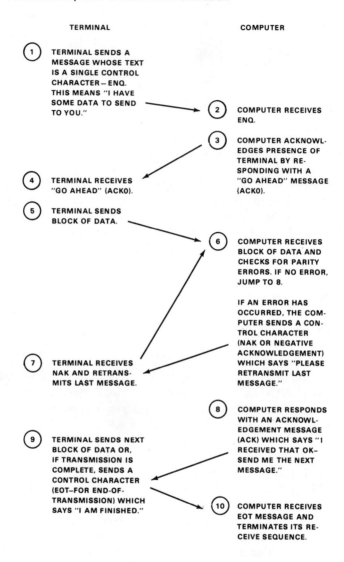

TERMINAL

COMPUTER

(1) TERMINAL SENDS A MESSAGE WHOSE TEXT IS A SINGLE CONTROL CHARACTER – ENQ. THIS MEANS "I HAVE SOME DATA TO SEND TO YOU."

(2) COMPUTER RECEIVES ENQ.

(3) COMPUTER ACKNOWL-EDGES PRESENCE OF TERMINAL BY RE-SPONDING WITH A "GO AHEAD" MESSAGE (ACK0).

(4) TERMINAL RECEIVES "GO AHEAD" (ACK0).

(5) TERMINAL SENDS BLOCK OF DATA.

(6) COMPUTER RECEIVES BLOCK OF DATA AND CHECKS FOR PARITY ERRORS. IF NO ERROR, JUMP TO 8.

IF AN ERROR HAS OCCURRED, THE COM-PUTER SENDS A CON-TROL CHARACTER (NAK OR NEGATIVE ACKNOWLEDGEMENT) WHICH SAYS "PLEASE RETRANSMIT LAST MESSAGE."

(7) TERMINAL RECEIVES NAK AND RETRANS-MITS LAST MESSAGE.

(8) COMPUTER RESPONDS WITH AN ACKNOWL-EDGEMENT MESSAGE (ACK) WHICH SAYS "I RECEIVED THAT OK-SEND ME THE NEXT MESSAGE."

(9) TERMINAL SENDS NEXT BLOCK OF DATA OR, IF TRANSMISSION IS COMPLETE, SENDS A CONTROL CHARACTER (EOT–FOR END-OF-TRANSMISSION) WHICH SAYS "I AM FINISHED."

(10) COMPUTER RECEIVES EOT MESSAGE AND TERMINATES ITS RE-CEIVE SEQUENCE.

Figure 17-2. Typical Data Exchange Using BISYNC

EOT—End of Transmission
EOT indicates the end of a message transmission which may contain a number of blocks, including text and headings. EOT is also used to respond "nothing to transmit" to a polling request and can also be used as an abort signal.

NAK—Negative Acknowledgement

NAK indicates that the previous block was received in error.

DLE—Data Link Escape

One of the uses of DLE is in the creation of WACK, ACK0, ACK1, and RVI, which are two-character sequences. In EBCDIC, for example, RVI is sent as DLE@. DLE is primarily used for control character sequences in transparent data transfer. The sequence DLE STX is used to initiate transparent text and DLE ETX, DLE ITB, and DLE ETB are used to terminate transparent text. In addition, DLE ENQ, DLE DLE, and DLE EOT are also used for control purposes during transparent text transmissions.

ENQ—Enquiry

ENQ is used to bid for the line when using point to point connections; it indicates the end of a poll or selection sequence. It is also used to request retransmission of the ACK/NAK response if the original response was garbled or not received when expected.

ACK0, ACK1—Affirmative Acknowledgement

These replies indicate that the previous block was accepted without error, and that the receiver is ready to receive the next block. ACK0 is used to acknowledge multipoint selection, point-to-point line bid, and even numbered blocks. ACK1 is used to acknowledge odd numbered blocks.

WACK—Wait before Transmit Positive Acknowledgement

A WACK reply indicates that the previous block was accepted without error, but that the receiver is not ready to receive the next block. The usual response from the transmitting station is ENQ and the receiving station continues to respond with WACK until it is ready to receive.

RVI—Reverse Interrupt

Like ACK0, ACK1, and WACK, RVI is a positive acknowledgement. However, it is also a request that the transmitting station terminate the current transmission as the receiving station has a high priority message which it wishes to send to the transmitting station and thus needs to turn the line around.

TTD—Temporary Text Delay (STX ENQ)

TTD is used by a transmitting station which is not quite ready to transmit, but wishes to retain the line. The receiving station responds with NAK and the transmitting station may again send TTD if it is still not ready.

To detect and correct transmission errors, BISYNC uses either Vertical/Longitudinal Redundancy Checks (VRC/LRC) or a Cyclic Redundancy Check (CRC) depending upon the information code being used. For ASCII, a VRC check is performed on each character (i.e., parity) and an LRC on the whole message. In this case, the block check in the trailer field of the message is a single eight bit character. If the code is EBCDIC or Six Bit Transcode, no VRC (parity) check is made; rather a CRC is calculated for the entire message. CRC-16 is used with EBCDIC. This results in a block check which is 16 bits long and is transmitted as two eight bit characters; the lowest order eight bits are transmitted first. With Six Bit Transcode, CRC-12 ($X^{12} + X^{11} + X^3 + X + 1$) is used, resulting in a block check character which is 12 bits long. This is transmitted as two six bit characters, lowest order bits first. If the block check character transmitted does not agree with the block check calculated by the receiver, or if there is a VRC error, then a negative acknowledge (NAK) sequence, such as that shown in Figure 17-2, is sent back to the data source. To correct errors, BISYNC requires the retransmission of a block when an error occurs. Retransmission will typically be attempted several times before it is assumed that the line is in an unrecoverable state.

When a transmitted block check does match the receiver's calculated block check, the receiver sends a positive acknowledgement: ACK0 for an even numbered block or ACK1 for an odd numbered block. This alternating between ACK0 and ACK1 checks for sequence errors to detect duplicated or missing blocks. The acknowledgement messages are sent as separate control messages rather than being incorporated in a data message.

The operation of the BISYNC protocol can best be appreciated from a state flow diagram, such as that shown in Figure 17-3. There are five states for transmission, two of which are applicable for transmission of ordinary data and three which are applicable for transmission of transparent data.

For ordinary non-transparent data, transmission begins in State 3 for the transmission of any header date or the ENQ control character. A header begins with SOH, which has some special rules associated with it. The first SOH or STX to follow a line turn-around causes the BCC to reset. All succeeding STX or SOH characters (until a line turn-around) are included in the BCC. The ITB, ETB, and ETX characters are always included in the BCC and are followed by the BCC. When an STX or ITB delimiter occurs in State 3, transmission progresses to State 4, the text transmission mode. When the transmitter has sent all of the data block, the character count (byte count) reaches zero and transmission returns to State 3 for transmission of the next data block.

For transparent data, transmission begins in State 0, where any ACK, RVI, or WACK control characters sent are prefixed with a DLE. The transmission of an STX is also prefixed with a DLE and shifts the transmission into State 1, the transparent data transmission state. The transmission stays

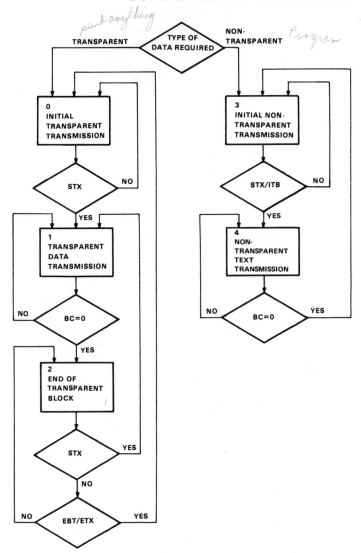

Figure 17-3. BISYNC Transmission Flow Diagram

in State 1 until all characters have been sent (character count/byte count reaches zero), and then switches to State 2, the end-of-transparent-block state. In State 2, the transmission of an ITB DLE STX sequence causes a return to State 1 for transmission of the remainder of the data block. Use of ETB or ETX in the above sequence causes a return to State 0 to enable transmission of the next data block.

Figure 17-4 is a state flowchart for the BISYNC reception control process. States 0 and 2 are used to handle ordinary data reception while States 3, 4,

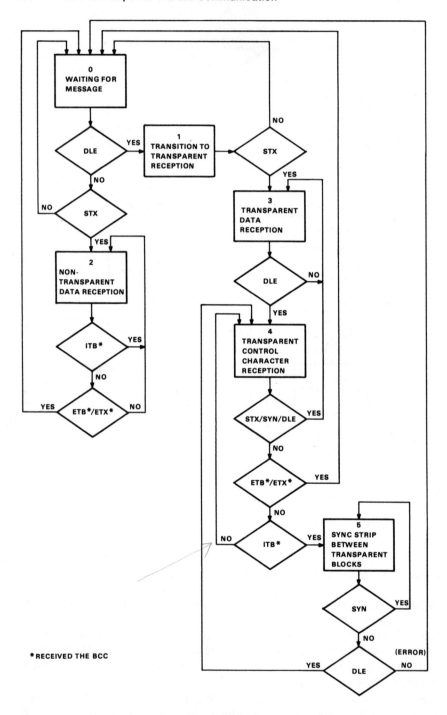

Figure 17-4. BISYNC Reception Flow Diagram

and 5 are used to handle transparent data reception. State 1 is a transition state between ordinary data reception and transparent data reception.

While waiting for a message, the receiver is in State 0. When the first control character arrives, the response of the receiver depends upon which control character is received:

> ENQ—Generate an interrupt to the computer to record the ENQ and to set up a buffer to store the expected data. Remain in State 0.

> DLE—Go to State 1 (transition to transparent reception).

> STX or SOH—Go to State 2 (ordinary data reception).

> EOT—Generate an interrupt to the computer to announce the end of message. Remain in State 0.

> NAK—Generate an interrupt to the computer to inform the program that it will have to retransmit. Remain in State 0.

The most interesting reception case is transparent data reception. As indicated in the above list, the first step toward transparent data reception is the receipt of DLE, placing the receiver into State 1. When a receiver is in State 1, the next character, in other than error situations, is STX. The receipt of the STX after DLE completes the entry into State 3, the transparent data reception state.

At this point it would be useful to compare State 2, ordinary data reception, with State 3, transparent data reception. In State 2, the following characters have significance: ITB, ETB, ETX, ENQ, and SYN. Reception of any of the first three is an indication to the receiver that it should notify the computer program by means of an interrupt, and that it should expect the block check next. Reception of ENQ is an error condition and reception of SYN is ignored. In State 3, on the other hand, all characters except DLE are received, stored, and included in the block check, as State 3 is transparent data reception. A DLE, if received is discarded, but accomplishes its purpose: changing the receiver to State 4.

Control characters received in the transparent data stream are processed in State 4. The usual control characters would be the block delimiters: ITB, ETB, or ETX; these are included in the block check, which is received immediately after them. The reception of the ITB causes a transition to State 5, whereas the ETB or ETX indicates the end of the transparent text block and sends the receiver back to the initial state, State 0. The other interesting characters to be received while in this state are DLE and SYN. A received DLE gets stored and included in the block check and returns the reception to State 3. This is how BISYNC solves the problem of sending a data pattern equivalent to DLE while in transparent mode. A DLE is "stuffed" in front of the data pattern to alert the receiver that a special character is coming and then the special character is checked. Upon finding it to be a bit pattern equivalent to DLE, the receiver treats it as a transparent data entry and returns to transparent data reception. Note that the "stuffed" DLE is not included in the block check, but the DLE-like data pattern is.

SYN received while the receiver is in State 4 is completely disregarded, except that the receiver is returned to State 3. Like the DLE-DLE combination, the use of DLE-SYN is a BISYNC special case. Earlier in the discussion of synchronous communications, it was mentioned that a transmitter which has no data to send must send something. The usual "something" is SYN, as that keeps the line in synchronism and is customarily discarded by the receiver. The problem arises when a transmitter is in the midst of sending transparent data and temporarily runs out of things to send. If the transmitter sends SYN, the receiver has every reason to believe that the bits which represent SYN are data. It will therefore include them in the stored buffer and in the block check, causing a block check error. The solution to this problem is for the transmitter, under such circumstances, to send DLE SYN, thus alerting the receiver via the DLE that something special is coming. The receiver can then recognize the SYN as SYN, discarding both the DLE and SYN and including neither of them in the block check. This problem and its solutions are important for two reasons. First, some of the ICs which are used to implement synchronous communications have a mechanism for automatically idling an SYN when the transmitter is not supplied with data at a sufficient rate; they do not provide, in all cases a mechanism for idling DLE SYN. Second, the idling of SYN or DLE SYN or anything else is fatal in byte count oriented protocols (DDCMP) or bit oriented protocols (SDLC). In short, allowing a transmitter to idle is only possible in a character oriented protocol like BISYNC and even then only if one is very careful.

The final reception state to be considered is State 5, which is used after the receipt of DLE ITB during transparent reception. This state is used to permit the syncs received between intermediate text blocks to be discarded without inclusion in the block check. The receipt of SYN is ignored, the receipt of DLE moves the reception back into State 4.

There are other protocols which computer users have developed that are character oriented like BISYNC, but which use different control characters or which use a subset of the BISYNC rules. The most commonly used subsets are those which leave out the transparent data transmission and reception features.

Readers interested in a more authoritative and complete explanation of BISYNC are referred to the reference listed below.

Reference

1. "Binary Synchronous Communications—General Information," (GA27–3004 File TP–09), IBM Corporation.

18
DDCMP and Byte Count Oriented Protocols

An examination of the BISYNC transmission and reception state flow diagrams in Chapter 17 reveals that much of the complication associated with that protocol is a result of the special procedures used to achieve transparent transmission and reception. Even with those procedures there are some difficult situations that arise. An example is the termination of transparent text containing bit combinations equivalent to DLE and ETX and being sent in the following order:

$$\text{DLE ETX DLE ETX DLE ETX} \qquad (1)$$

If the receiver is to interpret this data stream correctly, the transmitting unit must send:

$$\text{DLE DLE ETX DLE DLE ETX DLE DLE ETX} \qquad (2)$$

Since this is the end of the block, the transmitter also wishes to affix a "real" DLE ETX to indicate the end of the text. Thus, the final data stream, as it appears on the comunications facility, will be:

$$\text{DLE DLE ETX DLE DLE ETX DLE DLE ETX DLE ETX} \qquad (3)$$

A hardware or software system sending this message has to be quite careful, since the rules for sending the final "DLE ETX" are different from those for sending the others. No DLE is prefixed to DLE ETX the last time because that DLE ETX is supposed to be interpreted by the receiver as DLE ETX–only the first three are to have DLE stuffed in front of them. The only solution to this is to treat the last DLE ETX separately. It could be placed in a different message buffer. It could be sent after an interrupt indicating that the previous transparent text containing the three "DLE ETXs" had been sent, etc. If the "actual" DLE ETX is going to be kept in a separate buffer, and only sent when the block of transparent text has all been sent, how does the transmission software or hardware know when that is? The answer is by keeping track of the character count, referred to frequently as the "byte count" (because many computers store one character per eight bit "byte").

It is possible to devise a protocol which, by keeping track of byte count, solves the transparency problems without the use of DLE or other control characters. One of the widely used protocols that does this is Digital Equipment Corporation's DDCMP protocol, the format for which is shown in Figure 18-1.

DDCMP is a very general protocol; it can be used on synchronous or asynchronous, half- or full-duplex, serial or parallel, and point-to-point or multipoint systems. Most applications involving protocols are half- or full-duplex transmission in a serial synchronous mode; that operating environment will therefore be emphasized in this description.

As indicated in Figure 18-1, the format is somewhat similar to BISYNC in that the message is broken into two parts: a header containing control information and a text body. Unlike BISYNC, however, the header is not optional. It is the most important part of the message, as it contains the message sequence numbering information and the character count, the two most important features of DDCMP. Because of the importance of the header information, it merits its own CRC block check, indicated in the figure as CRC 1. Messages that contain data, rather than just control information, have a second section which contains any number of eight bit characters (up to a maximum of 16,363) and a second CRC indicated in the figure as CRC 2.

Before the message format is discussed in greater detail, the message sequencing system should be explained, as most of the header information is directly or indirectly related to the sequencing operation.

In the DDCMP protocol, any pair of stations that exchange messages with each other number those messages sequentially starting with message number 1. Each successive data message is numbered using the next number in sequence, modulo 256. Thus a long sequence of messages would be numbered 1,2,3,...254,255,0,1,.... The numbering applies to each direction separately. For example, station A might be sending its messages 6,7,8 to station B while station B is sending its messages 5,6,7 to station A. Thus, in a multi-

SYN	SYN	C L A S S	COUNT 14 BITS	FLAG 2 BITS	RESPONSE 8 BITS	SEQUENCE 8 BITS	ADDRESS 8 BITS	CRC 1 16 BITS	INFORMATION UP TO 16,363 8-BIT CHARACTERS	CRC 2 16 BITS

Figure 18-1. DDCMP Message Format

point configuration where a control station is engaged in two-way communication with 10 tributary stations, there are 20 different message number sequences involved—one for messages from each of the 10 tributaries to the control station and one for messages from the control station to each of the 10 tributaries.

Whenever a station transmits a message to another station, it assigns its next sequential message number to that message and places that number in the "Sequence" field of the message header. In addition to maintaining a counter for sequentially numbering the messages which it sends, the station also maintains a counter of the message numbers received from the other station. It updates that counter whenever a message is received with a message number exactly one higher than the previously received message number. The contents of the received message counter are included in the "Response" field of the message being sent, to indicate to the other station the highest sequenced message that has been received.

When a station receives a message containing an error, that station sends a negative acknowledge (NAK) message back to the transmitting station. DDCMP does not require an acknowledgement for each message, as the number in the response field of a normal header, or in either the special NAK or positive acknowledgement (ACK) message, specifies the sequence number of the last good message received. For example, if messages 4, 5, and 6 have been received since the last time an acknowledgement was sent, and message 6 is bad, the NAK message specifies number 5 which says "messages 4 and 5 are good and 6 is bad." When DDCMP operates in the full-duplex mode, the line does not have to be turned around; the NAK is simply added to the messages for the transmitter.

When a station receives a message that is out of sequence, it does not respond to that message. The transmitting station will detect this from the response field of the messages which it receives, and if the "reply wait" timer expires before the transmitting station receives an acknowledgement, the transmitting station will send a "REP" message. The REP message contains the sequence number of the most recent unacknowledged message sent to the distant station. If the receiving station has correctly received the message referred to in the REP message (as well as the messages preceding it), it replies to the REP by sending a positive acknowledgement (ACK). If it has not received the message referred to in sequence, it sends a NAK containing the number of the last message that it did receive correctly. The transmitting station will then retransmit all data messages after the message specified in the NAK.

The numbering system for DDCMP messages permits there to be up to 255 unacknowledged messages outstanding, a useful feature when working on high delay circuits such as those using satellites.

With this background, it is now time to explore the various DDCMP message formats in full detail, as shown in Figure 18-2. The first character of the

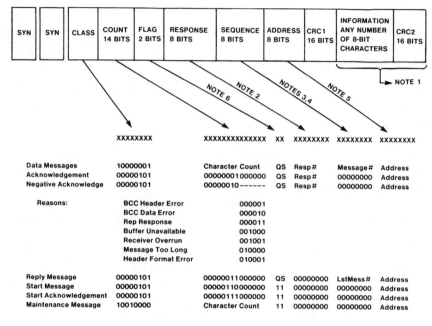

									INFORMATION	
SYN	SYN	CLASS	COUNT 14 BITS	FLAG 2 BITS	RESPONSE 8 BITS	SEQUENCE 8 BITS	ADDRESS 8 BITS	CRC1 16 BITS	ANY NUMBER OF 8-BIT CHARACTERS	CRC2 16 BITS

NOTE 6   NOTE 2   NOTES 3,4   NOTE 5   NOTE 1

XXXXXXXX   XXXXXXXXXXXXXX   XX   XXXXXXXX   XXXXXXXX   XXXXXXXX

Data Messages	10000001		Character Count	QS	Resp#	Message#	Address
Acknowledgement	00000101		00000001000000	QS	Resp#	00000000	Address
Negative Acknowledge	00000101		00000010------	QS	Resp#	00000000	Address

Reasons:		
	BCC Header Error	000001
	BCC Data Error	000010
	Rep Response	000011
	Buffer Unavailable	001000
	Receiver Overrun	001001
	Message Too Long	010000
	Header Format Error	010001

Reply Message	00000101	00000011000000	QS	00000000	LstMess#	Address
Start Message	00000101	00000110000000	11	00000000	00000000	Address
Start Acknowledgement	00000101	00000111000000	11	00000000	00000000	Address
Maintenance Message	10010000	Character Count	11	00000000	00000000	Address

Notes:

1. Only the Data Message and the Maintenance Message have character counts, so only these messages have the information and CRC2 fields shown in the message format diagram above.

2. "Resp #" refers to Response Number. This is the number of the last message received correctly. When used in a negative acknowledge message, it is assumed that the next higher numbered message was not received, was received with errors, or was unaccepted for some other reason. See "Reasons."

3. "Message#" is the sequentially assigned number of this message. Numbers are assigned by the transmitting station modulo 256; i.e., message 000 follows 255.

4. "LstMess#" is the number of the last message transmitted by the station. See the text discussion of REP messages.

5. "Address" is the address of the tributary station in multipoint systems and is used in messages both to and from the tributary. In point to point operation, a station sends the address "1" but ignores the address field on reception.

6. "Q" and "S" refer to the quick sync flag bit and the select bit. See text.

Figure 18-2. DDCMP Message Format in Detail

message is the class of message indicator, represented in ASCII with even parity. There are three classes of messages: Data, Control, and Maintenance. These are indicated by class of message indicators SOH, ENQ, and DLE respectively. The next two characters of the message are broken into a 14 bit field and a two bit field. The 14 bit field is used in Data and Maintenance messages to indicate the number of characters that will follow the header and will form the information part of the message. In Control Messages, the first eight bits of the 14 bit field are used to designate what type of control message it is and the last six bits are generally an all-zeros fill. The exception is in NAK messages where these six bits are used to specify the reason for the NAK. The two bit field contains the quick sync and select flags.

The quick sync flag is used to inform the receiving station that the message will be followed by sync characters; the receiver may wish to set its associated synchronous receiver hardware into "sync search" mode and "strip sync" mode. This will re-establish synchronization and syncs will be discarded until the first character of the next message arrives. The purpose of this is to permit the receiving station to engage any hardware sync-stripping logic it might have and prevent it from filling its buffers with sync characters. The select flag is used to indicate that this is the last message which the transmitting station is going to transmit and that the addressed station is now permitted to begin transmitting. This flag is useful in half-duplex or multipoint configurations, where transmitters need to get turned on and off.

The response field contains the number of the last message correctly received. This field is used in Data Messages and in the positive and negative acknowledge types of Control Message. Its function should be evident from the preceding discussion of sequence control.

The sequence field is used in Data Messages and in the REP type of Control Message. In a Data Message, it contains the sequence number of the message as assigned by the transmitting station. In a REP message, it is used as part of the question: "Have you received all messages up through message number (specify) correctly?"

The address field is used to identify the tributary station in multipoint systems and is used in messages both to and from the tributary. In point to point operation, a station sends address "1" but ignores the address field on reception.

In addition to the positive and negative acknowledgement and REP types of Control Message, there are also start and start acknowledge Control Messages. These are used to place the station which receives them in a known state. In particular, they initialize the message counters, timers, and other counters. The start acknowledge message indicates that this has been accomplished.

Figure 18-2 also shows the Maintenance Message. This is typically a bootstrap message containing load programs in the information field. A complete treatment of bootstrap messages and start up procedures is beyond the scope of this book.

DDCMP is able to do the following: run on full- or half-duplex transmission facilities; run on many existing hardware interfaces; support point to point and multipoint lines; run on synchronous, asynchronous, or parallel systems; and provide multiple acknowledgements per ACK message (up to 255 messages are acknowledged by one ACK message).

DDCMP has two drawbacks. First, the header is relatively short, and the higher level operating system must therefore have a buffer of the appropriate size ready on relatively short notice. Secondly, the transmitting station must not idle a sync in the middle of a message as that will cause the character count to come out wrong and produce a bad CRC check. The first of these problems is inherent in every protocol. Most get around it by agreeing that messages will not be more than "n" characters long; plainly, this can also be done in a DDCMP system. The second problem is shared by DDCMP, Transparent Mode BISYNC, and SDLC. In each case, the error detection and recovery systems will permit recovery and the only consequence will be an apparently higher line error rate than really exists. An error logging system that checks the Data Not Available flags in the synchronous transmitter units is able to detect the difference between this type of failure and a line error.

Reference

"Digital Data Communications Message Protocol," Digital Equipment Corporation.

19

SDLC and
Bit Oriented Protocols

It is not the intent of this chapter to be a definite source on SDLC, but rather to describe enough of its operation for the reader to get the general idea and to be able to more readily understand more detailed references on the subject.

First, a few definitions should be given. Any data communication link involves at least two participating stations. The station which has responsibility for the data link and which issues the commands to control that link is called the "primary station." The other station is a "secondary station." It is not necessary that all information transfers be initiated by a primary station. Using SDLC procedures, a secondary station may be the initiator.

The basic format for SDLC is a "frame," shown in Figure 19-1. The information field is not restricted in format or content and can be of any reasonable length (including zero). The maximum length is that which can be expected to arrive at the receiver error-free most of the time, and is hence a function of communication channel error rate.

The two flags which delineate the SDLC frame serve as reference points for the position of the address and control fields and initiate the transmission error checking. The ending flag indicates to the receiving station that the 16 bits just received constitute the Frame Check. The ending frame could be followed by another frame, another flag, or an idle. Note that this means that when two frames follow each other, the intervening flag is simultaneously the ending flag of the first frame and the beginning flag of the next frame. Since the SDLC protocol does not use characters of defined length, but rather works on a bit by bit basis, the 01111110 flag may be recognized at any time.

In order that the flag not be sent accidentally, SDLC procedures require that a binary 0 be inserted by the transmitter after any succession of five continuous 1s. The receiver then removes a 0 that follows a received succes-

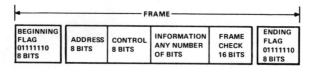

Figure 19-1. Basic SDLC Frame

sion of five 1s. Inserted and removed zeros are not included in the transmission error check.

The address field is eight bits long and designates the number of the secondary station to which the command from the primary station is being sent. The control field is an additional eight bits and can have three formats: "information transfer format," "supervisory format," and "nonsequenced format." The only thing in common between the three formats is the P/F (poll/final) bit. A frame with the P(poll) bit set is sent from a primary station to a secondary station to authorize transmission, and a frame with the F(final) bit set is sent by the secondary station in response to the poll. Typically, the primary station will send a number of frames to a particular secondary station, each frame having the P/F bit a 0, until the primary station is finished and ready for the secondary station to respond. At this time the primary station will send a frame having the P/F bit set to 1. The secondary station will recognize that the primary station desires a response and will reply, perhaps with a number of frames, each having the P/F bit a 0. Then, when the secondary station is completing its response to the "poll," it will send a "final" frame which has the P/F bit set to 1.

The three control formats are summarized in Table 19-1.

The information format is used for ordinary data transmission and is the only one of the three formats that uses frame sequence numbering. Each frame transmitted in this format is numbered so that the receiving station can tell if any are missing; when retransmission is required, the receiving station can tell the transmitting station which frame to start with in the retransmission. A station that transmits sequenced frames counts and numbers each frame. This count is known as Ns. A station receiving sequenced frames counts each error-free sequenced frame that it receives; the receiver count is called Nr. The Nr count advances when a frame is checked and found to be error-free; Nr thus becomes the count of the "next expected" frame and should agree with the next incoming Ns count. Returning to the format shown in Table 19-1, the initial 0 bit indicates that this control field is in information format, the three Ns bits are "this is the message number I am sending," the P/F bit is set if the station is concluding its poll or its response to a poll, and the three Nr bits are "this is the message number I am expecting next."

The supervisory format is used in conjunction with the information format to initiate and control information transfer in the information format. The

Table 19-1. SDLC Control Field Formats

Format		Bits			Acronym
Information	Nr	P/F	Ns	0	I
Supervisory	Nr	P/F	00	01	RR
	Nr	P/F	01	01	RNR
	Nr	P/F	10	01	REJ
Nonsequenced	000	P/F	00	11	NSI
	000	F	01	11	RQI
	000	P	01	11	SIM
	100	P	00	11	SNRM
	000	F	11	11	ROL
	010	P	00	11	DISC
	011	F	00	11	NSA
	100	F	01	11	CMDR
	001	1	00	11	ORP

Sent Last ⬑

Sent First ⬑

first two bits sent, 1 and 0, designate that this control field is in supervisory format. The next two bits indicate which command this is: RR, RNR, or REJ. An RR (Receive Ready) can be sent by either a primary or a secondary station, and indicates that all sequenced frames up through $Nr-1$ have been received correctly, and that the originating station is ready to receive some more. RNR (Receive Not Ready) can also be sent by either a primary or a secondary station, and also acknowledges messages up to $Nr-1$. Unlike RR, however, RNR indicates a temporary busy condition in which no additional frames that require buffer space can be accepted. REJ (Reject) is a command/response which may be transmitted to request transmission or retransmission. It acknowledges successful receipt of frames up through $Nr-1$ and requests Nr and following frames.

The nonsequenced format is used for setting operating modes, initializing stations, etc. As the name implies, nonsequenced communications are not sequence checked and do not use the Nr and Ns system. The first two bits sent, 11, indicate a nonsequenced format, the P/F bit has its usual meaning, and the remaining five bits in the control field are used for encoding the various commands and responses.

The commands and responses encoded in the nonsequenced format control field are listed below.

NSI (Nonsequenced Information)—This indicates that the information which follows in the variable length information field is being sent separately from any sequenced message presently in progress.

RQI (Request for Initialization)—This is transmitted by a secondary station when it wishes the primary station to send an SIM command. If the primary station sends something other than SIM, the secondary station sends another RQI.

SIM (Set Initialization Mode)—This command initiates system-specified procedures at the receiving secondary station for the purposes of initializing. Nr and Ns counts are set to 0 at both the primary and secondary stations. The expected response to SIM is NSA.

SNRM (Set Normal Response Mode)—This command subordinates the receiving secondary station to the transmitting primary station, and the secondary station is not expected to initiate any transmissions unless requested to do do by the primary station. The Nr and Ns counts at both the primary and the secondary stations are reset to 0. The secondary station remains in this mode until it receives a DISC or SIM. The expected response to SNRM is NSA.

ROL (Request On-Line)—This is transmitted by a secondary station to indicate that it is disconnected.

DISC (Disconnect)—This command places the secondary station effectively off-line. That station cannot receive or transmit information frames and remains disconnected until it receives an SNRM or SIM command. The expected response to DISC is NSA.

NSA (Nonsequenced Acknowledgement)—This is the affirmative response to SNRM, DISC, or SIM.

CMDR (Command Reject)—This is the response transmitted by a secondary station in normal response mode when it receives a non-valid command. A frame with CMDR in the control field has an information field following which is arranged in a fixed format which reports that station's present Ns, that station's present Nr, and four bits which indicate 1) an invalid or non-implemented command, 2) an information field associated with a command which isn't supposed to have one, 3) an information field that was so long it caused buffer overrun, or 4) the Nr received from the primary station does not make sense, given the Ns that was sent to it.

ORP (Optional Response Poll)—This command invites transmission from the addressed secondary stations.

While SDLC is simpler in most aspects than previously discussed protocols, the block check calculations are a good deal more complex. The first difference is that the transmitting station begins with a "remainder value" of all 1s rather than the customary all 0s. The binary value of the transmission is premultiplied by X^{16} and divided by the generating polynomial $X^{16}+X^{12}+X^5+1$. The quotient digits are ignored and the transmitter sends the complement of the resulting remainder value, with the high order bit first.

One other feature which should be discussed is the procedure for prematurely terminating a data link. This is called "abort" and is accomplished by the transmitting station's sending eight consecutive 1 bits. The abort pattern may be followed by a minimum of seven additional 1s to idle the data link, or it may be followed by a flag. The purpose of a flag following an abort is to clear the CRC function at the receiver.

The preceding has been a rather condensed description of SDLC, and the reader is advised to read the references listed below for further information about SDLC and about HDLC, a similar protocol.

References

1. "Synchronous Data Link Control—General Information," (GA27–3093 File GENL–09), IBM Corporation.
2. "High Level Data Link Control (HDLC)," DIS 3309.2 and DIS 4335, International Organization for Standardization (ISO).

20

A Single Line
Synchronous Interface for
Bit Oriented Protocols

The single line synchronous interface discussed in Chapter 15 has all of the receiver flag, receiver buffer, transmitter flag, and transmitter buffer features of a typical data communication interface. Added to those features were modem control and status signals that allowed the interface to play the role of "data terminal equipment" in data transmission involving both private line and switched network modems. A block diagram of the single line synchronous interface is shown in Figure 20-1. (Caution: The interface described is a hypothetical combination of two commercially available products.)

The simplest possible data communications interface has program addressable registers such as those shown in Figure 20-2.

Addition of the modem control and status features would expand the bit assignments to those illustrated in Figure 20-3. In addition to the modem control bits located in the Receiver Status Register, a Parameter Status Register has been added to permit the program to load a sync character into the interface. This sync character is used by the receiver logic to determine which eight bit groups constitute characters and is also used by the transmitter as an idling character. The Parameter Status Register also provides bits that permit the interface to operate in other than eight bit per character mode by selecting various settings for the Word Select (bits 10 and 11). Parity operation and parity sense are selected by various settings of bits 08 and 09. Finally, a maintenance system has been added due to the greater complexity of synchronous interfaces, and a Data Not Available flag has been added to indicate that the transmitter idled a character. A Transmitter Active bit (XMIT ACT) and a Send bit have also been added. A more complete

168

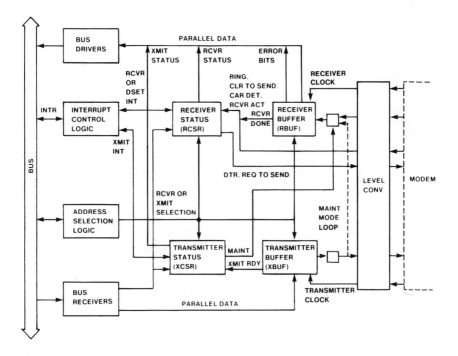

Figure 20-1. Single Line Synchronous Interface

review of the bit assignments for the single line synchronous interface shown in Figure 20-3 may be obtained by reading Chapter 15.

An interface designed to handle bit oriented protocols such as SDLC, HDLC, or ADCCP must have at least the bit assignments shown in Figure 20-3, except that Strip Sync, Search Sync, and, to some degree, the entire Parameter Status Register are unnecessary. In the interface to be discussed, Strip Sync and Search Sync will be retained, however, so that the interface may also handle character oriented and byte count oriented protocols. The Parameter Status Register will have a bit added (bit 15) whose state will determine whether the bits function as shown in Figure 20-3 or whether some of them are redefined for bit oriented protocol use. With these changes, the resultant interface will be able to handle all three types of protocol discussed in the past three chapters.

The new bit assignments and those old bit assignments that undergo a change of function are shown in heavy outline in Figure 20-4.

The first bit to be considered is the CRC Error bit, which is bit 12 in the Receiver Buffer Register. This is the bit position occupied in Figure 20-3 by the Parity Error bit. When a Flag character arrives in SDLC, the receiver is supposed to check the accumulated CRC to see if the CRC is

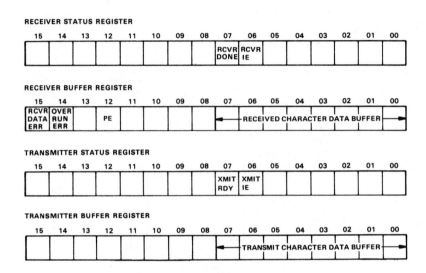

Figure 20-2. Program Addressable Registers—Simple Interface

0001110100001111 (X^{15} through X^0 respectively) indicating an error-free message. This requires that the receiver hardware accumulate a CRC calculation on the incoming data and be prepared to present it to a number comparison circuit when the message is complete. If the CRC does not equal 0001110100001111 at that time, the CRC Error bit in the Receiver Buffer Register is set along with an End of Message indication in bit 09 when the last data character of the message is presented. When the interface is being operated in this fashion, the setting of CRC Error also causes Receiver Data Error, bit 15, to be set. The End of Message, CRC Error, and Receiver Error flags remain set until the program reads the Receiver Buffer Register to obtain the final data character.

Since CRC calculation logic has been installed in the interface for the benefit of the SDLC protocol, a slight modification in bit definition can be made to permit use of the CRC logic with simplified versions of BISYNC and with byte count protocols such as DDCMP. This is done by redefining the function of the CRC Error bit when using protocols other than SDLC/HDLC/ADCCP. Under the new definition, in effect when the Byte Mode bit is set, the CRC Error bit is set whenever the accumulated CRC is equal to zero and the state of the CRC Error bit no longer affects the Receiver Data Error bit. When the receiver handling program wishes to check the received CRC, on the basis that either a special character has been received or the byte count has reached zero, it checks the CRC Error bit when the last character of the message (which has been stored in the interface while the CRC check takes place) is presented in the Receiver Buffer Regis-

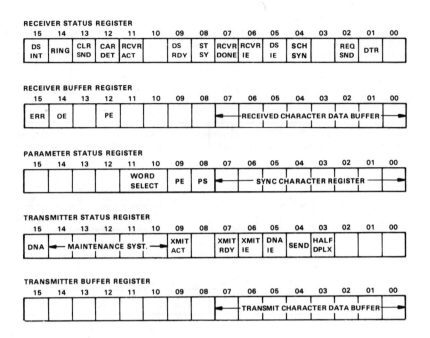

Figure 20-3. Program Addressable Registers—Complex Interface

ter. If the arrival of the CRC has caused the accumulated CRC to reach zero, the preceding message was error free. The sense of this bit may seem confusing in the "new definition," as the SET state is the "everything is OK" state. This choice of sense was done so that, in both SDLC and other protocols, characters received at times other than at the end of the message would have this bit and all other error bits clear. Only when the last portion of the message is being processed does this bit assume the "1" state. (There is some chance that the accumulated CRC will reach zero during a message, but this is very unlikely.)

It should be noted that, even with the definition flexibility of the CRC Error bit, this interface cannot perform CRC checking of messages in BI-SYNC. The rules regulating which characters are included in the CRC and which are not are so complicated that a more sophisticated interface, such as that described in Chapter 21, is required.

Bits 08, 09, and 10 of the Receiver Buffer Register are strictly associated with SDLC/HDLC/ADCCP protocols. The setting of the Received Abort (RCV ABRT) bit indicates that an abort sequence (eight or more consecutive 1s) has been received. (Receiver Data Error will also set.) The End of Message (EOM) bit indicates that a flag character has arrived, terminating the present message. It is then time for the program to look at the

RECEIVER STATUS REGISTER

15	14	13	12	11	10	09	08	07	06	05	04	03	02	01	00
DS INT	RING	CLR SND	CAR DET	RCVR ACT		DS RDY	ST SY	RCVR DONE	RCVR IE	DS IE	SCH SYN		REQ SND	DTR	

RECEIVER BUFFER REGISTER

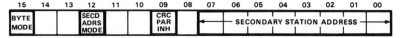

15	14	13	12	11	10	09	08	07	06	05	04	03	02	01	00
RCV DATA ERR	OVER RUN ERR		CRC PAR ERR		RCV ABRT	EOM	SOM	← RECEIVED CHARACTER DATA BUFFER →							

PARAMETER STATUS REGISTER

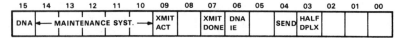

15	14	13	12	11	10	09	08	07	06	05	04	03	02	01	00
BYTE MODE			SECD ADRS MODE			CRC PAR INH		← SECONDARY STATION ADDRESS →							

TRANSMITTER STATUS REGISTER

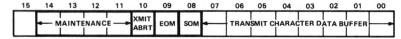

15	14	13	12	11	10	09	08	07	06	05	04	03	02	01	00
DNA	← MAINTENANCE SYST. →					XMIT ACT		XMIT DONE	DNA IE		SEND	HALF DPLX			

TRANSMITTER BUFFER REGISTER

15	14	13	12	11	10	09	08	07	06	05	04	03	02	01	00
	← MAINTENANCE →				XMIT ABRT	EOM	SOM	← TRANSMIT CHARACTER DATA BUFFER →							

Figure 20-4. Program Addressable Registers—Bit Oriented Protocol Interface

CRC Error bit. The Start of Message (SOM) bit indicates that the character presented in bits 00–07 is the first character of an SDLC/HDLC/ADCCP message. Of the three bits just described, Start of Message and End of Message are the only ones accompanied by valid data in bits 00–07.

It should be noted at this point that bits 08, 09, and 10 of the Transmitter Buffer Register in Figure 20-4 are also labeled Start of Message, End of Message, and Abort. When the program sets the Abort bit (as well as the Send bit described below) the transmitter unit in the interface sends an abort character (eight 1s) as soon as it has finished transmitting any character presently being serialized. When the program sets End of Message (and Send), the transmitter unit completes transmission of any characters it has, sends the accumulated CRC, and sends Flag characters until the next message is initiated. If the transmitter is not active, the program initiates messages by setting Start of Message, clearing End of Message and setting Send. If the transmitter is active (this includes sending flags), the next message is initiated by clearing End of Message and loading data into the Transmitter Buffer Register.

The Transmitter Buffer Register, as illustrated in Figure 20-4, also contains some additional maintenance bits. These are used to exercise the transmit and receive CRC logic.

The Parameter Status Register is next in line when discussion of the registers in top to bottom order is resumed. Bit 15 of this register is called "Byte Mode," and when set it conditions the interface logic to operate with character oriented and byte count oriented protocols. When this bit is clear, the interface is arranged to operate with bit oriented protocols. This bit affects the definition of the CRC Error bit, as previously discussed, and also influences the operation of the Start of Message bit in the Transmitter Buffer Register. When the Byte Mode bit is clear, the Start of Message bit operates as indicated above. When the Byte Mode bit is set, the Start of Message bit is used to facilitate the transmission of sync characters at the beginning of the message without including them in the transmitter CRC. This is done because the receiving station misses some syncs, uses some to synchronize, and only "receives" some number less than were transmitted. Thus the syncs at the beginning of a message are never included in CRC calculations at either the transmitting station or the receiving station. It is relatively easy for the receiving station logic to recognize the initial sequence of syncs at the beginning of a message and keep them out of the CRC calculation. Some method must be found, however, to insure that the transmitting apparatus also keeps the syncs out of its CRC calculation. This can be accomplished by the use of the Byte Mode bit along with the rule that a sync loaded into the transmitter buffer at the same time Start of Message is loaded is not included in the CRC. Further, as long as Start of Message remains set and a sync remains in the transmit buffer, syncs will continue to be transmitted. As soon as the program desires to send data, it loads the transmit buffer with that data and simultaneously loads a zero into the Start of Message bit.

The Secondary Address Mode Selection bit (Parameter Status Register bit 12) allows the interface to function as a secondary station in multipoint systems. When this bit is cleared, the interface operates as a primary station. All data subsequent to the last received flag character is presented to the program until the termination flag is received. Secondary station operation is in effect when this bit is set. In this mode, only messages that are prefixed with the correct secondary station address are presented to the program. The Secondary Station Address must have been loaded into the 00–07 bits of this register before the Receiver Enable bit was set by the program. The actual address character is not presented to the program in the secondary mode. If extended secondary addresses are used (i.e., 16 bit), the first eight bits of the address can be detected by the hardware. The software would have to confirm the second eight bits of the address.

The ninth bit of the Parameter Status Register is the CRC Inhibit bit. When that bit is set, transmission of the CRC is inhibited, and the CRC error detection logic is not operated during reception.

The function of the 00–07 bits has already been discussed in conjunction with Secondary Mode operation. When these bits are not used for that purpose and the Byte Mode bit is set, these bits are used to store the sync character that will be used to achieve line synchronization.

21

High Performance
Interfaces

So far, with the exception of the multiplexer in Chapter 12, each of the asynchronous and synchronous interfaces which has been discussed has utilized the computer's interrupt facilities in the process of character transfer. The interface interrupted the computer each time it had assembled a character from the communications line and each time it was ready to transmit another character. While this design is very flexible, since the computer program gets to look at each character before storing it in memory (reception) and again as the character is moved from memory to the interface's transmitter (transmission), a substantial amount of computer time is wasted.

In some computers, generation of an interrupt does not direct the computer program to a sub-program (service routine) appropriate to the particular interrupting device. Rather, the computer must address each device and sample the "done" bit to see if that is the interrupting device. In later computers, the generation of an interrupt from a particular device includes provisions to direct the computer program to a service routine appropriate to that particular device. In either case, however, the computer must stop its present activity, store various information necessary to return to that activity without loss of data or change in its operating state, and then enter the service routine. Depending upon the computer and the interrupting device, getting into the service routine and out of it again may take nearly as much time as the service routine itself. Furthermore, the interrupt service routines for typical communications interfaces take 25–200 microseconds. This limits the character throughput to 5,000 to 40,000 characters per second, even without considering the entry/exit time just described. At the end of this 25–200 microseconds, the received character has been deposited in the appropriate "message space" in memory or a character from a message in memory has been loaded for transmission.

If the communications interface were to keep track of the memory addresses for the message being received and for the message being transmitted, the interface could then load the received characters into memory and load the transmitter unit from memory without program attention, except when the end of the message or the end of the available storage space was reached. Interfaces which work in this fashion are called "Direct Memory Access" or DMA devices. Since the transfer of a character to or from memory takes only about a microsecond by this process, character throughput rates are substantially higher. They may reach a million characters per second if characters are stored one at a time, or even higher if characters are stored two or more at a time.

DMA, however, is not without its drawbacks. First, the hardware is generally more complicated because it must contain the necessary logic to perform transfers to and from memory. While it was implied above that the interface must store the addresses for the transfers, that information and the character transfer count could be stored in main computer memory and retrieved just before making the transfer to store or retrieve the character for the communications line. While this economizes on logic, it increases the number of transfers necessary on the computer's internal buses to store or retrieve a single character, and is probably not advisable with today's low logic prices. A second drawback of DMA is that devices with this capability are generally more complicated to program. In high throughput applications, however, these two drawbacks are relatively unimportant when compared with the truly outstanding speed advantage offered by DMA.

To obtain the full benefits of DMA transmission and reception, however, the communications interface must have some of the intelligence that the interrupt service routine has in the interrupt per character type of interface.

In asynchronous communication, particularly when it involves terminals on a time-sharing system, error detection codes are rarely used, so transmission to the terminals can easily be handled on a DMA basis. For the reception of characters from terminal keyboard, the interface is generally required to recognize some special characters that cause the computer to stop executing the user's program or stop the generation of output to the terminal. This can be handled by a character detection system that looks for special characters before depositing the typed characters into memory on a DMA basis. Alternatively, the reception portion of the communication interface could be designed to operate on an interrupt per character basis (possibly with a silo, see Chapter 7), since keyboards generate characters rather slowly.

In synchronous communication, use of DMA is a bit more complicated, but the rewards are very attractive. Most synchronous communication uses some type of error detection. As described in Chapter 13, error detection typically involves the calculation of a Cyclic Redundancy Check by the transmitting station while it is transmitting the characters and the sending of that check as a two-character group following the last character of the message. The receiving station performs a similar calculation, and the reception of the check character(s) should yield a zero result in the receiver calculation circuitry (except for SDLC/ADCCP-type protocols). This all seems simple enough, but the various protocols in use have special rules about which characters in a message are to be included in the block check calculation and which are not. Further, it is necessary for both the receiver and the transmitter to know where the messages start and end so that they can perform the check character calculations correctly. In addition to these problems with the block check calculations, there is often a requirement for special characters or sequences of characters to generate interrupts.

One method of accomplishing "intelligent" DMA is to use an associative memory in which are stored various special characters or two-character sequences. The incoming data stream is then compared with the contents of the associative memory; when a match is found, block check character calculation begins, ends, or skips these characters, as appropriate. Alternatively, the finding of a match might generate an interrupt. A similar system could also be used for transmission.

A second method of accomplishing "intelligent" DMA is to use the received characters as numerical offsets in a memory table. Such a table contains entries that indicate what to do when that character is received, such as include it in the block check or not, generate an interrupt or not, etc. This method is especially suited to detecting sequences of special characters. The received eight bit characters can have "mode bits" appended to stretch them into 9, 10, or 11 bit characters, thus permitting indexing into memory tables with different entries for the same character; the different entries are used depending upon what sequence of characters preceded the character in question.

This type of "intelligent" DMA is used in one of the 16 line synchronous multiplexers on the market; the basic operation of this multiplexer is shown in Figure 21-1.

Sixteen synchronous receivers assemble characters received from serial communications lines and assert a flag as each character is received. Sixteen synchronous transmitters disassemble characters and transmit them on serial communications lines and assert a flag whenever they can accept another character for transmission. The master scanner sequentially checks the synchronous receivers and transmitters for each line to see if a flag exists.

The microprocessor handles all characters received or transmitted. The microprocessor system includes a 128-character first-in/first-out storage buffer. While most characters received will propagate through this buffer and be directly transferred to memory by means of a DMA transfer, the occasion may arise when the attention of the computer program is required before this is done. To prevent the synchronous receivers from experiencing data overruns during the interval that the multiplexer is awaiting program attention, the microprocessor will continue to load the received characters into the

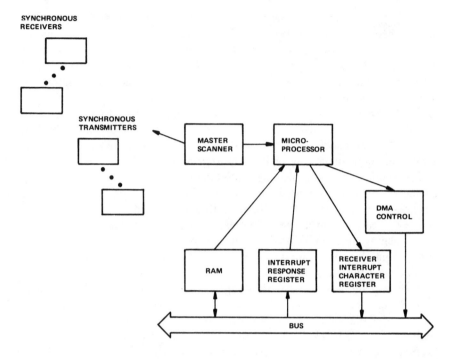

Figure 21-1. Basic Operation

first-in/first-out buffer. The action of the microprocessor in withdrawing characters from the buffer will cease, however, until the computer program responds to the interrupt caused by the special character at the bottom of the silo buffer. The character which requires program attention is copied into the Receiver Interrupt Character Register at the time the interrupt is generated.

The Receiver Interrupt Character Register is a computer-addressable register used by the microprocessor to show the computer program any received character, along with line number and error flags, for which the control logic requires assistance in processing.

The Interrupt Response Register is a computer-addressable secondary register used to instruct the microprocessor how to process the character in the Receiver Interrupt Character Register.

The DMA control is the hardware which is used to store received characters, obtain characters for transmission, and obtain control bytes that direct the character processing.

The microprocessor read/write random access memory (RAM) contains current addresses and byte counts used in the DMA transfers. The initial values are loaded by the computer program, and these values are subsequently updated by the microprocessor. The RAM also contains a line protocol word for each line by which the program can specify what action is to be taken when the byte count reaches zero and what type of block check polynomial should be used.

Reception is shown in greater detail in Figure 21-2. Line synchronization and character assembly are accomplished by synchronous receivers which initially compare groups of eight bits received on each line with the preselected sync character to achieve line synchronization. When line synchronization has been achieved, subsequently-received characters are placed into a first-in/first-out, 128-character silo storage buffer. Each line receiver appends the line number (four bits) and any error flags (two bits–parity error, overrun error) to the character prior to placing it in the receiver storage buffer.

The microprocessor removes characters from the silo along with their line number and error flags. If there is an error flag (as a result of the parity error or overrun error detected by the receiver) the character is placed in the Receiver Interrupt Character Register and an interrupt request is generated.

If there is no error flag, the processing depends on whether a character oriented protocol (example: BISYNC) or a byte count oriented protocol (example: DDCMP) is being used.

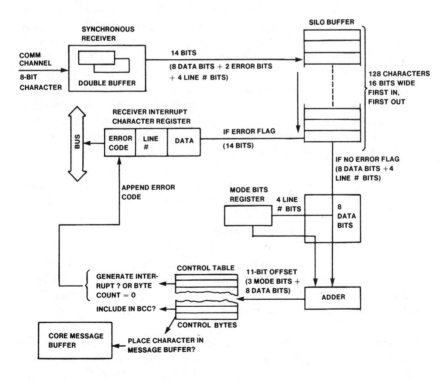

Figure 21-2. Reception

Character Oriented Protocol Reception
(Example: BISYNC)

If there is no error flag, the microprocessor affixes three mode bits at the high-order end of the received eight bit character. This 11 bit character is then used as an offset in the control table in main memory to obtain a control byte that will indicate to the microprocessor what mode is to be used for subsequent reception on this line and any special handling information appropriate to this character (such as whether or not to generate an interrupt, whether or not to include the character in a block-check computation, whether or not to store the character in a message buffer.)

If the generation of an interrupt is indicated, the character and the line number are moved to the Receiver Interrupt Character Register along with an error bit code. The error bit code indicates that this interrupt is being generated because a control table control byte has indicated that this is a special character.

If the control byte indicates that this character should be included in a block check, the microprocessor performs the appropriate calculation (LRC, CRC-16, or CRC-CCITT).

If the control byte directs that a received character be discarded, the character is discarded. If it indicates that the character be stored, the microprocessor obtains the current address from the RAM and uses that address to store the received character in a message buffer. The microprocessor then increments the current address for that line. In addition, the microprocessor increments the byte count for that line. If the storage of the character caused the byte count to reach its final value, the microprocessor checks to see whether special actions associated with byte count run-out have been requested. Having accomplished any actions requested, a copy of the character is moved to the Receiver Interrupt Character Register along with the error bits that indicate that a new receive message buffer must be established for this line. In all cases where a character is moved to the Receiver Interrupt Character Register, an interrupt is generated, and the microprocessor ceases to withdraw characters from the receiver silo storage buffer until the program indicates that such withdrawal can proceed again.

Byte Count Oriented Protocol Reception
(Example: DDCMP)

If a byte count oriented protocol is used, the microprocessor skips the control byte process described above, includes all characters in the Block Check Calculation, and stores all characters (except BCC1 and BCC2). Details of character storage are the same as indicated above.

The receiver throughput in the multiplexer is dependent on the number of characters identified in the control bytes as being special (interrupt generating) and the size of the message buffers for received characters. It is intended that the ability of control bytes to accomplish reception mode changes relieve the necessity for received special characters generating an interrupt. When a receiver interrupt is generated, received characters are accumulated in a 128-character first-in/first-out storage buffer until the interrupt is handled. Assuming arrival of characters at a 19,200-character-per-second rate, it would take approximately 6.6 milliseconds for a silo overflow to occur. Thus, substantial worst-case interrupt latency can be accommodated.

Character Oriented Protocol Transmission
(Example: BISYNC)

Transmission is shown in Figure 21-3. For each line there is a double-buffered serial transmitter. Whenever the transmitter buffer is empty, a flag is raised. The microprocessor scans for transmitter flags and when it finds one, it checks a "worksheet" to determine whether any special action must be taken (e.g., send a block check character). If no special action is required, the microprocessor checks to see if the transmitter "GO" bit for the line is set. If it is set, the microprocessor uses the transmitter current address register to perform a DMA transfer and obtain—from a message buffer—a character to be transmitted. The processing of this character depends on whether

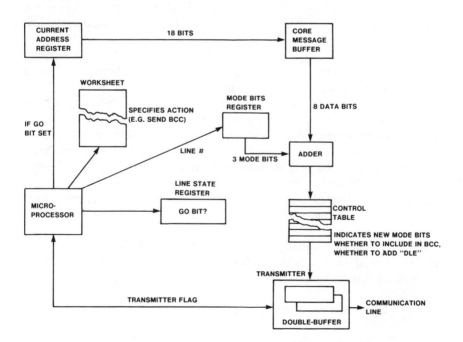

Figure 21-3. Transmission

a character oriented protocol (example: BISYNC) or a byte count oriented protocol (example: DDCMP) is being used.

Before transmitting the character, the microprocessor copies it, adds mode bits to the high-order end, and performs a DMA transfer to obtain a transmit control byte from a control table. This byte contains information indicating what new modes are to be used, whether to include the character in the block check, and whether to prefix the transmission of the character with a DLE (performed by the microprocessor).

Byte Count Oriented Protocol Transmission (Example: DDCMP)

If a byte count oriented protocol is used, the microprocessor skips the control byte process described above and includes all characters in the Block Check Calculation. The characters are transmitted as described below.

Transmission of Characters

The microprocessor then loads the character to be transmitted into the appropriate line transmitter and increments the byte count. It then checks the byte count to determine whether it has reached its final value. If it has, a check is made to determine whether any special action has been requested. Having accomplished any actions requested, the microprocessor will switch to a new transmit buffer. If the byte count of the new buffer is also 0, the microprocessor will clear "Transmit Go" in the Line State Register and idle sync (or 1s).

There are several ways of arranging transmit buffers such that a program can manage them conveniently, and a microprocessor in a high performance commmunications interface can progress from buffer to buffer without pause. One method is to alternate between two buffers—a "primary buffer" and an "alternate buffer." The program loads message text into each buffer and tells the microprocessor which one to start with. The microprocessor completes transmission from one buffer and proceeds to the other, generating an interrupt. The program now knows that it is safe to replace the text in the first buffer and establish a new byte count for that buffer. When the microprocessor finishes sending from the second buffer, it returns to the first, generating an interrupt. This process continues until there is no more text to send.

Another method of sending successive buffers involves the use of linked lists. In a linked list, blocks of memory are set aside for "linked list headers." A linked list header contains four pieces of information:

1. The address of the next header

2. The address of the message text buffer

3. The size of the message text buffer

4. Control bits indicating special actions to be taken before or during the transmission of the text.

When the microprocessor begins transmission of a text buffer, it picks up these four pieces of information and stores them in its memory. When the first text buffer has been completed, it uses the "address of next header" information to find the next header and repeat the process. If the "address of next header" is 0, the end of the list of buffers has been reached, and there is no more text to send.

Yet another method is the use of ring buffers. In the ring buffer system, a block of memory is set aside containing (for example) eight of the headers listed above. However, the "address of next header" is replaced with a status bit that is 1 if the microprocessor has not "picked up" the buffer information, and 0 if it has. Thus the microprocessor rotates through the header blocks, taking the information and acknowledging receipt of that information by changing status bits from 1 to 0. The computer program, managing the buffers, checks the status bits for changes from 1 to 0 and installs new headers upon discovering 0s.

22
Microprocessor Based Multiplexers

In Chapter 21, a multiplexer which employed a combination of a microprocessor and tables located in the memory of the main computer was described. There are at least two other ways in which microprocessors are being used to implement communication multiplexers. One of these methods is shown schematically in Figure 22-1.

In this implementation, each line unit is designed so that it can be used on the main computer bus if desired. Then, when dictated by throughput demands, the microprocessor system option can be added, creating a separate bus, similar to the main computer bus, upon which the line units would be placed. This method of building multiplexers has the advantage that a customer can start out on a small scale with just a few line units and later build on without having to throw away the original line units. The drawbacks lie in the design of the microprocessor assistance scheme. If this microprocessor uses main memory to keep track of various information used in its service of the line units, the main computer bus will still receive substantial traffic and the main computer memory, in particular, will be quite busy.

A second method for using microprocessors in multiplexer design is shown in Figure 22-2. In this implementation, each line unit is again designed so that it can be used on the main computer bus and, in fact, it is. When indicated by throughput demands, the microprocessor option is added. The microprocessor periodically scans the line units for "done" flags and services them when it finds them. Like the first method described, this method of building multiplexers has the advantage that a customer can start out with just a few line units and later build on without having to throw away the original units. Again the drawback is that the servicing of received and transmitted characters requires use of the computer bus. With the particular im-

184

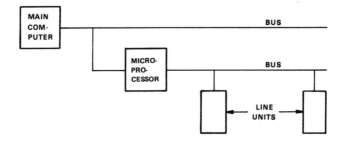

Figure 22-1. Microprocessor-Assisted Line Units on Separate Bus

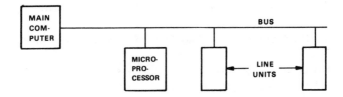

Figure 22-2. Microprocessor-Assisted Line Units on Main Bus

plementation presently used in the computer industry, the microprocessor illustrated in Figure 22-2 is much faster than that illustrated in Figure 22-1, and has local memory which radically reduces its computer bus utilization relative to the Figure 22-1 implementation.

The costs of single line units, smart multiplexers, and microprocessor-assisted line units are shown in Figure 22-3. Dollar prices and quantities of lines have been deliberately left out of the figure, as the prices are constantly changing.

As one might expect, building a system from single line units is very attractive in small line sizes. If you have no lines implemented you pay nothing, and the cost goes up linearly from there. In general, the cost of single line units will exceed the cost of a multiplexer after a dozen or so lines have been implemented. Even if the cost of single line units never reaches that of a multiplexer, the multiplexer will eventually be desirable because of the superior throughput of a multiplexer with silos or direct memory transfers or both. Microprocessor-assisted line units provide substantial throughput improvements compared to single line units, and are generally similar to multiplexers in performance, depending upon their bus utilization properties. The cost of microprocessor-assisted single line units tends to seesaw back and forth across the price lines of multiplexers depending upon what multiples of lines are available on the multiplexers. When the number of lines to be served is about 80–100 percent of the design size of a smart multiplexer, the lat-

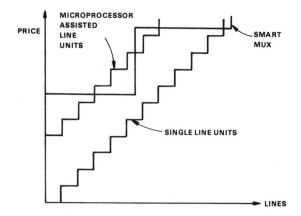

Figure 22-3. **Per-Line Costs of Various Types of Communications Interface**

ter is usually cheaper than any other solution. As soon as the number of lines to be served exceeds 100 percent of the design size, a second multiplexer is required. The price per line is generally unfavorable again until the number of lines to be served reaches 80–100 percent of the design size of *two* multiplexers.

In summary, the pricing of microprocessor-assisted single line units is a compromise between the linearity of single line unit pricing and the stepped nature of multiplexer pricing. Some manufacturers offer microprocessor-assisted small multiplexer systems in which simple-minded small multiplexers are used in small systems; then, when required for throughput improvement, a microprocessor assistance package is added to create the equivalent of a large smart multiplexer. The pricing of such an arrangement may

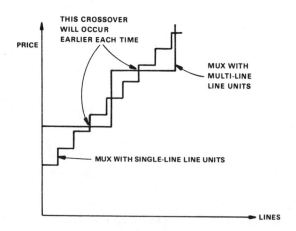

Figure 22-4. **Per-Line Costs of Various Kinds of Communications Multiplexers**

be envisioned from Figure 22-3 by imagining that the steps marked "micro-processor-assisted line units" extend further to the right (larger line size) but also further up (greater cost). Figure 22-4 illustrates this. Since there will be some economies from using large line units, the cost crossovers will occur "earlier" as the line sizes get larger; eventually the multi-line unit implementation will be consistently cheaper.

The declining price of microprocessors indicates that a possible direction for microprocessor/multiplexer systems may be a multiplexer which is, in fact, a plurality of single line units each with its own microprocessor. One manufacturer already offers a special case of this. It is called a "network link" and is described further in Chapter 23.

It should also be noted that microprocessor units such as those just described can also be used to assist devices other than simple multiplexers and single line units. They can be used to assist line printers, card readers, and other data handling devices.

23
Interprocessor Communication

In Chapter 1 it was noted that parallel communication is the usual method for transferring data between a computer and its peripherals due to the speed and simplicity of this type of operation. Increasing distance means not only more complicated interfacing due to the line driving and noise rejection circuitry required, but also increased expense due to the large number of conductors required for parallel data transfers. In these circumstances, serial data transmission becomes more attractive, despite the requirement of adding shift registers.

Communication between computer processors involves basically the same tradeoffs. Parallel transfer offers tremendous speed advantage and is very useful over short distances. Serial transfer is more useful as the distance increases and may also be useful over short distances as a solution to two frequent problems: hardware failure and software complication.

The use of serial communication to get around hardware failure is limited in application, but interesting nonetheless. When two or more processors are connected to a parallel bus structure, there is a chance that a failing processor will "bring down the bus" and make the entire system useless. This is likelier in some multi-processor systems than in others, and reducing this chance to near zero is a challenging system design problem. A serial connection is much less likely to fail in this way, as the control information is sent as structured words or messages rather than as assertions of an electrical signal on a specific lead.

Serial lines usually fail, or the devices driving them fail, in such a fashion that the line is held at a permanent MARK state or a permanent SPACE state, neither of which conveys information that is likely to confuse the receiving station. In fact it is quite simple to detect the long SPACE, and the long MARK is no different from an idle line. Thus, the surviving processor can easily ignore the failed processor. One of the disadvantages of this system is that the surviving processor cannot generally access the peripherals of the failed processor, which it would have had some chance of doing in the parallel bus connection scheme.

The use of serial communication to simplify software is motivated by the complications of designing software for multi-processor systems. One solution that can be used, particularly when a plurality of small computers gathers data for a larger computer is to arrange the system so that the small computers connect to the large computer by serial communications lines, even though they may be in the same room. The small computers will appear to the software of the large computer system as serial terminals such as teleprinters.

This latter application is often done with asynchronous communication lines, since it is desirable for the small computers to look like terminals to the large computer. While typical asynchronous systems do not employ error detection (a considerable oversight in cases where line errors are possible) it is presumed in this case that the distances are so short that errors are not of concern or else that there is some sort of protocol in use that will solve any error problems encountered. Given these assumptions, there is only one likely cause of problems, and that is clock skew between the transmitting and receiving stations.

Figure 23-1 shows an eight bit character as transmitted by a station which will be referred to as "station A." If this character is received by a "station B" whose clock is running somewhat slower than that of station A, the points at which station B samples the received character will be those indicated by the arrows in Figure 23-1. Note that the sampling points move gradually from the center of the bit (bit 1) to much later in the bit (bit 8). Since the sampling points are re-established with the 1-to-0 transition at the beginning of the next START bit, no errors will occur in this case (assuming no other distortion exists).

In Figure 23-2, station A is assumed to be transmitting at a rate of 1201 bits per second (0.083 percent fast). Characters arriving at station B are sampled as shown in Figure 23-1; the sampling of the last data bit is substantially beyond the center. However, as noted in conjunction with Figure 23-1, no data errors will occur, assuming that no other distortion is present.

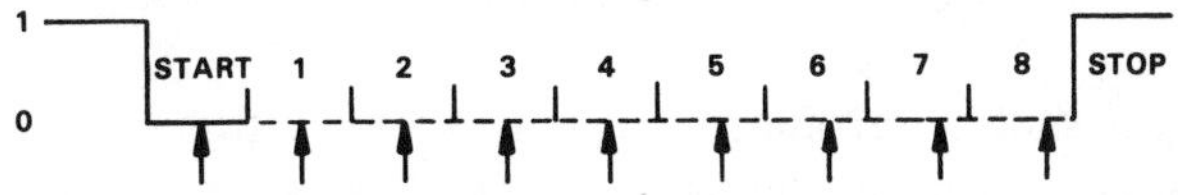

Figure 23-1. Sampling a Received Character by Means of a Clock Slower than That Used to Transmit the Character

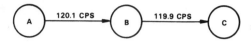

Figure 23-2. Relaying of Transmitted Characters by Stations Having Slightly Differing Clock Rates

The important part of the transmission from station A to station B is that, at a 1201 bit per second rate with 10 bits per character, characters are being delivered at a rate of 120.1 per second.

Now assume that the data is being transferred from station A to station B and thence to station C. If the transmitter in station B has a clock rate of 1199 bits per second (.083 percent slow), it will deliver characters to station C at a rate of 119.9 characters per second. Because of the speed difference between the station A clock and the station B clock, the station B receiver will believe that the station A transmitter is cheating slightly on the STOP bit lengths. This is because the 1-to-0 transition marking the beginning of the next character will come slightly early due to the higher character rate. Most asynchronous receivers are, however, willing to accept this and no data will be lost as a result of the apparent shortness of the STOP elements.

Instead, the sampling clock of station B's receiver will be re-established permitting it to sample the next character in accordance with Figure 23-1. Station B's transmitter is bound to send the correct number of bits as STOP elements, however, as any asynchronous transmitter must send proper STOP elements. Since station B's clock is slightly slow, bits are longer, and it will be sending longer STOP elements than it receives from station A. In fact, it will be sending longer characters, as its character transmission rate is less than that of station A.

By this time the problem should be evident. Station B is accumulating characters at a rate of 0.2 characters per second. After 10 seconds, two extra characters will have accumulated at station B, and this may be enough to cause an overrun condition. Regardless of the storage capacity of station B, there will be an overrun error condition eventually. The use of more accurate clocks helps only slightly. If the clocks used have an accuracy of .008 percent instead of .08 percent, the overrun error will occur in 100 seconds rather than in 10 seconds. There is only one sure solution that can be implemented in hardware and that is to provide progressively faster transmitter clocks with B faster than A, C faster than B, etc. If full-duplex transmission is envisioned, the receiver rates also have to be adjusted. This is shown in Figure 23-3.

To implement such an arrangement it is necessary to have control (in a management sense) of all of the hardware involved, to stock spare crystals for the various transmitters and receivers, and to be careful to put the right crystals in the right units.

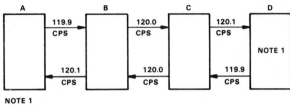

NOTE 1

IT IS ASSUMED THAT STATION D IS NOT ECHOING BACK DATA TO
STATION C. IF IT IS, A HIGHER RATE FOR STATION D'S
TRANSMITTER WOULD BE REQUIRED.

Figure 23-3. Relaying of Transmitted Characters by Stations Having Progressively Faster Clock Rates

A simpler scheme is to calculate a worst case overrun error frequency from the clock specifications of the hardware involved, and to arrange the software to provide an idle interval every so often that allows the intermediate stations to "catch up." Keyboard input automatically does this because humans type so slowly, but asynchronous interprocessor communication can easily run into the clock skew problem because of the processor's ability to send long messages at full speed. The simplest solution is to simulate the keyboard case by putting in an occasional idle period.

The use of synchronous communication for interprocessor communication solves both the error detection problem and the clock skew problem. The first is solved because all of the standard synchronous communication protocols contain some sort of error detection, and the second is solved by the inclusion of the transmitted clock with the transmitted data. The penalty for solving these problems is that execution of a synchronous communication protocol involves greater software complexity than that required for asynchronous communication. This is due to the existence of error detection systems and special characters or character counts. Chapter 14 described the general features of synchronous communications, and Chapters 16 through 19 described the various protocols that can be used. While it has been implied that serial synchronous communications links between processors are slow, relative to parallel data transfers, there are available short range modems with transmission speeds of 1 megabaud and more. With such a modem, one can transfer about 27,777 36-bit words per second, or 62,500 16-bit words per second. Actual throughput would of course depend upon the error rate and length of message blocks as well as the required software overhead.

Returning to the concept of microprocessor-assisted single line units, it is possible to simplify the software associated with interprocessor communication by building a "network link" consisting of a pair of microprocessors, a pair of line units, a pair of line drivers, and a line. The configuration is shown in Figure 23-4.

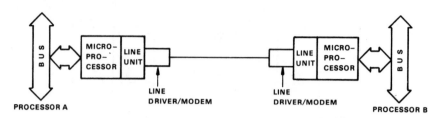

Figure 23-4. Microprocessor-Implemented Network Link

To use the network link, a program in processor A tells its network link microprocessor the starting address of the message stored in main memory and the length of the message. The microprocessor then sends that message in blocks to the microprocessor at the other end of the link. The transmission is done in one of the standard synchronous communication protocols and includes error detection. When the receiving microprocessor detects an error, it requests the transmitting microprocessor to retransmit the block in which an error was detected, which it does without bothering processor A. When the transmission has been completed and accepted, processor A is then notified. In addition to performing error detection tasks, the microprocessor at processor B, which is receiving the message, alerts processor B when the message begins to arrive, telling it to prepare a buffer area. In protocols such as BISYNC, standard buffer size must be used; in DDCMP, the buffer size required is included in the header information.

24

Digital Transmission And Packet Switching Networks

In previous chapters, the electrical properties of telephone switching networks and transmission systems have been discussed. As is evident from these discussions, the electrical properties of existing telephone systems have been optimized for the transmission of voice signals. While modems have made data transmission over the telephone system very workable, there are nonetheless certain properties of the telephone network which will always work against its complete usefulness in data transmission. Chief among these are high error rate, long call set-up time, unavailability of speeds above 9600 baud, and unavailability of full-duplex service above 1200 baud. Private lines solve some, but not all, of these problems.

Interestingly enough, while digital data transmission has been using modems to transfer signals over the analog telephone network, the analog telephone network has been turning increasingly to the use of digital techniques to transfer analog signals (voices).

Until relatively recently, all amplifiers in telephone transmission systems worked similarly to the amplifiers used in home high fidelity systems. As anyone who owns some scratchy records knows, amplifiers make the noise louder at the same time they make the signal louder. In any analog telephone transmission system, the received signal differs from the transmitted signal because of crosstalk, noise, intermodulation, and other distortion. Once the disturbance has been introduced, it cannot be eliminated, and the information content of the signal is thus degraded. Ultimately, the system performance is limited by these degradations. In a digital transmission system, however, a receiver needs only to decide whether the signal present on the line at a given moment is a one or a zero. This task is very easy unless there is a great deal of noise. Most important, however, is the fact that a digital signal can be regenerated before signal degradation becomes so severe that the receiver will be unable to discern the ones and zeros. Thus, while an analog amplifier cannot improve the quality of a signal passing through it, a digital amplifier can restore the signal to an exact replica of the transmitted signal. Thus, with digital regenerative repeaters, there is no limit to the transmission distance, and the signal to noise ratio of the facility over which the system is operating may be as poor as 12 db. (An analog system would require 60 db.)

The Western Electric T1 carrier system is an excellent example of a digital transmission system. If one wishes to transmit an analog signal with a bandwidth of 4000 Hertz, Nyquist's Sampling Theorem says that a sampling rate of 8000 samples per second (2 × 4000) will produce enough information to completely reconstruct the original signal. Sending analog samples will not produce the noise resistance desired, however. First the samples must be encoded. After assigning the amplitude of the sample a seven bit code representing one of 128 distinct amplitude values, the T1 system adds an eighth bit to indicate whether the channel is on-hook or off-hook. After each sequence of 24 eight bit words, an additional bit, called the framing bit, is added to supply synchronizing information for the receiver system. The 24 eight bit words represent one sample from each of 24 voice grade (4000 Hertz) lines, and these 192 bits plus the framing bit are called a "frame." Because frames occur 8000 times per second, the system bit rate is 193 times 8000 or 1,544,000 bits per second. This bit stream is transmitted over lines which use one cable pair for each direction of transmission and which have regenerative repeaters spaced approximately every 6000 feet. In addition to the T1 system, there are other larger digital transmission systems in the "T" series and numerous systems made by other transmission system suppliers. Some international standards are being developed and may be found in the G.700 series of CCITT Recommendations.

In present communications systems, it is possible for digital data from a computer to get converted into analog signals by a modem only to be converted to digital by a T1 terminal. It would then be converted back to analog by another T1 terminal, converted to digital by another modem, and then used by a second computer. This situation, together with competition from non-Bell carriers in the United States, has caused the evolution of a Bell System offering called the Digital Data System. In Canada, the Trans Canada Telephone System offers Data-Route and a nationwide packet switching service called DataPac. Packet switching will be discussed at the end of this chapter.

The Digital Data System is a private line, two-point or multi-point, full-duplex transmission offering. Synchronous data rates of 2400, 4800, 9600, and 56,000 bits per second are available. A Data Service Unit provides the customer interface to this system and is designed to provide plug for plug interchangeability with existing modems using the EIA RS-232-C interface at speeds of 2400, 4800, and 9600 bits per second. It also provides plug for plug interchangeability with existing modems using the CCITT Recommendation V.35 interface at a speed of 56,000 bits per second. The Digital Data System takes advantage of the existing and planned digital hierarchy of T1, T2, and similar systems. Bell System Technical Reference Manual PUB 41450 describes the specifications of the Data Service Unit interface in greater detail, but it resembles the synchronous modem interfaces discussed in Chapter 14 at speeds of 9600 bits per second and below. It is similar to the Bell System 303 modem when operated at 56,000 bits per second.

A switched 56,000 bit per second service is offered as the Switched Digital Data System. This service uses a Data Service Unit described in Technical Reference Manual PUB 41452 ("Dataphone Switched Digital Data Service Unit Interface Specifications"). It also uses the CCITT V.35 interface and offers connections for automatic calling units, multi-line hunting group arrangements, and other features.

While digital transmission systems are an impressive technical accomplishment, they are not of great interest to the programmer or the computer interface designer. They have been made intentionally to look exactly like their modem predecessors so that a minimum software and hardware impact is noted by the customer. The digital transmission service offerings are of interest to the system designer, however, as their cost/benefit tradeoffs, error rates, system availability, and other factors offer new system configuration possibilities.

The most exciting communications advance in the area of new configuration possibilities is packet switching. The best way to explain packet switching and its pros and cons is to contrast it with other methods.

Telephone systems and telex (switched teleprinter) systems use circuit switching. In circuit switching a person or terminal places a call by entering into the switching system the directory listed number of the person or terminal to be called; the switching system then sets up a connection. Every piece of information entered at the calling point is immediately conveyed to the called point with a delay equal only to the speed of light in the transmission medium used. Furthermore, the connection between the two points is used solely by the two communicating parties; although some multiplexing may take place in portions of the transmission system, the parties will not notice this. The connection will exist for use by the two communicating parties until they decide to "hang up."

Message telegram systems use message switching, in which a message is sent to a switching center where it is stored. When facilities become available to send it on to another switching center closer to the destination, the message is forwarded over those facilities to be stored at the next point. The storing and forwarding process continues until the message reaches its destination. Message switching is also called "store and forward" switching.

Circuit switching has several advantages over message switching. First of all, it is interactive. If a person asks a question, the other person answers right away. In addition, each person can tell immediately if the other person is happy or sad or angry. Secondly, it is full-duplex for low speed data transmission. Finally, the speed of service is nearly immediate, except for occasional blocking in the switching systems involved, and connection to the distant party is confirmed when that party answers.

Message switching is more efficient than circuit switching, however. Because a switched circuit is in place between the two conversing parties or terminals throughout the conversation, there are frequent intervals in which little is being said or little data is being transferred. Thus the use of the information capacity of the channel is not very efficient. A message could have been sent over that channel occupying the channel at full capacity just long enough to send the message; the channel could then have been made available for some other use. The ability of a message switching system to store messages during traffic peaks and send them on their way later also makes a message switching system much more efficient. There are no traffic peaks that must be taken care of immediately as there are in circuit switching. Since all service requests are handled on a "blocked calls delayed" basis rather than a "blocked calls lost" basis, the service can be offered at far less cost than that of a system that must be designed for busy hour loads. Since a higher percentage of attempted calls is completed, more revenue is collected for a given capital investment.

There are some other factors involved in contrasting telephone systems with telegram systems: the greater ease of using the telephone terminal apparatus and the emotional appeal of a loved one's voice compared with his or her typed words. While these two factors cited make a case for the telephone, the value of a written record that can be passed around to several people, and the ease of operating written message systems across half a world of time zones, make a strong case for the telegram in many applications. None of these factors is a strong influence in the discussion of circuit switching versus message switching for data switching, however, as both methods involve the same apparatus and written communications.

The critical points of comparison for data transmission systems are speed of operation and cost. The efficiencies of line time utilization and the traffic peak smoothing effects inherent in message switching make message switching very attractive from a cost standpoint. If only the speed of operation could be improved... .

A message switching system which is operating at 100 percent of design capacity will have very substantial delays, regardless of message length. A message switching system operating at 80 percent of design capacity will have very short delays providing there are no long messages in the system which might block certain routing paths and delay other messages. If all messages are limited to 1000 information bits and 9600 bit per second transmission facilities are used, no message occupies the line for more than about 100 milliseconds. Application of this rule requires that messages longer than 1000 bits be broken up into separate messages or "packets," hence the term "packet switching." Each packet must have some additional bits added for address and administrative purposes.

By designing the message switching system so that it never has to operate at or near design capacity, and by limiting the length of the messages, packet switching systems provide speed of service close enough, for data communications purposes, to that of circuit switching, and do so at an attractive cost. There are some drawbacks however. The principal one is that long messages must be broken up into a great many packets, each of which has its own address/administrative header. Had that long message been sent through a circuit switching system, the addressing information would only have been presented once and the "overhead" would have been much less. Thus packet switching is most effective when most of the messages handled fit in a small number of packets, preferably one.

Very short messages also have a high overhead, as the addressing information is required for a message comparable in length to the address. Very short messages have high overhead in a circuit switching system also, hence they are not a worthwhile item of comparison between the two systems. While on the subject of short messages, it is worthwhile to note that 1000 bit packets or similar size packets are too short to be effectively circuit switched because of the time taken within circuit switching systems and between circuit switches (signaling) to set up a call. The call set up period involves the greatest utilization of elaborate and expensive equipment, particularly in common control switching systems. The call set up period also makes the most demands on the signaling equipment. Because of the high cost of setting up a call and the lack of revenue accrual during this period, most common carriers and telecommunications authorities charge more for the initial connection period of a call than for subsequent equal intervals of time. For this reason, transmission of data as separate short calls is not economical, and the packet concept is applied only to networks of message switching processors connected by private lines. Some packet switching systems have access ports which are reached by dialing numbers in the circuit switched telephone network, but these are provided principally as a convenience for low utilization terminal users.

While the most commonly cited packet switching network is the ARPANET, one of the first packet switching systems offered as a service to the general public is Trans Canada Telephone System's DataPac. The DataPac system uses a protocol called SNAP (Standard Network Access Protocol) which is essentially equivalent to the protocol contained in CCITT Recommendation X.25. A copy of the SNAP specification may be purchased from:

SNAP Distribution Centre
Room 940
160 Elgin Street
Ottawa, Ontario, Canada
K1G 3J4

A brief review of SNAP is included here, but the reader is cautioned that this is not a complete presentation.

Recommendation X.25 transfers packets only in frames in the High level Data Link Control (HDLC) format, which is equivalent to the SDLC protocol described in Chapter 19. SNAP, however, permits packets to be sent in the frame formats of HDLC or transparent BISYNC, as shown in Figure 24-1.

The packets are sent from the customer's Data Terminal Equipment (typically a computer, programmable terminal controller, or intelligent terminal) to the DataPac network over a point to point private line operating in synchronous mode at 1200, 2400, 4800, or 9600 bits per second. While asynchronous operations and dial-in facilities are also available, only the synchronous private line service will be discussed here. The line from the Data Terminal Equipment to the DataPac network is time division multiplexed to provide the capability of handling traffic on a number of virtual circuits. A "virtual circuit" is a bi-directional association between a pair of Data Terminal Equipments over which all data transfers take the form of packets. Transmission facilities are only assigned when data packets are actually being transferred. The association between two Data Terminal Equipments may either be a permanent one (a "permanent virtual circuit") or a temporary one (a "switched virtual circuit"). The only important difference between these two types of virtual circuits is that the switched virtual circuit requires that the Data Terminal Equipments and the DataPac network exchange call set-up packets to establish the call and call clearing packets to take down the connection when the call is complete. This process will be explored in greater detail below, but first a closer look will be taken at the transmission facility between a typical Data Terminal Equipment installation and the DataPac network.

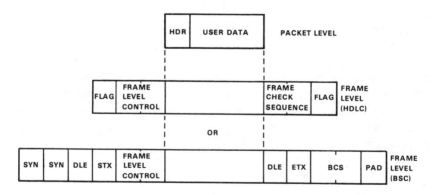

Figure 24-1. Framing Formats in SNAP

In most time division multiplex systems, the transmission facility transmits a sample of one channel for a moment, then the next channel, then the next, and so on until all channels have been sampled. At that time it starts over again with the first channel. Each channel is sampled and the result of that sample placed on the line whether the channel is handling traffic or not. The DataPac network does not do this. Instead, Asynchronous Time Division Multiplexing is used. In this system, the fact that a typical virtual circuit to a remote Data Terminal Equipment may actually be carrying data only a small percentage of the time is exploited by dynamically allocating the transmission facility to an active virtual circuit. The bit rate of the physical circuit must be chosen based on queuing delay considerations to handle the average busy period loads for the virtual circuits being multiplexed. The Asynchronous Time Division Multiplexing of virtual channels is shown in Figure 24-2.

The logical channel identifiers shown in Figure 24-2 are used only between the Data Terminal Equipment and the Network Node to which it is connected. In the example shown, logical channel identifiers 1 and 2 are in permanent use for permanent virtual circuits to Data Terminal Equipments B and C respectively. Identifiers 3 and 4 are in use only as long as the switched virtual circuits to Data Terminal Equipments D and E are in use. When either of those connections is released, the associated virtual circuit number will be available for other outgoing or incoming calls.

The establishment of a connection between two Data Terminal Equipments over switched virtual circuits in the DataPac network is accomplished by the calling station sending a Call Request packet which the network sends on to the called station. If the called station accepts the call, it sends a Call Accepted packet back to the network. This is forwarded to the calling station as a Call Connected packet (assuming there is no network congestion). Data

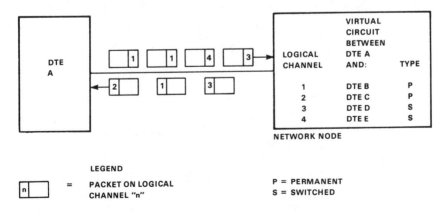

Figure 24-2. Packet Flow

transfer can then take place. At the conclusion of data transfer, either station can cause the connection to be taken down by sending a Clear Request packet into the network. The network responds by giving a Clear Confirmation packet back. The network also sends a Clear Indication packet to the other station and that station in turn responds with a Clear Confirmation packet. This is summarized in Figure 24-3.

The packets used in Figure 24-3 to establish and clear calls over switched virtual circuits have prescribed formats consisting of three or more eight bit groupings called "octets" rather than characters. Bits of an octet are numbered 0 to 7, where bit 7 is the low order bit and is transmitted first. Octets of a packet are numbered consecutively starting from 1 and are transmitted in that order. The Call Request packet format is shown in Figure 24-4. Note

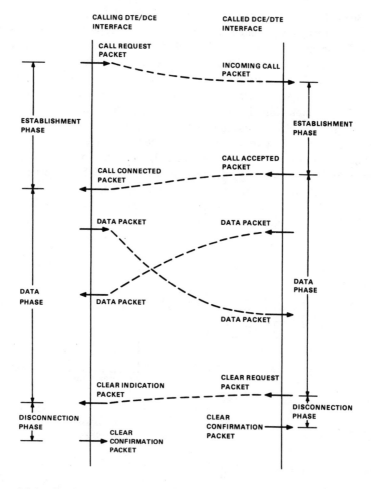

Figure 24-3. Packet Transmissions in SNAP Protocol

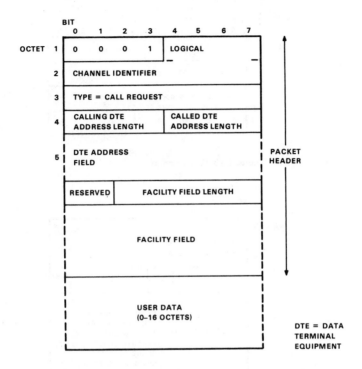

Figure 24-4. Call Request Packet Format

that this format contains some of the features of the DDCMP protocol discussed in Chapter 18, in that Octet 4 contains the length of the address field. This is followed by the address field. The same procedure is used again with the facility field. This is somewhat similar to the character count in DDCMP which is followed by an information field of the length specified by the count.

The facility field provides for some interesting features. Codes may be placed there which indicate that the call is "collect," i.e., that the recipient pays the telecommunications costs. Codes may also be placed there which identify the calling Data Terminal Equipment as part of a closed user group; the called terminal might only accept calls from members of that group.

While the size of the packet header in Figure 24-4 may seem quite large, the packet headers for the other types of signaling packets used, such as Clear Request, are typically much smaller (see Figure 24-5).

The packet header for data packets, shown in Figure 24-6, is the shortest header of all, as might be expected. This permits minimum overhead. The Data Qualifier bit is used to distinguish between data and control information which is destined to a terminal controller. The More Data bit indicates that there is an additional packet following which contains more of the same message. P(R) and P(S) are the Packet Receive Sequence number and Packet Send Sequence number respectively. Their function is similar to the Re-

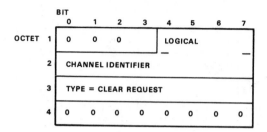

Figure 24-5. Clear Request Packet Format

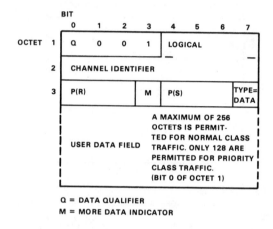

Q = DATA QUALIFIER
M = MORE DATA INDICATOR

Figure 24-6. Data Packet Format

sponse and Sequence fields in DDCMP and identical to the Nr and Ns sequence numbers in SDLC.

In addition to the packets shown here, there are a number of flow control, restart, and reset packets designed for use in special circumstances. These are beyond the scope of this text, but they are described completely in the SNAP specification.

The packets are transmitted in HDLC or BISYNC frames (see Figure 24-1) and the SNAP specification reviews the appropriate procedures, especially with regard to HDLC. A reader familiar with SDLC (Chapter 19) will find that familiarity a great help.

25

Parallel
Communication

The remarks in some of the preceding chapters may have given the impression that all short distance communication involving computers and peripheral equipment is done in parallel, and that all communication done over medium to long distances is done in serial form. This is not quite the case, as the signals on a group of wires representing a parallel data transfer can be encoded into separate tones, transmitted over a single pair of wires, and then decoded by tone receivers which assert the appropriate states on a group of parallel leads at the receiving station. One of the most widespread examples of this type of data transfer is dual tone multifrequency (DTMF) signaling between a telephone subscriber's telephone and the local telephone exchange. American Telephone and Telegraph and its associated companies refer to this as Touch Tone (a registered trademark). Other companies refer to it by a variety of names combining the words touch, push-button, tone, calling, dialing, etc.

DTMF signaling is accomplished by using the arrangement of frequencies shown in Table 25-1. When the "1" button is depressed, an oscillator generates two tones: 697 Hertz and 1209 Hertz. When "9" is depressed, 852 Hertz and 1477 Hertz signals are generated. The column associated with the 1633 Hertz frequency is used for special functions. For example, when DTMF signaling is used in the AUTOVON military voice network, these buttons are used to establish the priority of this call relative to other calls. The button marked "a" in this figure is marked "FO" for "Flash Override" and the button marked "d" in this figure is marked "P" for priority. If none of these buttons is depressed after the desired number is dialed, the call is treated as Routine, and Priority, Immediate, Flash, or Flash Override calls may "bump" it to obtain transmission facilities necessary for completion of those calls. This telephone could not be used in such a way on the ordinary voice

Table 25-1 Touch Tone® Frequency Assignments

	1209	1336	1477	1633
697	1	2	3	a
770	4	5	6	b
852	7	8	9	c
941	*	0	#	d

telephone DDD network, however, since the ordinary DDD network does not include such priority features. Even in the AUTOVON network, the usability of the various buttons is limited by the "class of service" assigned to the line upon which the telephone is located.

The * and # buttons are generally used for special services available in areas served by Electronic Switching System (ESS) offices. The special services include the ability to have calls transferred to another number on a temporary basis, the ability to dial frequently dialed numbers by using special two-digit codes, etc. As was the case with the priority features in AUTOVON, the mere possession of a telephone set with these buttons is not sufficient; the telephone switching equipment must have been "told" that your telephone line is entitled to these features—that your line has this "class of service."

Telephones installed in residences and businesses have only the buttons 1 through 0 and * and #. Most telephone companies charge a modest additional charge per month for DTMF signaling rather than conventional rotary dial signaling. This charge controls the market demand (so that customers will not demand the new service at a rate faster than the rotary dial telephones wear out) and compensates for the cost of making the necessary changes in the telephone central office switching equipment. These changes are substantial in the case of Strowger (step-by-step) systems, where the tones received from the subscribers must be converted to dial pulses to operate the switches.

The changes are minor in the more advanced electromechanical systems such as #5 Crossbar, where tone decoders are added to the existing dial-pulse counting devices (originating registers). In fact, due to the much shorter time it takes to address the switching equipment with tones rather than dial pulses, the number of originating registers required is smaller in a telephone switching office with a substantial number of DTMF subscribers than it would be in an office with only rotary dial subscribers, assuming all of the originating registers were equipped with tone decoders.

Despite the charge for DTMF signaling, the cost of the service is sufficiently low that one may expect a fair fraction of the population in the more prosperous countries to have this service by the year 2000. The prospect of a low cost terminal in a great many homes makes parallel data transmission by DTMF signaling an area of great growth potential in data communications.

There are two factors which may adversely affect those growth prospects, however. One is the limited range of characters available on the "dial." Some DTMF tone pads have the traditional letters ABC above the number 2, DEF above the 3, etc., but many others do not. Even if the letters are present, some elaborate procedure involving the * and # buttons is necessary to tell the computer that you wish to have it interpret a particular set of two received tones as a letter rather than as a number. About 15 years ago, an engineer from Western Union proposed such a scheme in an article for *Datamation* magazine. For the letters ABC above the number 2, for example, one would depress *2 to indicate "A," *#2 to indicate "B," and #2 to indicate C. The three letters above each of the other digits could be accessed similarly. To send a number, one would press the appropriate number button without using a * or # prefix. This system has not come into any substantial use. A system that is more common, but still very limited in scope, is the use of pieces of plastic which fit over the tone pad and assign certain functions to certain buttons. The caller reaches a voice response unit which asks questions and then interprets the replies as either numbers or special functions, depending upon the question asked. A Seattle bank terminated an experimental banking service using such a system, however, probably due to a customer acceptance problem.

The customer acceptance problem is the second limitation to the use of DTMF signaling. People would certainly be unwilling to use the *# prefix system for transmitting more than a very few characters. Thus, the use of DTMF for data input is limited to cases where the data is mostly numerical or where there is a very small number of functions to be performed, such as turning something on and off. The use of DTMF for a customer to transfer his funds at a bank or from the bank to creditors is an application where a mainly numeric input is involved. However, people like to receive paper receipts and to have faith that the person with whom they are dealing will do the right thing or at least remember them. DTMF banking does not provide slips of paper, at least not on the spot, and involves dealing with "the computer," and every consumer has been told at one time or another that "our computer made an error in your account." In summary, DTMF signaling for financial transactions requires both training and faith.

The training and faith problems are substantially solved when the employees of a bank or store use a DTMF system for inquiry purposes to secure credit approvals or similar information. Their faith is particularly fortified if the voice response unit repeats the account number to confirm the keyed input, although an employee may re-try if there are problems.

Telephones with DTMF capability are widely used in banks to secure customer balance figures and in other businesses for inventory control, dictation machine operation, and other tasks. The AT&T Transaction® telephone system for credit authorization is another interesting application.

® Transaction is a Registered Trademark of the American Telephone and Telegraph Company.

In the Transaction® system, a special telephone is used which has a slot for reading the magnetic stripe on credit cards, a Touch Tone® DTMF keypad, and a display or indicator lamp panel.

The user applications of the Transaction® system include credit authorization, check verification, account transfer, reservation systems, audit trails, inventory control, quotation systems, retrieval, and monitoring systems.

To begin the transaction, the user presses the "ON" button and listens for dial tone. A dialing card, containing the telephone number to be dialed, the merchant identification code, and some other information is inserted into the telephone. This information is on a magnetic stripe which is read by a reader in the telephone. The credit card of the customer that the merchant is checking is next inserted into the telephone. The telephone number from the dialing card is then automatically dialed, while the rest of the information is buffered in the telephone and formatted appropriately. Additional information such as the amount of the sale can be entered from the manual entry pad on the telephone. The user then depresses the "END" key and the message is sent on its way. When the credit verification or other inquiry has been completed, the results are returned by voice answer back, tone signals, and indicator lamp display, or a character display, depending upon the specific system configuration.

The materials listed below are suggested for further information on DTMF systems and the Transaction® system in particular.

References

1. Bell System Technical Reference—Data Set 407A Interface Specification, PUB 41408.
2. Bell System Technical Reference—Switched Network Transaction Telephone System, PUB 41804.
3. Bell System Technical Reference—Switched Network Transaction Telephone System Interfacing with Transmission Control Units, PUB 41805.
4. Bell System Technical Reference—Transaction III Terminal, PUB 41806.

26

Special
Problems

There is a children's story which tells how the lack of a nail in a horseshoe caused the horseshoe to be lost and how the loss of the horseshoe caused the horse to be lost. This in turn led to the loss of the knight on the horse, which led to the loss of a critical battle and the loss of a kingdom.

It is possible to call a nail a form of connector, since it connects the horseshoe to the horse. Thus the king who lost his kingdom did so because of a connector problem. Men no longer ride to battle on horses, but connector problems are still with us, especially when setting up data communication systems.

Data communication interfaces, especially multiplexers, are generally designed to connect to modems. The connectors used are 25-pin male connectors that present data to be transmitted on pin 2 and expect to receive data on pin 3. This type of connector (in the U.S., a DB25-P) is shown in abbreviated form in Figure 26-1. A full list of DB25-P pinning is given in Appendix G.

Terminals are also generally designed to plug into modems and also use a connector as shown in Figure 26-1. In most computer installations, however, there are some terminals which are located close to the computer and need to be connected to the same multiplexer that has the modem equipped lines connected to it. The problem is shown schematically in Figure 26-2. Not only is there a problem with the sex of the connectors (both male), but there is also a problem with the pinning, as both connectors deliver data to be transmitted on pin 2.

Figure 26-3 shows one solution to this problem, the "null modem," and indicates how its use is similar to that of actual modems. In both Figure 26-3a and Figure 26-3b the "modem facility" provides a female connector for the

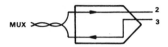

Figure 26-1.   Pin Utilization of DB25-P Connector

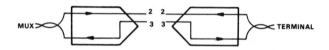

Figure 26-2.   Attempted Connection of Multiplexer and Terminal Using DB25-P Connectors

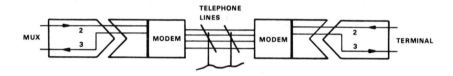

Figure 26-3a.   Connection with Actual Modems

Figure 26-3b.   Connection with Null Modem

mux to plug into and a female connector for the terminal to plug into. Furthermore, data applied to pin 2 of one of those connectors comes out pin 3 of the other.

The "null modem" may be implemented either as a length of cable with leads 2 and 3 (and some others) transposed, or as a cigarette box size container with a terminal board inside and female connectors at the ends. The cable implementation is much neater and provides some additional cable length. Many computer companies sell cables which accomplish this function without referring to them as "null modems" but rather as "cable for connection terminal to computer interface." As can be deduced from Figure 26-2, either the cable from the mux or the cable from the terminal can be altered to solve the connector problem.

The cigarette box type of null modem offers some advantages over the cable type, however. With a terminal strip inside the box a number of different wiring arrangements are possible. Figure 26-4 shows a typical terminal block.

The dashed lines indicate the connections usually provided. The two Signal Ground leads (pin 7) are connected together and the Transmitted Data lead (pin 2) on each side is connected to the Received Data lead (pin 3) on the other side to accomplish the transposition described in conjunction with Figure 26-3b. The remaining cross-connections involve control leads. To convince the devices connected to the null modem that they are dealing with a real modem, a lead is provided which causes the assertion of Request to Send by the device to be returned as an assertion of Clear to Send by the null modem. Since, under these circumstances, a real modem would send carrier to the distant device (i.e., the other device attached to the null modem), a lead is also provided which causes the assertion of Request to Send by one device to assert Carrier Detect at the other device. Finally a cross connection between Data Terminal Ready of one device and both Ring Indicate and Data Set Ready of the other device permits the assertion of Data Terminal Ready (indicating a willingness to transfer data) to show as a call arrival (assertion of Ring and Data Set Ready) at the other device.

The cross connections of the control leads permit the turning on of the terminal to look like a call arrival to the multiplexer and hence elicit the appropriate software response.

The interconnection of synchronous hardware by means of null modems is slightly more complicated than the case just described, due to the presence of clock leads. Many synchronous modems provide both a transmitter clock, which tells the synchronous transmitter unit when to apply data to the Transmitted Data lead, and a receiver clock, which tells the receiver unit when to

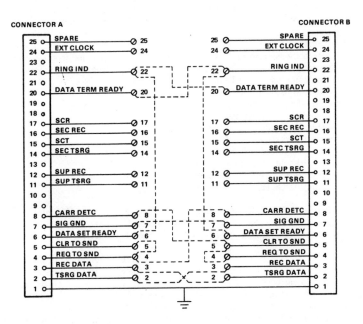

Figure 26-4. Null Modem Wiring Diagram

sample the data on the Received Data lead. Other modems provide only the receiver clock and require the synchronous transmitter unit to supply its own timing information along with the data.

Frequency accuracy of clocking provided by the data communications equipment is generally required to be .005 percent or .01 percent depending on the modem. The modem then uses phase lock loop techniques to keep in step with the clock being provided.

Pin 15 of the interface connector is used for the Transmitter Signal Element Timing when it is being provided by the modem (CCITT Circuit 114). Pin 17 is used for the Receiver Signal Element Timing when it is being provided by the modem (CCITT Circuit 115). When the data terminal equipment provides the Transmitter Signal Element Timing (CCITT Circuit 113), pin 24 is used. Receiver Signal Element Timing using the data terminal equipment as a source (CCITT Circuit 128) is done so infrequently that there is no "commonly used" pinning convention.

EIA RS-232-C Definitions	CCITT V.24 Definitions
Circuit DB—Transmitter Signal Element Timing (DCE Source) (CCITT 114) Direction: From data communication equipment	*Circuit 114*—Transmitter Signal Element Timing (DCE Source) Direction: From DCE
Signals on this circuit are used to provide the data terminal equipment with signal element timing information. The data terminal equipment shall provide a data signal on Circuit BA (Transmitted Data) in which the transitions between signal elements nominally occur at the time of the transitions from OFF to ON condition of the signal on Circuit DB. When Circuit DB is implemented in the DCE, the DCE shall normally provide timing information on this circuit whenever the DCE is in a POWER ON condition. It is permissible for the DCE to withhold timing information on this circuit for short periods provided Circuit CC (Data Set Ready) is in the OFF condition. (For example, the withholding of timing information may be necessary in performing maintenance tests within the DCE.)	Signals on this circuit provide the Data Terminal Equipment with signal element timing information. The condition on this circuit shall be ON and OFF for nominally equal periods of time. The Data Terminal Equipment shall present a data signal on Circuit 103 (Transmitted Data) in which the transitions between signal elements nominally occur at the time of the transitions from OFF to ON condition of Circuit 114.
Circuit DD—Receiver Signal Element Timing (DCE Source) (CCITT 115) Direction: From data communication equipment	*Circuit 115*—Receiver Signal Element Timing (DCE Source) Direction: From DCE
Signals on this circuit are used to provide the data terminal equipment with received signal element timing information. The transition from ON to OFF condition shall nominally indicate the center of each signal element on	Signals on this circuit provide the Data Terminal Equipment with signal element timing information. The condition on this circuit shall be ON and OFF for nominally equal periods of time, and a transition from ON to OFF condition shall nominally indicate the centre of

EIA RS-232-C Definitions	CCITT V.24 Definitions

Circuit BB (Received Data). Timing information on Circuit DD shall be provided at all times when Circuit CF (Received Line Signal Detector) is in the ON condition. It may, but need not be present following the ON to OFF transition of Circuit CF.

Circuit DA—Transmitter Signal Element Timing (DTE Source) (CCITT 113)
Direction: To data communication equipment

Signals on this circuit are used to provide the transmitting signal converter with signal element timing information.

The ON to OFF transition shall nominally indicate the center of each signal element on Circuit BA (Transmitted Data). When Circuit DA is implemented in the DTE, the DTE shall normally provide timing information on this circuit whenever the DTE is in a POWER ON condition. It is permissible for the DTE to withhold timing information on this circuit for short periods provided Circuit CA (Request to Send) is in the OFF condition. (For example, the temporary withholding of timing information may be necessary in performing maintenance tests within the DTE).

There is no EIA RS-232-C equivalent to Circuit 128.

each signal element on Circuit 104 (Received Data).

Circuit 113—Transmitter Signal Element Timing (DTE Source)
Direction: To DCE

Signals on this circuit provide the date communications equipment with signal element timing information. The condition on this circuit shall be ON and OFF for nominally equal periods of time, and the transition from ON to OFF condition shall nominally indicate the centre of each signal element on Circuit 103 (Transmitted Data).

Circuit 128—Receiver Signal Element Timing (DTE Source)
Direction: To DCE

Signals on this circuit provide the data communications equipment with signal element timing information. The condition on this circuit shall be ON and OFF for nominally equal periods of time. The Data Communication Equipment shall present a data signal on Circuit 104 (Received Data) in which the transitions between signal elements nominally occur at the time of the transitions from OFF to ON condition of the signal on Circuit 128.

The problem when connecting two synchronous terminals (or a terminal with one or two multiplexers) together without modems is that with no modems there is no source of clock. It is therefore important when contemplating such a configuration to insure that there is at least one device involved that contains a clock source and preferably two such devices. Manuals describing modems refer to clocks located outside the modems as "external clocks," despite the fact that these clocks may be internal to the data terminal equipment; therefore the term "external" may often be confusing.

It may be best to substitute mentally the phrase "non-modem clock" whenever one sees the phrase "external clock."

Returning to Figure 26-4, the device which contains the non-modem clock delivers that clock signal on lead 24. By wiring the lead 24 containing the clock signal to leads 15 and 17 of both devices connected to the null modem, operation of two synchronous devices without a modem is possible. This arrangement is rather risky, however, since one EIA/CCITT driver, that associated with lead 24, is driving four EIA/CCITT receivers. A better arrangement is where both devices have clocks in them producing signals on lead 24 of each device. For this configuration, a wire is run from lead 24 of one device to lead 15 of that same device and lead 17 of the other device. In this way, the "external clock" of a given device drives that device's transmitter and the other device's receiver. The major benefit of this scheme is that each EIA/CCITT driver involved drives only two EIA/CCITT receivers. Even with this arrangement, cable lengths add up quickly; the capacitance of the leads from the driver to the null modem and from the null modem to each of the two clock receivers may become excessive.

The problems of interconnection are not limited to devices with EIA/CCITT voltage level interfaces. The same types of problems exist when dealing with current loop devices such as teleprinters. Figure 26-5 indicates schematically the problems of trying to connect two teleprinters to each other. Figure 26-6 indicates similar problems trying to connect two single line interfaces (see Chapter 2) or multiplexers together.

Not only do the two teleprinters in Figure 26-5 both have male connectors, but neither has the current sources necessary to make a current loop interface work. The multiplexers in Figure 26-6 (in each of which only one line is shown) have a similar problem since both have female connectors. In the latter case, however, there is a surplus of current sources rather than a lack. In both the Figure 26-5 and the Figure 26-6 configurations, a transposition of the receiver leads and the transmitter leads is required to connect the keyboard of one teleprinter to the printer of the other and to connect the transmitter section of one multiplexer to the receiver section of the other. This is analogous to the transposition of the Transmitted Data lead and Received Data lead in the null modem, except that, in this case, two pairs of wires are involved rather than two wires. The device shown in Figure 26-7 will solve the problem shown in Figure 26-5, and the device shown in Figure 26-8 will solve the problem shown in Figure 26-6.

The devices shown in circles are optical couplers, which were explained in greater detail in the latter part of Chapter 3. The connectors shown in both figures are chosen to mate with the connectors shown in Figures 26-5 and 26-6, and a transposition of the leads is provided on the right hand side of Figures 26-7 and 26-8 to connect transmitters of one unit to receivers of the other. Figure 26-7 includes current sources to supply the 20 milliampere signal-

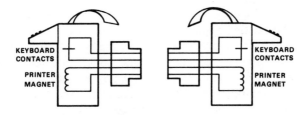

Figure 26-5. **Connection Problem: Two Teleprinters**

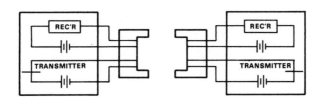

Figure 26-6. **Connection Problem: Two Interfaces**

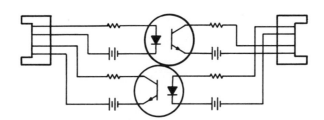

Figure 26-7. **Use of Optical Coupler to Solve Connection Problem of Two Terminals**

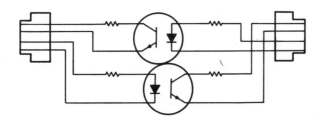

Figure 26-8. **Use of Optical Coupler to Solve Connection Problem of Two Interfaces**

ing current while Figure 26-8 provides isolation between the current loops powered by the existing Figure 26-6 current sources. It is to be understood that these figures are conceptual only, as the use of batteries as current sources is not customary practice in data communication. Likewise, the simple optical coupler circuit of Figure 26-8 might not be suitable if the voltages used in the multiplexers were high. Also the light emitting diodes may not accommodate currents of 20 milliamperes or more, so a bypass transistor circuit (not shown) is often used.

27

CCITT Recommendations X.20 and X.21

The introduction of the RS-422 and RS-423 standards, discussed in Chapter 5, brought an increase in the number of interface leads used. The additional leads provided a capability for putting local and remote modems into various test modes and improved the electrical characteristics of the interface. While this capability reduced the cost of troubleshooting, it increased the number of level converters and connector pins required.

An increased number of level converters is a much more serious problem than an increased number of logic gates, flip-flops, or memory bits. Level converters have substantial power dissipation and sink a great deal of current into their ground leads; thus, they are unsuited to most LSI density improvement techniques. The number of level converters per integrated circuit package has remained constant while the numbers of gates, flip-flops, and memory bits housed in a single integrated circuit package have risen by orders of magnitude.

An increase in the number of connector pins affects price in four ways. First, more level converters are required, as mentioned above. Second, use of a larger connector means that fewer connectors can be mounted in a given space. Where large numbers of communications lines are brought together, more sheet metal and more rack space are required to mount the connectors. Third, more connector pins means more wires in the cables, and fourth, more connector pins means more gold plating.

All four of these costs have remained constant or risen during the same period that logic costs have steadily declined. This suggests that an interface that uses fewer connector pins and more logic would be attractive. The CCITT Recommendation X.20 and X.21 interfaces are steps in that direction because they use only a 15-pin connector.

The X.21 interface has additional features beyond economy, however. While it does not utilize the large connectors associated with RS-422, it does use the superior electrical characteristics of that interface. Furthermore, X.21 provides automatic calling in the same interface as the data transfer, with automatic calling features far more sophisticated than those outlined in Chapter 11. Call progress signals, calling and called line identification information, and call failure cause codes are included.

For data communications over public telephone networks, and for point-to-point privately owned circuits, the advanced call control features of the X.20 and X.21 interfaces cannot be implemented or are unnecessary. Thus, the large number of modems that have already been installed utilizing the RS-232-C/V.24 interface will remain. However, the X.21 automatic calling and call progress features are especially attractive to telecommunications authorities operating or planning to operate public data networks, and a familiarity with these interfaces will be helpful to data communication hardware and software designers. Therefore, they are summarized below:

X.20   Interface Between Data Terminal Equipment (DTE) and Data Circuit-Terminating Equipment (DCE) for Start-Stop Transmission Services on Public Data Networks.

The interface consists of:

G	Signal Ground	
Ga	DTE Common Return	(from DTE to DCE)
Gb	DCE Common Return	(from DCE to DTE)
T	Transmit	(from DTE to DCE)
R	Receive	(from DCE to DTE)

The electrical characteristics may be according to Recommendations X.26 (similar to RS-423), X.27 (similar to RS-422) without cable termination in the load, or V.28. A 15-pin connector is used.

When a call is being established, the sequence of operations starts with the Ready state, wherein both the T and R circuits are binary 0. To enter the Call Request state, the T circuit is changed to 1 (similar to going off-hook with a telephone). The call enters the Proceed to Select state when the R circuit changes to 1 (similar to getting a dial tone). The Data Terminal Equipment then sends a specially formatted string of "selection characters" over the T circuit; this is the Selection Signals state (similar to dialing a telephone). In some implementations, the Data Circuit-Terminating Equipment now sends "Called Line Identification" information to the Data Terminal Equipment by signaling on the R circuit. If the call is successful, the Data Circuit-Terminating Equipment then sends an ACK character on circuit R. Twenty milliseconds later, data transfer can begin.

For the station receiving the call, call arrival is announced by circuit R changing to 1. The station can accept the call by changing the T circuit to 1 and then sending an ACK character 10–100 milliseconds later. As was the case with call origination, 20 milliseconds after the receipt of the ACK, data transfer can begin.

The Data Terminal Equipment can request that a connection be cleared by holding the T circuit in the binary 0 condition for more than 210 milliseconds.

Recommendation X.20 contains additional information about call clearing, information about the sequence of events of unsuccessful calls, and formats for the call selection signals.

X.21 General Purpose Interface Between Data Terminal Equipment (DTE) and Data Circuit-Terminating Equipment (DCE) for Synchronous Operation on Public Data Networks.

The interface consists of:

G   Signal Ground
Ga   DTE Common Return   (from DTE to DCE)
T   Transmit   (from DTE to DCE)
R   Receive   (from DCE to DTE)
C   Control   (from DTE to DCE)
I   Indication   (from DCE to DTE)
S   Signal Element Timing   (from DCE to DTE)
B   Byte Timing (optional)   (from DCE to DTE)

The electrical characteristics depend upon the operating speed. Below 9600 bits per second, the circuits at the DCE are according to Recommendations X.27 (similar to RS-422) without cable termination in the load. The circuits at the DTE can be the same, or can be X.26 (similar to RS-423) subject to some restrictions. Above 9600 bits per second, both the DCE and DTE must use Recommendation X.27 with cable termination in the load. In both cases, a 15-pin connector is used.

The X.21 interface is similar to the X.20 interface in that call control information is passed serially over the T and R circuits. However, unlike X.20, the X.21 interface is a synchronous interface (See Chapters 14 and 15) and thus utilizes a clock lead, referred to in the above list as Circuit S, Signal Element Timing. Furthermore, like other synchronous interfaces, X.21 requires that the call control information bits be aligned into characters. This is done via the transmission of SYNC characters or by manipulation of Circuit B, Byte Timing, depending upon the wishes of the organization providing the data transmission service.

Operation of an X.21 interface involves more states than operation of an

X.20 interface, but the following paragraphs will deal only with those states which have parallels in X.20, so that the two interfaces can be conveniently compared.

When a call is being established, the sequence of operations starts with the Ready state, wherein both the T and R circuits are binary 1, and both the C and I circuits are OFF. To enter the Call Request state, the T circuit is changed to 0 and the C circuit is changed to ON within the same bit interval. The call enters the Proceed to Select state when the Data Circuit-Terminating Equipment sends two or more SYNC characters followed by continuous "+" characters on the R circuit. The Data Terminal Equipment then causes entry into the Selection Signals state by sending a specially formatted string of "selection characters" over the T circuit. In some implementations, the Data Circuit-Terminating Equipment now sends "Called Line Identification" information to the Data Terminal Equipment by signaling on the R circuit. If the call is successful, the Data Circuit-Terminating Equipment then asserts the R circuit to a binary 1 while simultaneously turning the I circuit ON. Data transfer can now begin.

For the station receiving the call, call arrival is announced by the Data Circuit-Terminating Equipment sending two or more SYNC characters followed by continuous "BEL" characters on the R circuit with the I circuit OFF. The station can accept the call by changing the T circuit to 1 and the C circuit to ON within 500 milliseconds. The 500 millisecond number may be reduced to 100 milliseconds in the future. As was the case with call origination, data transfer can begin after the Data Circuit-Terminating Equipment asserts the R circuit to a binary 1 while simultaneously turning the I circuit ON.

The Data Terminal Equipment can request that a connection be cleared by holding the T circuit in the binary 0 condition with the C circuit OFF.

Recommendation X.21 contains additional information about call clearing, information about the sequence of events of unsuccessful calls, and formats for the call progress and selection signals.

For the sake of completeness, two other X-series interfaces should be mentioned. These interfaces, X.20 *bis* and X.21 *bis* are interim interfaces that allow connection of conventional modem interfaces to public data networks. They are *not* serial control interfaces.

X.20 *bis*   **V.21 Compatible Interface Between Data Terminal Equipment (DTE) and Data Circuit-Terminating Equipment (DCE) for Start-Stop Transmission Services on Public Data Networks.**

(Recommendation V.21 is "200-baud Modem Standardized for Use in the General Switched Telephone Network," which includes 300 baud operation.)

The interface consists of:

102 Signal Ground or Common Return
103 Transmitted Data
104 Received Data
106 Ready for Sending
107 Data Set Ready
108/x
    108/1 Connect Data Set to Line, or
    108/2 Data Terminal Ready
109 Data Channel Received Line Signal Detector
125 Calling Indicator

The electrical characteristics are according to Recommendation V.28 and a 25-pin connector is used.

These are the familiar RS-232-C/V.24 signals, and they are used in the same way as described in Chapters 5, 9, and 14 of this book, with very minor definition and timing changes appropriate to electronic data network operation instead of switched telephone network operation. Note that X.20 *bis*, unlike X.20, does not include call selection, calling line identification, or called line identification.

X.21 *bis* Use on Public Data Networks of Data Terminal Equipments (DTEs) Which Are Designed for Interfacing to Synchronous V-Series Modems.

The interface consists of:

102 Signal Ground or Common Return
103 Transmitted Data
104 Received Data
105 Request to Send
106 Ready for Sending
107 Data Set Ready
108/x
    108/1 Connect Data Set to Line, or
    108/2 Data Terminal Ready
109 Data Channel Received Line Signal Detector
114 Transmitter Signal Element Timing (DCE)
115 Receiver Signal Element Timing (DCE)
125 Calling Indicator
142 Test Indicator (DCE)

The electrical characteristics of the Data Communication Equipment are according to Recommendation V.28 and a 25-pin connector is used. The electrical characteristics of the Data Terminal Equipment may be according to Recommendation V.28 or Recommendation X.26.

When X.21 *bis* is used at a rate of 48,000 bits per second, the Data Circuit-Terminating equipment will use a 34-pin connector and the Data Terminal Equipment interface will follow Recommendation V.35.

The call establishment and disconnection phases are controlled by Circuit 107, Data Set Ready, and either Circuit 108/1, Connect Data Set to Line, or Circuit 108/2, Data Terminal Ready, according to the following tables:

Circuit 107—Data Set Ready

ON   Ready for Data
OFF   DCE Clear indication
OFF   DCE Clear confirmation

Circuit 108/1—Connect Data Set to Line (an alternative to 108/2)

ON   Call Request
ON   Call Accepted
OFF   DTE Clear indication
OFF   DTE Clear confirmation

Circuit 108/2–Data Terminal Ready (an alternative to 108/1)

ON   Call Accepted
OFF   DTE Clear indication
OFF   DTE Clear confirmation

Recommendation X.21 *bis* specifies that the automatic placement of calls over a switched network using addressed calling (i.e. dialing) should use the 200-series interface circuits described in Recommendation V.25 (See Chapter 11). If an automatic "direct call" (no dialing required) facility is provided, the assertion of Circuit 108/1 can be used to automatically originate a call, as is indicated in the table above, where an ON condition of Circuit 108/1 is labeled "Call Request." If the 200-series circuits are not used, or if a direct call facility is not provided, call origination must be done manually. Successful call completion is indicated when the Data Circuit-Terminating Equipment asserts Circuit 107, Data Set Ready, to the ON condition.

For the station receiving the call, call arrival is announced by the Data Circuit-Terminating Equipment asserting Circuit 125, Calling Indicator. The station can accept the call by asserting Circuit 108/1 or Circuit 108/2, as indicated by the "Call accepted" entries in the above tables. This must be done within 500 milliseconds after the assertion of Calling Indicator. As was the case with call origination, data transfer can begin after the Data Circuit-Terminating Equipment asserts Circuit 107, Data Set Ready to the ON condition.

Data transmission can now begin, using Circuits 102, 103, 104, 105, 106, 109, 114, and 115. These are the familiar Recommendation V.24 signals, and they are used in the same way as described in Chapters 5, 9, and 14 of this book, with very minor definition and timing changes appropriate to electronic data network operation instead of switched telephone network operation.

The Data Terminal Equipment can request that a connection be cleared by dropping Circuit 108/1 or 108/2 to the OFF condition. The Data Circuit-Terminating Equipment will respond by dropping Circuit 107, Data Set Ready. The Data Circuit-Terminating Equipment can request that a connection be cleared by dropping Circuit 107, Data Set Ready. The Data Circuit-Terminating Equipment will respond by dropping Circuit 108/1 or 108/2 to the OFF condition.

Note that X.21 *bis*, unlike X.21, does not include call selection, calling line identification, or called line identification.

Recommendation X.21 *bis* contains a number of notes about alternative arrangements of interchange circuits. These notes are not provided here, as this is only a summary.

Readers desiring to implement any of the Recommendations discussed in this chapter should purchase the appropriate Recommendation from the UN Bookstore or International Telecommunications Union at the addresses given in Chapter 5.

28
Local Area Networks

In early computer systems, users brought their problems to a computer by carrying punched cards or paper tape to the computer room and submitting the cards or tape to computer operators. It was considered a great advance when timesharing systems and data communications made it possible for computer users to sit in a "terminal room" and deal with the computer on an interactive basis.

The preceding chapters have discussed several methods of data communication between terminal users and computers. Specifically, Chapter 3 discussed the 20 milliampere current loop, and Chapter 5 discussed various EIA RS-series interfaces. The speed versus distance performance for these interfaces is given in Appendix A, "How Far—How Fast?" The tables in that appendix indicate that for 9600 baud communication, RS-422, 20 milliampere current loop, RS-423, and RS-232-C, provide satisfactory operation for distances of 4000, 1000, 375, and 250 feet, respectively. As noted in the text accompanying the tables, these figures depend upon the type of cable used, the proximity of the cable to electrical noise sources, and (in the case of RS-232-C) the ground potential differences between the transmitting and receiving sites. Unfortunately, factors of history and economy have caused the interface with the poorest performance, RS-232-C, to be the one most commonly used. In addition to the various performance characteristics of these interfaces, cited in Appendix A, additional physical and electrical problems are cited in Chapter 26. In summary, the connection of terminals to computers at rates of 9600 baud and above, over distances of 250 feet and beyond, remains problematic.

222

The difficulties encountered connecting terminals to computers at higher speeds over greater distances have become more important because:

1. An increasing percentage of the terminals sold have been high speed terminals, and they are being installed in locations hundreds of feet from the computer.

2. There has been an increasing need for terminals to access more than one computer.

3. There has been an increase in the number of terminals that are themselves computers. Such terminals, being true computers, require high speed access to central files and require access to specialized printing services. In the remainder of the chapter such terminals will be referred to as "personal computer terminals." They will be called "personal" because they are used 99 percent of the time by the same person, "computer" because they contain a computer, and "terminals" because they are most useful when connected to a communications facility.

The increased percentage of terminals that are high speed terminals has been due to a decline in price of all terminals and a decrease in the price spread between low speed and high speed terminals. In addition, there has been an increase in the number of people who have used high speed terminals in terminal rooms. Once someone has used a high speed terminal, they wish to retain the high speed performance when they obtain a terminal for their office. This poses a data communications problem because the distance from an office to a computer is usually greater than the distance from a terminal room to a computer.

The increased need for multi-computer access is principally the result of the increased number of computers in the world. In some corporations, program development, word processing, and corporate message switching are services provided on different computers. A single terminal user may wish to access all of these services. While the proliferation of computers in the past decade has made the need for multi-computer access more pressing recently, the problem has existed for a long time, and a number of solutions have been applied.

Telephone switching equipment has been used to provide access to multiple computers since at least 1964. In that year, terminal users at MIT could access either the MIT Computation Center or the Project MAC computer by placing a call through a telephone switching system (PBX) that used conventional switching components, but was designed for high density data traffic. A few years later, a similar system was installed to provide access to a dual processor IBM 360/67 system at MIT Lincoln Laboratory. Modems capable of 300 baud full-duplex operation were used in both cases.

Since that time, many companies have used their office telephone systems for data communication, usually by equipping terminals with acoustic couplers. There are several advantages to such an arrangement:

1. Flexibility—one can reach the desired computer by dialing the appropriate number.

2. Portability—the terminal and acoustic coupler can be moved and used in another office without rewiring.

3. Low entry cost—acoustic couplers are inexpensive.

There are also several disadvantages:

1. Congestion—excessive use of a telephone system for data communication may block voice calls, since conventional telephone systems are not designed for a large number of simultaneous calls (see Chapter 8).

2. Need for second telephone—if people use their office telephone for data transmission a large portion of the time, callers will be unable to reach them. A second telephone will need to be installed.

3. High real cost—individual acoustic couplers may be inexpensive, but equipping an entire company with them is expensive. Also, modems must be supplied at the computer end of the connection.

4. Poor performance—the maximum baud rate for dial-up telephone connections is typically 1200 baud full-duplex, with many acoustic couplers limited to 300 baud full-duplex.

A second alternative for multi-computer access is the use of a patchfield where terminal lines get connected to computer lines in much the same fashion as an old-fashioned telephone switchboard. Unlike a switchboard, there are no bandwidth-limiting transformers or other audio equipment in the circuit, so only the electrical properties of the wire used limit the transmission speed. A typical speed is 9600 or 19,200 baud full-duplex (two wires and ground for EIA, four-wire loops for 20 milliampere operation). Like a switchboard, however, an operator is required, so a patchfield is only attractive when the changing of associations between terminals and computers is infrequent.

A third alternative is the electronic data switch, such as the time division switching systems made by Gandalf and the digital PBXs made by Exxon, Rolm, Datapoint, and others.

In the Gandalf PACX-series data switches, connections can be made automatically by the terminal user, who types commands to a controller in the switch. After the connection is set up, a sampling system transfers data from the terminal line to the computer line. The building wiring and the switch's sampling rate typically limit the speeds used to 9600 baud full-duplex. In contrast, the digital PBXs use ordinary dialing techniques to set up both voice and data connections. They also use improved wiring interface techniques and higher sampling rates to obtain speeds of 56,000 baud or more.

The advantages of both the data switches and digital PBXs are use of telephone wiring, flexibility, and an operating speed that exceeds that available with conventional analog telephone switching. The disadvantages are the cost of the switch, insuring proper software handshaking between the switch and the computer, and inability to handle very high peak data rates for file transfers to and from personal computer terminals.

A fourth alternative is the local area network. A local area network is a data communications network that spans a physically limited area (generally less than a mile or two), provides high bandwidth communication over inexpensive media (generally coaxial cable or twisted pair), provides a switching capability, and is usually owned by the user (i.e., not provided by a common carrier).

Table 28-1 compares the distance, bandwidth, and cost characteristics of local area networks with those of other communications techniques.

In a local area network, the relatively short distance spanned, the high bandwidth provided, and the low cost media used create an operating environment where "bandwidth is cheap," a substantial contrast to the traditional common carrier environment described in the rest of this book. An important consequence of these differing environments is that there are radical differences between the network topology (and the routing of traffic within that topology) for a telephone network and that for a local area network. While a telephone network generally has a hierarchical form with links placed between nodes according to traffic and cost, a local area network usually has a very regular form that is either a star (Figure 28-1a), a ring (Figure 28-1b) or a bus (Figure 28-1c). Further, the nodes of a telephone network route traffic according to complex rules (see Figure 8-1), but the nodes of a local area network do very little (if any) routing.

**Table 28-1. Comparison of Alternative
Communications Techniques**

Distance	Bandwidth	Cost	Example
Short	Low	Low	Ordinary Wire
Short	High	Low	Local Area Networks, Busses
Long	Low	Low	Public Telephone Network
Long	High	High	Satellite, Microwave

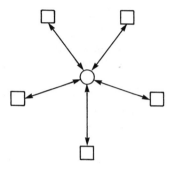

Figure 28-1a. Local Area Network with Star Topology

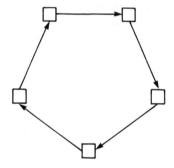

Figure 28-1b. Local Area Network with Ring Topology

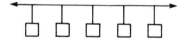

Figure 28-1c. Local Area Network with Bus Topology

Each topology shown in Figure 28-1 is best suited to particular media types, has an optimum routing strategy, and has identifiable reliability characteristics, as will be described in the following paragraphs.

The star is a convenient topology for transmission media that are inherently simplex or cannot easily be tapped. The star permits exceptionally easy routing, as the central node knows the path to the other nodes. Since there is a central control point, access to the network can be easily controlled and priority status can be given to selected nodes. With the centralization of control come the requirements that the central node be exceptionally reliable and have the computational capacity to route all of the network traffic.

A ring is another attractive topology for transmission media that are simplex or difficult to tap. The ring also permits easy routing, as each node decides whether to pass on a message or to accept it, although that is a slight over-simplification. A ring may at first seem less robust than a star, as every node of a ring must work in order that the network function correctly. In practice it is possible to design rings that allow a failed node to be bypassed via relays. This concept is shown in Figure 28-2a. It is also possible to extend the bypass concept one step further and utilize bypass relays and duplex connections between the nodes. Such an arrangement allows a failed node or failed ring segment to be bypassed and is shown in Figure 28-2b. The addition of a node to a ring network does pose a problem, however, in that the ring must be broken for the node to be inserted, causing the network to be out of service while such changes are made.

A bus requires a medium in which signals can flow in either direction, i.e., a full-duplex medium. Unlike the star or ring topologies, nodes associated with a bus do no routing at all. That is because the bus is a broadcast medium in which all nodes receive all transmissions. Furthermore, in many bus systems the nodes contend with each other for use of the medium, a scheme

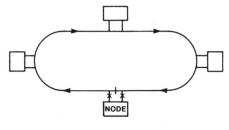

NOTE:
In the figure, the connections for one node have been enlarged to show the bypass relay wiring. All nodes are similarly wired.
Connections shown "X" are closed in normal operation.

Figure 28-2a.   Ring Network with Bypass Relays

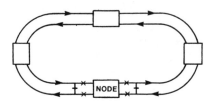

NOTE:
In the figure, the connections for one node have been enlarged to show the bypass relay wiring. All nodes are similarly wired.
Connections shown "X" are closed in normal operation.
Connections shown "+" are closed in bypass operation.

Figure 28-2b.   Ring Network with Bypass Relays Between Nodes

which distributes the control of the medium to the nodes. The lack of routing and the lack of centralized control provide substantial reliability. A major attraction of a bus is that nodes can fail and traffic can still be passed over the network, providing the node failure is not of the "babbling tributary" type (in which random signals are applied to the line). Also, the addition of nodes can be accomplished without disrupting network traffic.

Busses do have a drawback, however. The impedance irregularities caused by the installation of taps will cause signal reflections that can interfere with data transmission if the taps are placed too close to each other. Thus, bus systems often have a minimum distance between taps specified in their installation manuals.

While the above paragraphs have hinted at methods of controlling access to the media for various topologies, no control systems have been discussed in detail because there is not a one-to-one relation between control schemes and local area network topology. Some schemes are more widely used with certain topologies than others, so the following discussion of control schemes will emphasize the most popular control/topology combinations.

All three topologies described above were used in teleprinter networks for military, weather, and airline reservation systems long before their appearance in local area networks. A widely used control scheme for such networks was "polling," in which a master station queried each slave station inquiring whether or not it had traffic to send. A polling system has the advantage that all stations can receive equal access, or priority stations can be given preference by having them polled more often. Further, a polling system can be arranged to function well over extremely long distances, as it can be adjusted to compensate for long propagation delays. Polling is extremely time consuming, however, as a substantial number of the messages on the medium are polling messages from the master station. The success of a polling system is also highly dependent upon the reliability of the master station.

An efficient variation of polling, especially suitable for the ring topology, is the use of tokens. In a token system, a special bit pattern referred to as the "token" circulates around the ring. If a node has no traffic, it allows the token to pass. If the node does have traffic, it takes the token, inserts a message in front of the token, and then re-inserts the token. The token system provides the fairness and distance insensitivity of the polling system, while also providing far more efficient utilization of the medium. It relies upon the correct performance of the nodes, however, and provision must be made to recover gracefully from failures that have caused the token to disappear. There are a number of variations of the token scheme, many of them described in the references.

Another control technique is the use of contention. While this technique is most suitable for a bus topology, the classic use of contention was the ALOHA network in Hawaii, a star topology. The ALOHA network used radio communications from the nodes around the base of a mountain to a central node atop the mountain. While the central node could communicate with the nodes at the base of the mountain, those nodes could not communicate with each other. The control system chosen was that the nodes at the base would transmit whenever they wished. If no one else was transmitting during that time, the central node would receive the message correctly; otherwise, the reception would be garbled by a transmission from some other node, an occurance referred to as "collision." A possible analog of this is a meeting in which all of the participants talk to the chairman whenever they want. As might be imagined, the throughput of such a scheme is quite low—the medium is used for successful transmissions less than 20 percent of the time.

In the "talk whenever you want to" contention scheme, often referred to as "pure ALOHA," it is possible that a collision will occur at any time during a transmission. A collision can even occur at the very end of an otherwise good message, wasting the channel time it took to send that message. A substantial improvement in channel time utilization was accomplished by creating the "slotted ALOHA" contention scheme. In slotted ALOHA, the nodes are synchronized and only begin transmissions at the beginning of a time slot and can only transmit for at most the length of the slot time. As a result, some time slots contain a jumble of simultaneous transmissions, some contain no transmissions, and some contain the transmission from just one node—the successful transmissions. Returning to the meeting analogy, it is as if the chairman only allowed people to talk for less than a minute, starting exactly on a minute boundary. Slotted ALOHA provides roughly twice the capacity of pure ALOHA.

The contention systems described for the ALOHA network may seem strange, but the limitation that the nodes cannot hear each other is a severe constraint. If that constraint is removed, a number of more attractive techniques can be used, the simplest of which is "carrier sense multiple access," abbreviated CSMA. In CSMA, a node listens to the medium before transmitting, and if nothing is heard, begins transmitting. There is, however, a finite probability that some other node will come to the same decision at the same time, and two (or more) transmissions will commence simultaneously. The likelihood of such an event increases on long busses, because a transmission can commence at one end of the bus and not propagate to the distant end of the bus before a node at the distant end decides to transmit. Thus an additional feature, collision detection, is usually added to CSMA systems to create "carrier sense multiple access with collision detection," or CSMA/CD. The collision detection may be accomplished by comparing transmitted data with received data to see if the message on the medium matches the one being transmitted or by techniques which detect the presence of other transmissions by direct electrical means. Returning to the analog of a meeting, the comparison of transmitted and received data is the method actually used by meeting participants. A person listens to see if anyone else is talking. If not, he begins to talk while listening to see if the sounds in the room contain voices other than his. If another voice is heard, each speaker will usually "back-off" by being silent for a few seconds, and then will try to start talking again. In a CSMA/CD system, backing-off when a collision is detected is also used. The amount of time before a retry can be random or can follow the "exponential back-off" rule. In random retry, a transmitting node which has encountered a collision will wait a random amount of time and then retry. If the retry encounters a collision, the process will be repeated using another random time interval. In exponential back-off, the first retry occurs after a random time interval, but if collision occurs again, the node will wait twice as long before retrying. This procedure is continued until either a collision-free transmission is accomplished or a maximum retry limit is exceeded. The optimum strategy for backing-off has been the subject of a number of papers.

The most famous implementation of CSMA/CD contention is the Ethernet™ system, and its advantages and disadvantages have become well known. In addition to its simplicity, CSMA/CD has the advantage that control is distributed to the nodes, and in the bus topology, where the nodes are not part of the medium, a high degree of reliability is possible. CSMA/CD is more efficient than polling and does not require the "lost token recovery" features of a token system. However, use of CSMA/CD on its best-suited topology, a bus, is not without drawbacks. As mentioned above, two nodes that are beginning to transmit may not recognize each other's presence (i.e., detect collision) for some time, because of the amount of time (about 5 nanoseconds per meter) that it takes signals from each to reach the other. If the messages are short enough, a collision may occur without either node knowing about it. Thus, there is a requirement in CSMA/CD that messages not be less than a minimum length which is a function of the transmission speed and the length of the medium. Thus, this relationship places practical limits on the packet size and the medium length. Another problem in CSMA/CD is that the amount of time required to gain access to the medium is highly variable; in fact, there is theoretically no guarantee that a node will ever get a chance to transmit. This problem is generally overcome by not trying to carry more than about 50 percent of the theoretically possible traffic.

Local area networks are an attractive solution to the problem of connecting high speed terminals to host computers over distances of several thousand feet and to the problem of allowing terminals access to multiple computers. The terminals need only be connected to a nearby "terminal concentrator" situated on the local area network. This arrangement reduces the transmission distance requirements to a range suitable for RS-232-C, allows the terminals to be connected to any host on the network, and (in the case of a sophisticated terminal concentrator) can provide character echoing and text editing services with minimal host processing overhead. Local area net-

™ Ethernet is a trademark of Xerox Corporation.

works are, however, an expensive solution to those problems and provide far more bandwidth than is needed for terminal communications. There must be additional reasons for wanting a local area network.

It is the local area network attributes of high bandwidth and low delay that make them especially attractive, as those attributes permit file transfers over the communication network at practical and attractive rates, an essential feature for the connection of personal computer terminals. While personal computer terminals can operate in a stand-alone mode, the ability to access files, down-line load programs, and utilize the services of a high quality printer make connection to a network that provides these services (in addition to more traditional services like mail) essential.

The advantage of allowing personal computer terminals access to a file system by means of a local area network is partly economic. There have always been advantages to storing data on the largest disks available because of the economies of scale in the construction of large disks. Also, it is simpler to update and backup a single large disk system than to update and backup a plurality of small disk systems. Finally, some data files just won't fit on a small disk. A non-economic advantage to access to a common file system is that a number of users can, if desired, retrieve data from and add updates to a common file, simplifying data base management problems. The disk-equipped node which provides the aforementioned filing services for a local area network is called a "file server."

To some degree, the arguments in favor of sharing a central file also favor the sharing of a central printer. Truly high quality printers are expensive and it is easier to repair and maintain supplies for one or two central printers than for a dozen printers widely distributed. However, a printer produces output that must be picked up or delivered. Hence a tradeoff must be made between the advantages of a central printer and the advantages of convenient access by the users. The best solution is probably to provide several low cost, medium quality printers close to the users, and provide one or two central high quality printers. The printer-equipped node which provides the aforementioned central printing services for a local area network is called a "printer server."

Finally, a local area network can provide common access to a long distance communications facility such as a satellite link or a connection to a public packet network. Such access is achieved via a "gateway." A gateway typically provides protocol translation and message buffering services, and can be thought of as a "communications server."

The preceding discussion of local area network applications, topologies, and control systems is intended only as an outline. The references listed below and the proceedings of recent conferences should be consulted for a complete and up-to-date view of progress in local area networks. It should also be noted that local area networks are not the solution to all data communication problems. The direct connection of terminals to large computer systems, particularly for news services, stock exchanges, and other users of data communication over long distances, will be an important part of data communication for the rest of the century and beyond.

References

1. Thurber, Kenneth J. and Freeman, Harvey A., *Tutorial—Local Computer Networks,* (IEEE Catalog No. EHO 163-6), IEEE Computer Society, New York (1980).

Reference 1 contains reprints of the following references, in addition to others not listed here:

2. Clark, David D. et al., "An Introduction to Local Area Networks," *Proceedings of the IEEE,* November 1978, pp. 1497–1517.
3. Fraser, A.G., "Spider—An Experimental Data Communications System," *Conference Record,* International Conference on Communications, 1974, pp. 21F1–21F10.
4. Rawson, Eric G. and Metcalfe, Robert M., "Fibrenet: Multimode Optical Fibers for Local Computer Networks," *IEEE Transactions on Communications,* July 1978, pp. 983–990.
5. Farber, David J., "A Ring Network," *Datamation,* February 1975, pp. 44–46.
6. Binder, R. et al., "ALOHA Packet Broadcasting—A Retrospect," *Proceedings,* National Computer Conference, 1975, pp. 203–215.
7. Metcalfe, Robert M. and Boggs, David R., "ETHERNET: Distributed Packet Switching for Local Computer Networks," *Communications of the ACM,* July 1976, pp. 395–404.
8. Gordon, R. L. et al., "Ringnet: A Packet Switched Local Network with Decentralized Control," *Proceedings,* 4th Conference on Local Computer Networks, 1979, pp. 13–19.

Appendix A

How Far—
How Fast

"How far—how fast?" is one of the most difficult questions to answer in data communications. Intuition suggests that it would be possible to draw a curve similar to that in Figure A-1 and from it tell anyone who asked how far they could transmit a data signal at a particular signaling rate.

In practice, such a curve can be drawn. However, the position of the curve is different for each hardware configuration. The use of various line driver circuits and various line receiver circuits will influence the position of the curve, as will external influences such as noise. When signaling which relies on various voltage levels representing "1" and "0" states (such as EIA RS-232-C) is used, differences in ground potential between the transmitting and receiving stations become important. For example, if the transmitting station applies +5 volts to a line to represent a "0," but the receiving station measures the voltage on the line relative to a "ground" that is ten volts "higher" than the ground at the transmitting station, the voltage on the line will appear to be −5 volts. The receiving station will interpret that as a "1." This problem is partially alleviated by running a Signal Ground lead between the transmitting and receiving stations to provide a common ground reference. This solution is not entirely adequate because, if current flows in the Signal Ground wire, the resistance of the wire will permit a voltage difference between the two ends of the wire.

While the most common cause of ground potential differences is imbalances in the power distribution systems supplying the transmitting and receiving stations, the use of voltage interfaces between different buildings brings special problems during lightning storms; entire buildings will assume varying potentials, even if no direct lightning strikes occur to those buildings.

The best way to avoid ground potential problems is to make sure that the

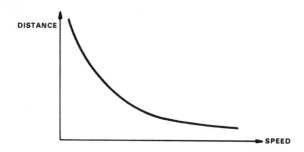

Figure A-1. Idealized Speed Versus Distance Performance Curve

equipment at the transmitting station and the equipment at the receiving station are powered from the same power distribution system. Using the same outlet box is ideal; using the same circuit breaker panel is almost as good; using the same step-down transformer/voltage distribution panel is quite good; using the same building distribution system is fair; using any other arrangement is risky, but may well work.

A more satisfactory method of transmitting information than the voltage-relative-to-ground method just described is differential transmission. In this type of transmission, two conductors are used for each data path, and the information to be conveyed is expressed as the difference in voltage between the two conductors. It does not matter what the ground potential difference is as long as it is not so high as to cause electrical breakdown in the receiver circuitry. The receiver only needs to determine whether the relative voltage between the two conductors is that appropriate to a "0" or that appropriate to a "1." Interfering signals are generally voltages relative to ground and will affect both conductors equally. Assume that a noise voltage V_n is applied to two conductors, one carrying a voltage $+V$ and the other carrying a voltage $-V$. The resultant voltages will be $+V+V_n$ and $-V+V_n$. However, the receiver will take the difference between the two voltages, which is 2V, just as it was before the noise was added. Noise of this kind is called "common mode" noise, and the differential properties of the receiver produce what is called "common mode rejection." EIA Standard RS-422 is an excellent example of a differential transmission system.

In Chapter 5, it was mentioned that the RS-232-C specification places a limit of 2500 picofarads on the capacitance of the receiving station's receiver system, including the capacitance of the cable from the transmitting station to the receiving station. The consequence of violating this specification is that the amount of time needed to accomplish a transition from the MARK state to the SPACE state and vice versa will be increased from the 4 percent of a bit time allowed by the RS-232-C standard. Since it is also likely that the resistance of the driver and receiver circuitry is different for the MARK-SPACE transition than for the SPACE-MARK transition, there will be a different amount of time required to charge the cable capacitance in the two transitions; the increased capacitance created by going beyond 2500 pico-farads of cable capacitance will make that difference more dramatic. The result will be that the receiver circuits will produce MARK bits that are longer than SPACE bits ("Marking Distortion") or SPACE bits that are longer than MARK bits ("Spacing Distortion"). This type of distortion, called "bias distortion," can cause characters to be received incorrectly, especially if clock speed distortion, noise, or other effects are present.

While this effect was discussed both here and in Chapter 5 with respect to EIA Standard RS-232-C interfaces, cable capacitance and the differing resistances of cable drivers in the "1" and "0" states will cause bias distortion in 20 milliampere and other information transmission systems, although differential transmission systems are much less inclined toward this type of distortion.

To further complicate the speed versus distance problem, circuit design practices that improve noise immunity may contribute to distortion. For example, the use of shielded cable is highly recommended in noisy environments, but it has a higher capacitance per foot than unshielded cable, hence the operating speed may have to be reduced. This effect is shown in the speed versus distance charts which follow, as curves are plotted for both shielded and unshielded cables.

A second circuit design practice that is a mixed blessing is hysteresis. Consider the pulse shown in Figure A-2. The resistance, capacitance, and inductance of the transmission facility have "smeared" the square pulse that entered the transmission facility into a barely discernible hump. A receiver circuit can recover the pulse, however, by asserting a high level whenever the "hump" exceeds a certain voltage and asserting a low level at all other times. This is demonstrated in Figure A-3.

There is a very good possibility, however, that there will be noise on the transmission facility. If the noise occurs just as the output voltage from the transmission facility is reaching the decision threshold of the receiver circuit,

Figure A-2.   Effect of Cable Capacitance on Transmitted Signal

Figure A-3.   Reception of Signal Distorted by Cable Capacitance

the receiver output will produce extraneous pulses. This is shown in Figure A-4. A common way to solve this problem is to add hysteresis to the receiver circuit. With hysteresis, as illustrated in Figure A-5, the receiver circuit will not recognize an input as being "high" until it passes threshold T1 and will not recognize it as being "low" until it passes threshold T2. This prevents noise near a single threshold point from producing extraneous pulses unless that noise is of quite substantial magnitude. Since T1 is higher than the old threshold point by the same amount that T2 is lower than the old threshold point, the length of the pulse coming from the receiver output is unchanged from that shown in Figure A-3, *provided that the waveform coming from the transmission facility has equal rise and fall times.*

Assume, however, that the output of the transmission facility has unequal rise and fall times. This is a quite likely case and is usually caused by driver circuits which do not have equal resistance in the ON and OFF states. As a result of the unequal resistances, the "time constant" of the signal differs for the rise time and the fall time, as the time constant is the product of the driver/line resistance and the driver/line capacitance. The effect on a non-hysteresis receiver is shown in Figure A-6 and on a hysteresis receiver in Figure A-7. Note that the pulse at the receiver output has been lengthened, thus causing bias distortion.

This example is not intended to imply that hysteresis is undesirable. On the contrary, it is a very useful technique for rejecting noise. The objective of

Figure A-4. Reception of Signal Distorted by Cable Capacitance and Noise

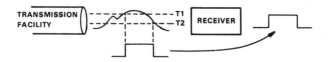

Figure A-5. Use of Hysteresis in Reception of Signal Distorted by Cable Capacitance

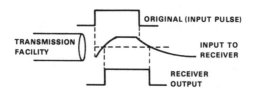

Figure A-6. Effect of Unequal Rise and Fall Times of Signal at Ordinary Receiver

this example is to indicate that, as cable lengths reach large values, the capacitance of the cable also reaches large values, and large values of capacitance accentuate distortion-causing phenomena.

So far, distortion has been claimed to be evil, but no proof has been offered. Back in Chapter 1 the sampling process by which an asynchronous receiver detects the 1-to-0 transition signifying the arrival of a START bit was described. In that description, it was noted that typical receiver circuits sample the communication line at a rate 16 times the bit arrival rate. Thus it is possible that a START bit which arrives just after a sample point would not be detected until the next sample point, 1/16th of a bit time later. This would introduce a 1/16th of a bit time (6.25 percent) error in the subsequent sampling times—i.e., they would all be 6.25 percent of a bit time past the center of the bit being sampled. In theory, the sampling of a bit can be off by 50 percent of a bit time before an error occurs. That is because there is a half bit time between the sampling point at the center of a bit and the "edge" of the bit time, where the line changes state to the appropriate value for the next bit. Thus, distortion of $50 - 6.25$ or 43.75 percent can be accommodated by a receiver sampling at 16 times the bit rate. This is shown in diagram form in Figure A-8.

The use of a $16 \times$ clock in receivers using UART LSI chips is the reason such receivers typically contain the phrase "Receiver Distortion Tolerance: 43.75 Percent" in their specifications.

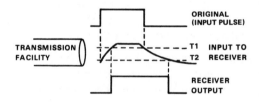

Figure A-7.   Effect of Unequal Rise and Fall Times of Signal at Hysteresis Receiver

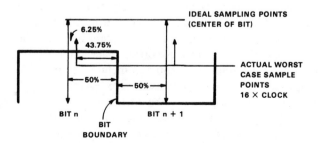

Figure A-8.   Calculation of Distortion Tolerance of Receiver Using $16 \times$ Clock

Assuming no noise effects, error free reception requires that the sampling of the STOP element to check for Framing Error not occur too early (so that it happens in part of the last data bit) or too late (so that it happens in part of the next START element). The time at which the sampling occurs is based on the detection of the 1-to-0 transition of the START element which began the character. That transition occurred 9-1/2 bit times before the sampling of the STOP bit, so any clock speed distortion must be multiplied by 9-1/2 and deducted from the 43.75 percent distortion tolerance described above. For example, a 2 percent clock distortion would cut the distortion tolerance to 24.75 percent.

The other distortion left to be tolerated is bias distortion. Figure A-8 assumes that the transition point between the two bits shown occurs where it should. Marking distortion will cause bit n to last longer, moving the bit boundary to the right; spacing distortion will move the bit boundary to the left, as bit n+1 will be lasting longer (both beginning earlier and terminating later). In this way, the bias distortion caused by the various cable capacitance effects discussed previously will add to the other distortions and possibly produce errors. In the example just cited, a 6.25 percent sampling error combined with 2 percent clock distortion (2 percent times 9-1/2 equals 19 percent) and 24.75 percent bias distortion would produce marginal results, as the sampling of the STOP element would occur on the edge of that STOP element.

NOTE
Percent distortion is the difference between the time
that an event occurs and the time that it should occur
expressed as a percentage of a bit time.

All of the preceding discussion of distortion, noise, ground potential differences, etc. is an introduction to the data presented in the following figures. Figures A-10 through A-12 were developed on the basis of experiments performed by the Data Communications Engineering Group at Digital Equipment Corporation. The experiments were conducted using the wire types indicated, which were strung about a building rather than being kept on a reel. Noise effects were not measured quantitatively, but it was noted that signals within the same cable were a far more important noise source than any noise picked up from electrical machinery or fluorescent lighting. The building in which the wire was strung was used for office space and light manufacturing, although a medium size machine shop was included in the cable route.

The transmitter and receiver units used were UART LSI chips which tolerate 43.75 percent distortion. On the assumption that user applications might not have such a good distortion tolerance, or that user applications might involve clock speed error of greater than 2 percent, an arbitrary limit of 10 percent was chosen for bias distortion. It was this limit which determined the position of the first two curves shown. The third curve was positioned based on crosstalk considerations.

For the EIA RS-232-C interface tests, 1488 drivers and 1489 receivers (not 1489A) were used, with a ground potential difference of less than two volts between the transmitting and receiving stations. Since the 1488 and 1489 are widely used in the electronics industry, and the electrical properties of the RS-232-C drivers and receivers are quite closely controlled by the specification, the curve given is probably applicable for products made by companies other than Digital Equipment Corporation.

The curves for 20 milliampere transmission are based upon the circuit described in Chapter 3, which is a circuit unique to Digital. In the discussion of this circuit, it was mentioned that other circuits which did not limit line charging current caused crosstalk from transmitter units to their associated receiver units ("near end crosstalk"). This effect is demonstrated in the third chart, where that crosstalk introduced errors before the 10 percent distortion limit was reached.

The curves given in these figures are very conservative, as no errors were permitted. In contrast, on standard switched telephone network lines, an error rate of one bit in 10^5 is tolerable. Furthermore, the arbitrary limit of 10 percent on bias distortion is fairly conservative. The reason for the conservative approach is best demonstrated by consulting Figure A-9, which is very similar in concept to Figure A-1.

The outermost curve in Figure A-9 shows outstanding speed versus distance performance, but only 10 percent of all system builders will have conditions (ground potential difference, noise, etc.) ideal enough to obtain this performance. The innermost curve shows the speeds and distances that will yield satisfactory results for 99 percent of the systems built, assuming conditions similar to the test conditions in terms of noise environment and grounding conditions. Figures A-10, A-11, and A-12 are 99 percent curves.

Figures A-13 and A-14 are speed versus distance curves from RS-422 and RS-423 respectively. The Figure A-13 curve is based on empirical data using a 24 gauge twisted-pair telephone cable terminated in a 100 ohm resistive load. The signal quality requirements for determining the position of the curve were that the rise and fall times should not exceed one half of a bit

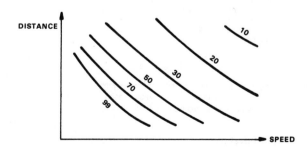

Figure A-9. Idealized Speed Versus Distance Performance Curves for Various Percentages of Satisfied Users

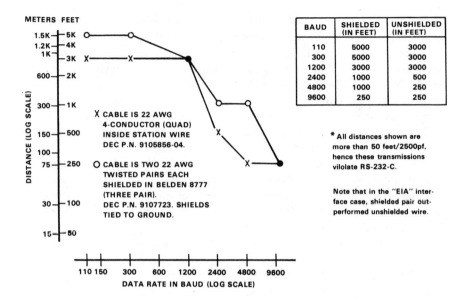

BAUD	SHIELDED (IN FEET)	UNSHIELDED (IN FEET)
110	5000	3000
300	5000	3000
1200	3000	3000
2400	1000	500
4800	1000	250
9600	250	250

X CABLE IS 22 AWG
4-CONDUCTOR (QUAD)
INSIDE STATION WIRE
DEC P.N. 9105856-04.

O CABLE IS TWO 22 AWG
TWISTED PAIRS EACH
SHIELDED IN BELDEN 8777
(THREE PAIR).
DEC P.N. 9107723. SHIELDS
TIED TO GROUND.

* All distances shown are
more than 50 feet/2500pf,
hence these transmissions
vilolate RS-232-C.

Note that in the "EIA" interface case, shielded pair out-
performed unshielded wire.

Figure A-10. EIA Interface

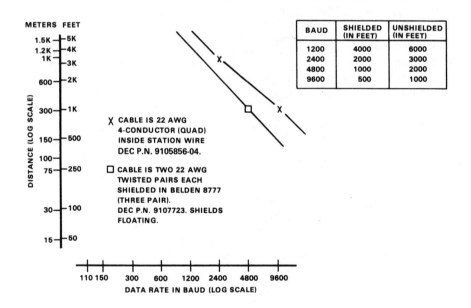

BAUD	SHIELDED (IN FEET)	UNSHIELDED (IN FEET)
1200	4000	6000
2400	2000	3000
4800	1000	2000
9600	500	1000

X CABLE IS 22 AWG
4-CONDUCTOR (QUAD)
INSIDE STATION WIRE
DEC P.N. 9105856-04.

□ CABLE IS TWO 22 AWG
TWISTED PAIRS EACH
SHIELDED IN BELDEN 8777
(THREE PAIR).
DEC P.N. 9107723. SHIELDS
FLOATING.

Figure A-11. 20 ma Interface

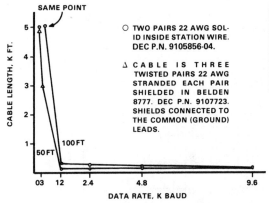

BAUD	SHIELDED (IN FEET)	UNSHIELDED (IN FEET)
150	5000	5000
300	3000	5000
1200	50	100
2400	50	100
4800	50	100
9600	50	100

○ TWO PAIRS 22 AWG SOL-ID INSIDE STATION WIRE. DEC P.N. 9105856-04.

△ CABLE IS THREE TWISTED PAIRS 22 AWG STRANDED EACH PAIR SHIELDED IN BELDEN 8777. DEC P.N. 9107723. SHIELDS CONNECTED TO THE COMMON (GROUND) LEADS.

Figure A-12. 20 ma Interface Without Current Limiting Feature

time and that the amplitude of the signal at the load should be no more than 6 dBV (a factor of two) below the voltage at the generator. The signal amplitude requirement is the limiting factor below 90,000 baud and accounts for the flat section at the left of the figure. Above 90,000 baud, the rise time requirement is the limiting factor and the curve then begins to decline toward the lower part of the figure, reaching 40 feet at 10 megabaud. The figure does not account for cable imbalance or common mode noise beyond seven volts (sum of ground potential difference, generator offset voltage, and externally introduced noise) that may be introduced between the generator and the load by exceptionally long cables, but it is nonetheless quite conservative, especially at the low baud rate end.

Figure A-14 is based on calculations and empirical data using twisted pair telephone cable with a shunt capacitance of 16 picofarads per foot, a 50 ohm source impedance, and a 12 volt peak-to-peak source signal, and allowing a maximum near-end crosstalk of one volt peak. The rise time of the source signal at modulation rates below 900 baud is 100 microseconds and above 900 baud is 0.1 bit time. The figure does not account for cable imbalance or common mode noise beyond four volts (sum of ground potential difference, generator offset voltage and externally introduced noise).

In addition to the various types of line drivers described here, there are other high baud rate, short distance line drivers commercially available that cover distances of a mile or more.

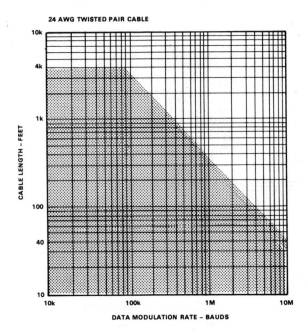

Figure A-13. **Data Modulation Rate Versus Cable Length for Balanced Interface, RS-422**

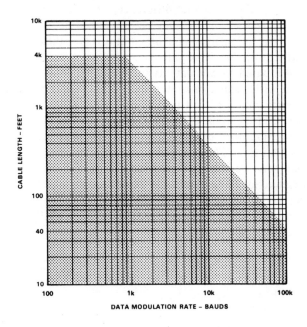

Figure A-14. **Data Modulation Rate Versus Cable Length for Unbalanced Interface, RS-423**

Appendix B

Modem
Options

The tables which follow are extracted from information provided in Bell System Technical References. These technical references are available from:

Publisher's Data Center, Inc.
P.O. Box C738
Pratt Street Station
Brooklyn, New York 11205

All requests should include both billing and shipping addresses. A recommended minimum set of references is listed below.

PUB40000　Technical Reference Catalogue

PUB41004　Data Communications Using Voiceband Private Line Channels

PUB41005　Data Communications Using the Switched Telecommunications Network

PUB41106　Data Set 103J, 113C, 113D-type Interface Specification

PUB41209　Data Set 208A Interface Specification

PUB41211　Data Set 208B Interface Specification

PUB41212　Data Sets 202S and 202T Interface Specification

PUB41213   Data Set 209A Interface Specification

PUB41214   Data Set 212A Interface Specification

PUB41216   Data Set 201C/L1C Interface Specification

This collection of 9 technical references and a catalogue will cost over $160, but will give anyone an excellent picture of the Bell System modem offerings. Because of the high cost of these references, a visit to a corporate library is recommended.

Modem	Option	Description	Preferred Arrangement
103J	Receive Space Disconnect (Yes/No)	With this option installed, the modem will disconnect a call after receiving a SPACE signal of approximately two seconds duration.	*Yes*, is preferred.
	Send Space Disconnect (Yes/No)	With this option installed, the modem, upon receiving a negation of Data Terminal Ready, sends approximately three seconds of SPACE signal and then disconnects. Without this option, the modem, upon receiving a negation of Data Terminal Ready, disconnects immediately.	*Yes* is preferable. This permits the modem at the distant end to disconnect from the line without special action by the modem control. It insures that the distant modem will be available for future calls and will not appear "off-hook" to the telephone switching equipment.
	Loss of Carrier Disconnect (Yes/No)	With this option installed, a loss of received carrier for about 275 milliseconds will cause the modem to terminate the call.	*Yes*, except that some operating systems, such as Digital's RSTS-11, prefer to do their own timing. In those cases, *No* is preferred.
	CC Indication (Early/Delayed)	For incoming calls and for originating calls when the CC Indication Early option is installed, circuit CC (Data Set Ready) comes On when the modem enters the data mode. For originating calls when the CC Indication Delayed option is installed, circuit CC does not come On until carrier is detected from the called modem.	*Early* is preferred unless the system software assumes otherwise.

Modem	Option	Description	Preferred Arrangement
103J (Cont)	CB and CF Indication (Common/ Separate)	When the CB/CF Separate option is provided, Clear to Send remains On despite loss of carrier. With CB/CF Common, performance mimics the earlier models of the 103, such as the 103A2, and Clear to Send turns Off if Carrier Detect turns Off. On the other hand, when the call is being established, the CB/CF Common option will not allow either to turn On until carrier has been received *and* the Clear to Send timer has run out.	*CB/CF Common* is preferred to make the newer modems appear the same to the software as the 103A2. Some operating systems, such as those for Digital's PDP-11, prefer the added flexibility of *CB/CF Separate*.
	CC Indication for Analog Loop (On/Off)	This option determines whether Data Set Ready is asserted or negated when the modem is in analog loop test mode.	*On* is preferred because some software and some hardware requires that Data Set Ready be asserted before data can be sent.
	Fail Safe State of CN Circuit (On/Off)	This option determines whether the modem assumes the CN Circuit (Make Busy/Analog Loop) is On or Off when there is no signal driving this circuit. The intent of this option is to provide a means to make the telephone line busy when the interface connector is loose or disconnected. There are problems with this, however; these are described in the column to the right.	*Off* is preferred because some data terminal equipment does not provide an interface driver for this circuit. In those cases, selection of *On* as the fail-safe condition for this circuit would cause the modem to make the associated telephone line busy at all times.
	Automatic Answer (Yes/No)	The Auto-Answer option provides the appropriate wiring for the modem to answer any calls received while Data Terminal Ready is asserted.	*Yes* unless it is desired that all calls be answered manually.
	Common Grounds (Yes/No)	When the Common option is provided, Protective Ground (Circuit AA, Pin 1) is connected to Signal Ground (Circuit AB, Pin 7).	*Yes* is the preferred arrangement unless local procedures and conditions dictate otherwise.

Modem	Option	Description	Preferred Arrangement
108F 108G	Local Copy in Digital Loop Test Mode (Yes/No)	When a remote test center is sending data to the modem and that data is being looped back for retransmission to the test center, this option allows a copy of the data being passed to appear on Circuit BB (Received Data).	*No* is preferred. Since this modem is commonly used with printing terminals, provision of the option would consume a great deal of paper. Also, to make use of the option, the terminal speed would have to match the speed of the signals being sent from the test center.
	Hold State (MARK/SPACE)	This option determines whether loss of received carrier produces a steady MARK signal or a steady SPACE signal.	*MARK* is preferred.
	Carrier Control (Always On/ Controlled by Received Carrier/ Controlled by Request to Send/ Always Off)	This option determines whether the carrier is always On, comes On in response to received carrier (an arrangement that can only be used at one end of the connection), is controlled by the Request to Send lead, or is always Off.	*Always On* is permissible in a two-point system. *Controlled by Request to Send* is permissible in a two-point system and is required in slave stations of a polling network. *Always Off* is required in all stations (except the master) in a broadcast system.
	Clear to Send (None/ Controlled by Request to Send/Controlled by Received Carrier)	This option determines whether or not a Clear to Send Signal is provided, and if so, whether it is a delayed version of Request to Send or is controlled by received carrier.	*None* is permissable in a two-point system, unless software requires a response to assertion of Request to Send. In that case *Controlled by Request to Send* would be appropriate. The delay between assertion of Request to Send and the response by Clear to Send is normally zero unless a "data auxiliary set" is added. The *Controlled by Received Carrier* option is appropriate when the terminal software is arranged to monitor Clear to Send rather than monitoring Carrier Detect.
	Ground Wire Connected to Signal Ground (Yes/No)	This option determines whether or not the signal ground of the interface circuits is connected to power outlet ground.	*Yes* is the preferred arrangement unless local procedures and conditions dictate otherwise.

Modem	Option	Description	Preferred Arrangement
108H 108J	20 mA Current Loop Interface (2-wire/ 3- or 4-wire Without Local Copy/ 3 or 4-wire With Local Copy)	Local copy is always provided on 2-wire connections. This option allows one to have it as an option on 3- and 4-wire connections.	For full-duplex operation, local copy is usually not desired if the distant station (a computer) echoes the characters, thus *3- or 4-wire Without Local Copy* is preferred.
	Local Copy in Digital Loop Test Mode (Yes/No)	When a remote test center is sending data to the modem and that data is being looped back for retransmission to the test center, this option allows a copy of the data being passed to appear on Circuit .BB (Received Data).	*No* is preferred. Since this modem is commonly used with printing terminals, provision of the option would consume a great deal of paper. Also, to make use of the option, the terminal speed would have be match the speed of the signals being sent from the test center.
	Hold State (MARK/SPACE)	This option determines whether loss of received carrier produces a steady MARK signal or a steady SPACE signal.	*MARK* is preferred.
	Carrier Control	Carrier in the 108H and 108J is always on.	
	Ground Wire Connection	The signal ground in the 108H and 108J is not connected to the power line ground.	
113A	CD Lead Control (Enabled/ Disabled)	When Enabled, the CD (Data Terminal Ready) lead can be controlled at the interface connector. When Disabled, the CD lead is not controlled at the interface, but rather is always asserted.	*Enabled* is preferred because any device that wishes to control Data Terminal Ready will require the Enabled option. Devices that do not control Data Terminal Ready generally provide a means of holding it asserted and thus do not require the *Disabled* option.
	Data Lamp (Enabled/ Disabled)	When Enabled, the Data Lamp lights whenever the 113A is in data mode.	*Enabled* is preferred.
113C	Receive Space Disconnect (Yes/No)	With this option installed, the modem will disconnect a call after receiving a SPACE signal of approximately two seconds duration.	*Yes*

Modem	Option	Description	Preferred Arrangement
113C (Cont)	Send Space Disconnect (Yes/No)	With this option installed, the modem, upon receiving a negation of Data Terminal Ready, sends approximately three seconds of SPACE signal and then disconnects. Without this option, the modem, upon receiving a negation of Data Terminal Ready, disconnects immediately.	*Yes* is preferable. This permits the modem at the distant end to disconnect from the line without special action by the modem control. It insures that the distant modem will be available for future calls and will not appear "off-hook" to the telephone switching equipment.
	Loss of Carrier Disconnect (Yes/No)	With this option installed, a loss of received carrier for about 275 milliseconds will cause the modem to terminate the call.	*Yes*, except that some operating systems, such as Digital's RSTS-11, prefer to do their own timing. In those cases, *No* is preferred.
	CC Indication (Early/Delayed)	For incoming calls and for originating calls when the CC Indication Early option is installed, circuit CC (Data Set Ready) comes On when the modem enters the data mode. For originating calls when the CC Indication Delayed option is installed, circuit CC does not come On until carrier is detected from the called modem.	*Early* is preferred unless the system software assumes otherwise.
	CB and CF Indication (Common/Separate)	When the CB/CF Separate option is provided, Clear to Send remains On despite loss of carrier. With CB/CF Common, performance mimics the earlier models of the 103, such as the 103A2, and Clear to Send turns Off if Carrier Detect turns Off. On the other hand, when the call is being established, the CB/CF Common option will not allow either to turn On until carrier has been received *and* the Clear to Send timer has run out.	*CB/CF Common* is preferred to make the newer modems appear the same to the software as the 103A2. Some operating systems, such as those for Digital's PDP-11, prefer the added flexibility of *CB/CF Separate*.
	CC Indication for Analog Loop (On/Off)	This option determines whether Data Set Ready is asserted or negated when the modem is in analog loop test mode.	*On* is preferred because some software and some hardware requires that Data Set Ready be asserted before data can be sent.

Modem	Option	Description	Preferred Arrangement
113C (Cont)	Fail Safe State of CN Circuit	In the 113C, the absence of a signal applied to circuit CN leaves the modem in the normal mode.	
	Common Grounds (Yes/No)	When the Common option is provided, Protective Ground (Circuit AA, Pin 1) is connected to Signal Ground (Circuit AB, Pin 7).	*Yes* is the preferred arrangement unless local procedures and conditions dictate otherwise.
113D	Receive Space Disconnect (Yes/No)	With this option installed, the modem will disconnect a call after receiving a SPACE signal of approximately two seconds duration.	*Yes*
	Send Space Disconnect (Yes/No)	With this option installed the modem, upon receiving a negation of Data Terminal Ready, sends approximately three seconds of SPACE signal and then disconnects. Without this option, the modem, upon receiving a negation of Data Terminal Ready, disconnects immediately.	*Yes* is preferable. This permits the modem at the distant end to disconnect from the line without special action by the modem control. It insures that the distant modem will be available for future calls and will not appear "off-hook" to the telephone switching equipment.
	Loss of Carrier Disconnect (Yes/No)	With this option installed, a loss of received carrier for about 275 milliseconds will cause the modem to terminate the call.	*Yes*, except that some operating systems, such as Digital's RSTS-11, prefer to do their own timing. In those cases, *No* is preferred.
	CC Indication	In the 113D, circuit CC (Data Set Ready) comes On whenever the modem enters the data mode for incoming calls or originating calls.	
	CB and CF Indication (Common/ Separate)	When the CB/CF Separate option is provided, Clear to Send remains On despite loss of carrier. With CB/CF Common, performance mimics the earlier models of the 103, such as the 103A2, and Clear to Send turns Off if Carrier Detect turns Off. On the other hand, when the call is being established, the CB/CF Common option will not allow either to turn On until carrier has been received *and* the Clear to Send timer has run out.	*CB/CF Common* is preferred to make the newer modems appear the same to the software as the 103A2. Some operating systems, such as those for Digital's PDP-11, prefer the added flexibility of *CB/CF Separate*.

Modem	Option	Description	Preferred Arrangement
113D (Cont)	CC Indication for Analog Loop (On/Off)	This option determines whether Data Set Ready is asserted or negated when the modem is in analog loop test mode.	*On* is preferred because some software and some hardware requires that Data Set Ready be asserted before data can be sent.
	Fail Safe State of CN Circuit (On/Off)	This option determines whether the modem assumes the CN circuit (Make Busy/Analog Loop) is On or Off when there is no signal driving this circuit. The intent of this option is to provide a means to make the telephone line busy when the interface connector is loose or disconnected. There are problems with this, however; these are described in the column to the right.	*Off* is preferred because some data terminal equipment does not provide an interface driver for this circuit. In those cases, selection of *On* as the fail-safe condition for this circuit would cause the modem to make the associated telephone line busy at all times.
	Automatic Answer (Yes/No)	The Auto-Answer option provides the appropriate wiring for the modem to answer any calls received while Data Terminal Ready is asserted.	*Yes,* unless it is desired that all calls be answered manually.
	Common Grounds (Yes/No)	When the Common option is provided, Protective Ground (Circuit AA, Pin 1) is connected to Signal Ground (Circuit AB, Pin 7).	*Yes* is the preferred arrangement unless local procedures and conditions dictate otherwise.
201C		NOTE: The 201C is available in two versions, the 201C/L1C for switched network service and the 201C/L1D of private line service. In the option list below, options which apply to only one of these are marked "L1C only" or "L1D only."	
	Grounding Option (AB Connected to AA/AB Not Connected to AA)	When provided, this option connects Protective Ground (Circuit AA, Pin 1) with Signal Ground (Circuit AB, Pin 7).	*AB Connected to AA* is the preferred arrangement unless local procedures and conditions dictate otherwise.

Modem	Option	Description	Preferred Arrangement
201C (Cont)	Clock Source (Internal/ External)	When Internal clocking is selected, the modem supplies the clocking for data transfer between the data terminal equipment and the modem. When External clocking is selected, the data terminal equipment provides the clocking. When External clocking is used, the clock in the data terminal equipment must conform to the distortion accuracy of EIA RS-334 which requires peak individual distortion of no greater than 0.5 percent. Frequency accuracy must be ±0.005 percent.	*Internal* clocking is preferred for convenience.
	Automatic Calling Unit	If this modem is used in conjunction with a Bell System 801 Automatic Calling Unit, certain wiring changes must be made within the modem and a cable to the 801 installed.	*No*, unless an automatic calling unit is being used, in which case, *Yes*.
	Automatic Answer (Selective/ Permanent/ None)	The Automatic Answer option provides the appropriate wiring so that the modem will automatically answer any calls received while Data Terminal Ready is asserted, except that when Selective is chosen, both Ready and Data Terminal must be asserted. Ready is a special lead described in greater detail in the 201C Technical Reference.	*Permanent* automatic answering is preferred, since, without any automatic answering, manual answering would be required on all calls. The *Selective* option requires an interface to the Ready lead and provides little if any additional capability.
	Electrical Interface (EIA/Contact)	In the early days of modems, some modems used Contact interfaces rather than EIA RS-232, hence this choice.	*EIA* is preferred.
	Alternate Voice Capability (Yes/No) (L1D only)	This option is applicable only in dedicated private wire service. It permits the use of the line for voice communication or data communication but not simultaneously.	*Yes* is preferable because it could be of assistance to maintenance personnel. This is not a strong preference, and many users may prefer *No*.

Modem	Option	Description	Preferred Arrangement
201C (Cont)	Switched Network Backup (Yes/No) (L1D only)	Switched Network Backup provides some additional hardware to permit use of the 201C to be transferred from the private line to the DDD network in the case of a private line failure. One DDD call is made to back up a two-wire private line; two calls are required to back up a four-wire private line.	*Yes* is preferable if the criticality of the application and the anticipated failure rate of the private line overcome the additional costs.
	Data Set Line Interface (Two-Wire/ Four-Wire) (L1D only)	This option determines whether one uses Two-Wire facilities or Four-Wire facilities. On switched network (DDD) service, it must be Two-Wire.	*Four-Wire* is preferable, as the additional cost is modest compared to the increased throughput available from full-duplex operation. If switched network service or half-duplex must be used, *Two-Wire* is sufficient.
	Carrier Control (L1D only) (Continuous/ Switched)	This option determines whether the modem transmitter operates all the time (Continuous) or whether it is under the control of the Request to Send lead.	For four-wire point-to-point circuits, choose *Continuous*, unless it is desired that voice communication use the circuit alternately. For multipoint configurations, or half-duplex service, use *Switched (Request to Send Controlled)*.
	Request to Send, Clear to Send Delay (150 msec/7 msec/0 msec)	This option determines the delay between the time that the data terminal equipment asserts Request to Send and the time that the modem asserts Clear to Send.	For Switched Network (201C/L1C) use or for two-wire private line use, the *150 Millisecond Delay* is necessary to permit the direction of transmission to be "turned around." This involves echo suppressors in some cases; in all cases it involves a time allowance for letting echos decay on two-wire lines. For four-wire lines operated in switched carrier mode, the *7 Millisecond Delay* is necessary to allow the distant modem to synchronize to the carrier after it is switched on. For four-wire lines operated in continuous carrier mode, either the *7 Millisecond* or the *0 Millisecond Delay* may be used. The *0 Millisecond* option may be used for

Modem	Option	Description	Preferred Arrangement
201C (Cont)			the master station in a polling system only if a "split bridge" configuration is used. For more detail, refer to the 201C Technical Reference Manual.
	New Sync (With/ Without) (L1D only)	This option may be used, on four-wire private multi-point lines, at the master station of a polling network to assure rapid resynchronization of the receiver on a sequence of messages from several different remote transmitters. This feature is necessary because the receiver clock maintains the timing information of the previous message for some time interval (no more than 10 milliseconds) after it has ended; this may interfere with resynchronization on receipt of the next message. An On condition should be applied to this lead for a millisecond or more after detection of End of Message and after Received Line Signal Detect (Carrier Detect) has gone off. At all other times the data terminal equipment must hold New Sync Off. CAUTION Data terminal equipment which uses silo buffers or similar systems where characters are processed substantially after they are received must use New Sync very cautiously, as leaving it On too long will damage the next data message, which may arrive within 7 milliseconds of the previous message.	*Without* is preferred unless one has both the exact application described at left and a modem control which can control this lead. In the application described, this option is required in those cases where intermessage intervals of incoming messages at the master station are 10 milliseconds or less. The intermessage interval consists of the time from the end of one message to the beginning of the next. It is thus the sum of the Request to Send/Clear to Send delay of the master station as it prepares its next poll, the length of time required to transmit that poll, and the Request to Send/Clear to Send delay of the remote station as it begins its reply to the poll. If the Request to Send/Clear to Send delay in the master station is 7 milliseconds and the delay used in the remote station is also 7 milliseconds, the master station will not require the New Sync option, as the intermessage interval will be at least 14 milliseconds. If the master station uses a 0 millisecond Request to Send/Clear to Send delay, New Sync will be required.
	CC Indication for Analog Loop (On/Off)	This option determines whether Data Set Ready is asserted or negated when the modem is in analog loop test mode.	*On* is preferred because some software and some hardware requires that Data Set Ready be asserted before data can be sent.

Modem	Option	Description	Preferred Arrangement
201C (Cont)	Satellite Option (Yes/No) (L1C only)	Inhibits Request to Send at the called modem for 275 milliseconds to allow echo suppressors to function properly when the call is first set up.	*Yes* is preferred if usage over satellite links is envisioned. It may also be used on land links, but at the expense of slightly slower initial call set-up.
	Function of Pin 18 (Initiates Loopback/ Provides DCR)	Pin 18 can be either an input for controlling the Analog Loop test feature or an output of the Receiver Symbol Clock (DCR).	The preferred arrangement will depend upon whether the data terminal equipment provides a driver or receiver on pin 18.
	Receiver Signal Element Timing Signal (Clamped/ Continuous)	The receiver clock signal can be present even when there is no carrier or it can be clamped On when Carrier Detect is Off.	*Clamped* is probably preferable.
202S 202T	Received Data Squelch (156 msec/9 msec/ 0 msec)	The Squelch option prevents the demodulator (receiver) of a station which has been transmitting from delivering spurious data on the Received Data circuit when the Request to Send lead is turned off. Spurious data is a possibility because in half-duplex operation on two-wire facilities, the telephone line may reflect echos back to the transmitting station for as long as 100 milliseconds after the Request to Send lead has been turned off. NOTE Talkback is an arrangement available in four-wire multipoint configurations. When this feature is installed, the bridge circuit associated with each modem's connection to the transmission facility that constitutes the backbone of the multi-point line is arranged to repeat what the modem transmits back to the modem.	*156 Milliseconds* is recommended for switched network (DDD) service, two-wire private lines, and four-wire private lines that have been arranged for "talkback." *9 Milliseconds* may be used on two-wire private lines less than 50 miles in length at the customer's risk. *0 Milliseconds* is recommended for four-wire private lines. The *9 or 0 Millisecond* options can be used on two-wire private line facilities over any distance if the system software uses Start of Message codes or some other method of ignoring echo-induced spurious data. Use of 9 or 0 Millisecond options in switched network service is not recommended because the varying call routing produces varying propagation delays. In addition, these options are not recommended because of the possible existence of echo suppressors (which require 100 milliseconds to "turn around"). Use of these options may, however, be attempted at customer risk, if the system software can ig-

Modem	Option	Description	Preferred Arrangement
202S 202T (Cont)			nore the echo-induced spurious data and can also use the reverse channel to keep the echo suppressors disabled, and if the modems used at each end of the line have compatible options.
	Request to Send, Clear to Send Delay (180 msec/ 60 msec/30 msec/8 msec)	This option determines the delay between the time that the data terminal asserts Request to Send and the time that the modem asserts Clear to Send.	The Clear to Send delay option must be chosen to be compatible with the remote modem's Squelch and Receive Line Signal Detect acquisition timing and for soft carrier turn-off options on two-wire applications. The *180 Millisecond Delay* is required in applications where the remote modem has 156 millisecond Squelch installed and is recommended for all switched network (DDD) applications, two-wire private lines, and four-wire private lines equipped for "talkback." The *60 and 30 Millisecond* options are preferred for four-wire point to point and multi-point lines requiring fast start-up. The *60 Millisecond* option is compatible with the Received Line Signal Detector turn-on time of 202C, 202D3, and 202D4, and the 40 millisecond Receive Line Signal Detector option of 202D5, 202D6, and 202R. The *30 Millisecond* option is compatible with the 20 millisecond Receive Line Signal Detector option of 202D5, 202D6, and 202R and with the Fast Carrier Detection out mode of 202S and 202T. The 8 *Millisecond* option is preferred for use in the 202T for duplex multipoint systems requiring fast start up. This option is only usable with a 202S or 202T at the other end with Fast Carrier Detection In. When this option is used, the data terminal equipment must

Modem	Option	Description	Preferred Arrangement
			maintain a MARK on the Transmitted Data circuit when Request to Send is On and until the Clear to Send indication is given.
	Fast Carrier Detection (In/Out)	This option provides either a normal or a fast response time for the Received Line Signal Detector. When In, the Signal Detector turns on in approximately 7 milliseconds when a MARK signal is received and off in approximately 5 milliseconds when it detects soft carrier turn-off. If turn-on is done with other than MARK and turn-off is done with other than soft carrier turn-off, the normal response times occur. The normal response times are: on in approximately 23 milliseconds when data signals are received and off in approximately 10 milliseconds when data signals are no longer received. These are the times used when the Fast Carrier Detection option is Out.	*Out* is preferred, except for the use of 202S and 202T on duplex multi-point systems requiring fast startup and using the 8 millisecond Clear to Send delay, in which case *In* is required.
	Soft Carrier Turn-Off (In[8]/ In[24]/Out)	When In, this option causes the modem to transmit 8 or 24 milliseconds of a soft carrier frequency (typically 900 Hertz) after the Request to Send lead has been turned off. This prevents the distant modem from seeing possible spurious SPACE signals as the carrier turns off. When this option is Out, the carrier is turned off within 1 millisecond after Request to Send is turned off.	*In (24)* is preferred, except that *In (8)* should be used when the distant modem is a 202S or 202T with Fast Carrier Detect. In two-wire applications, use of this option influences the Clear to Send delay option needed at the distant modem. In all applications, this option should be used with the Received Data Clamp option (to produce a steady MARK on the Received Data lead of the distant modem when the local modem turns off its carrier). *Out* is preferred only when the Carrier Detector Reset option is used in the distant modem in applications requiring fast start up.

Modem	Option	Description	Preferred Arrangement
202S 202T (Cont)	Received Data Clamp (In/Out)	When In, this option causes Received Data to be clamped to a MARK state when Carrier Detect is Off.	*In* is preferred.
	Local Copy Primary Channel (In/Out)	When this option is In, and the modem is being used on two-wire facilities, the receiver section of the modem monitors the line signals at all times and thus reproduces the transmitted data on the Received Data lead.	*Out* is preferable, unless the system software wants it otherwise.
	Reverse Channel (In/Out)	When this option is In, and the modem is being used on two-wire facilities, a 5 baud reverse channel is available. The Secondary Request to Send circuit and the Secondary Line Received Signal Detector are used for the transmission and reception of reverse channel data respectively. Chapter 9 discusses the reverse channel in greater detail, but it should be noted here that the 202S and 202T are the first Bell System modems to use Secondary Request to Send and Secondary Received Signal Detector for the 5 baud reverse channel. Previous Bell System modems used Secondary Transmitted Data and Secondary Received Data for this purpose, hence many modem controls refer to the reverse channel leads by these terms. The pinning used on the 202S and 202T is compatible with the previous 202-series modems, so it is only a matter of terminology.	Application determines the preferred arrangement. If the modem control will control these leads and the system software will control them, *In* is preferred. The reverse channel may be used to provide a break feature, circuit assurance, or as part of an error detection and request for retransmission system. It can also be used to hold echo suppressors disabled on switched network applications. (See discussion of Received Data Squelch, Preferred Arrangement, last few sentences.)

CAUTION
Request to Send must be On in order to receive data on the Secondary Channel Received Line Signal Detector circuit.

Modem	Option	Description	Preferred Arrangement
202S 202T (Cont)	Local Copy of Reverse Channel (In/Out)	When this option is In, and the modem is being used on two-wire facilities, the Secondary Received Line Signal Detector circuit follows the state of the Secondary Request to Send lead.	*Out* is preferable, unless the system software wants it otherwise.
	Grounding (AB Connected to AA/AB Not Connected to AA)	When provided, this option connects Protective Ground (Circuit AA, Pin 1) with Signal Ground (Circuit AB, Pin 7).	*AB Connected to AA* is the preferred arrangement unless local procedures and conditions dictate otherwise.
	Automatic Calling Unit (Yes/No)	If this modem is used in conjunction with a Bell System 801 Automatic Calling Unit, certain wiring changes must be made within the modem and a cable to the 801 installed.	*No*, unless an automatic calling unit is being used, in which case, *Yes*.
	Automatic Answer (Yes/No)	The Automatic Answer option provides the appropriate wiring so that the modem will automatically answer any calls received while Data Terminal Ready is asserted.	*Yes*, unless one wants *all* calls to be answered manually.
202T Only	Data Set Line Interface (Two-Wire/ Four-Wire)	This 202T option determines whether the modem is arranged to operate on two-wire facilities or four-wire facilities. The two-wire mode permits operating in either simplex or half-duplex mode. The four-wire arrangement permits full-duplex in addition to these.	*Four-Wire* is preferable, as the additional cost is modest compared to the increased throughput available from full-duplex operation. Plainly, the choice is dependent upon the transmission facilities available and the software system operating methods.
	Carrier Detector Reset (In/Out)	This option is intended to be used in a 202T receiver at a master station of a four-wire multipoint system to permit rapid acquisition of incoming signals from different remote transmitters. An assertion of 0.2 milliseconds or more should be applied to the Carrier Detector Reset lead from the Data terminal	*Out* is preferable, unless the modem control implements an interface to this lead, the system software supports the control of this lead, and the application demands use of this lead. If all of those conditions are satisfied, then *In*.

Modem	Option	Description	Preferred Arrangement
202T Only (Cont)		equipment to the modem after the End of Message has been detected. This circuit should be held off at all other times.	
	Continuous Carrier (In/Out)	When this option is *In*, the modem produces carrier at all times. When this option is Out, carrier is turned on by asserting the Request to Send lead. When the option is In, the Clear to Send lead is permanently held on.	*In* is preferred for four-wire facilities and transmit-only service over two-wire facilities. *Out* is required for half-duplex operation over two-wire facilities, any system where it is desired to use lack of carrier as an out-of-service indicator, or non-master stations in a polling network. Carrier is transmitted in less than one millisecond after the Request to Send circuit is turned on.
	Received Data Clamp (In/Out)	When installed, this option causes the Received Data lead to be clamped to a MARK state when the Received Line Signal Detector is off.	*In* is preferred.
	Alternate Voice Capability (Yes/No)	This option is applicable to the 202T. It permits the use of the line for voice communications or data communications, but not both simultaneously.	*Yes* is preferable, because it could be of assistance to maintenance personnel. This is not a strong preference, and many users may prefer *No*.
	Switched Network Backup (Yes/No)	Switched Network Backup provides some additional hardware to permit use of the 202T to be transferred from the private line to the DDD network in case of a private line failure. One DDD call is made to back up a two-wire private line; two calls are required to back up a four-wire private line.	*Yes* is preferable if the criticality of the application and the anticipated failure rate of the private line overcome the additional costs.

The modem options listing resumes on page 264 with options for the 208 series. The following tables (B-1, B-2, B-3, and B-4) are reproduced from the Bell System Technical Reference on the 202S and 202T.

Table B-1. 202S/T Option Summary Table

Feature	Options		
Line Interface	Switched Network	Private Line Two-Wire	Private Line Four-Wire
Received Data Squelch	156 msec 9 msec* 0 msec		
Clear to Send Delay	180 msec 60 msec 30 msec 8 msec		
Fast Carrier Detection	In (Turn On—7 msec; Turn Off—5 msec) Out (Turn On—23 msec; Turn-Off—10 msec)		
Soft Carrier Turn-Off	24 msec* 8 msec Out (Quick Turn-Off)		
Received Data Clamp	Not Applicable	In (BB Clamped MARK Whenever CF is Off) Out	
Local Copy of the Primary Channel	In Out		Not Applicable
Reverse Channel	In Out		Not Applicable
Local Copy of the Reverse Channel	In Out		Not Applicable
Groundings	AB Connected to AA AB Not Connected to AA		
Automatic Calling Unit	No Yes	Not Applicable	
Automatic Answer	In (Controlled by CD) Out	Not Applicable	
Alternate Voice	Not Applicable	No Yes	
Dial Backup	Not Applicable	No Yes	
Carrier Detector Reset	Not Applicable	In Out	
Continous Carrier	Not Applicable	In (Carrier Transmitted Continuously) Out (Carrier Under Control of CA)	

*The combination of 9 msec received data squelch and 24 msec soft carrier turn-off is not available.

Table B-2. Recommended Customer Options for Switched Network Service with Data Set 202S*

Received Data Squelch	156 msec
Clear to Send Delay	180 msec
Fast Carrier Detection (Received Line Signal Detector Timing)	Out (normal—23 msec)
Soft Carrier Turnoff	24 msec
Received Data Clamp	Always in
Reverse Channel	Optional**
Local Copy—Primary Channel	Optional
Local Copy—Reverse Channel	Optional**
Automatic Calling Unit	Optional**
Automatic Answer	Optional
Grounding	AB connected to AA

*It is assumed that the remote data set (202C, 202D with 804 Data Auxiliary Set, 202R, or 202S) uses the recommended options shown below:

	202C and D	202R	202S
Squelch	In	In	156 msec
Clear to Send	200 msec	200 msec	180 msec
Received Line Signal Detector Timing (Fast Carrier Detection)	40 msec (Note 1 for 202C)	40	Out (normal—23 msec)
Soft Carrier Turnoff	In	In	24 msec
Received Data Clamp	In	In	In
Reverse Channel	Optional	Not available	Optional
Local Copy—Primary Channel	In (Note 1)	In (Note 1)	Optional
Local Copy—Reverse Channel	In (Note 1)	Not available	Optional
Automatic Calling Unit	Optional (Note 2)	Not available	Optional
Automatic Answer	Optional	Not available	Optional

NOTES
1. Standard arrangement; not a customer option.
2. Not available with 202D.

**The Reverse Channel and Automatic Calling Unit Options should not be used with a remote 202R Data Set.

Table B-3. Recommended Customer Options for Data Set 202T*
with Two-Wire and Four-Wire Private Lines with Talkback

Line Interface	Two-wire or four-wire
Received Data Squelch	156 msec
Clear to Send Delay	180 msec
Fast Carrier Detection (Received Line Signal Detector Timing)	Out (normal—23 msec)
Soft Carrier Turnoff	24 msec
Received Data Clamp	In
Reverse Channel	Optional in two-wire private lines
Carrier Detector Reset	Out (not used)
Continuous Carrier	Out (Carrier under control of CA)
Local Copy—Primary Channel	Optional in two-wire private line
Local Copy—Reverse Channel	Optional
Alternate Voice	Optional
Dial Backup	Optional
Grounding	AB connected to AA

*It is assumed that the remote data set (202C, 202D, 202R, or 202T) uses the recommended options shown below:

	202C and D	202R	202T
Squelch	In	In	156 msec
Clear to Send	200 msec	200 msec	180 msec
Received Line Signal Detector Timing (Fast Carrier Detection)	40 msec	40 msec	Out (normal—23 msec)
Soft Carrier Turnoff	In	In	24 msec
Received Data Clamp	In	In	In
Dial Backup	Optional	Optional	Optional
Reverse Channel	Optional for two-wire	Not available	Optional for two-wire
Carrier Detector Reset	Not available	Not available	Out (not used)
Local Copy—Primary Channel	In for two-wire	In for two-wire	Optional for two-wire
Local Copy—Reverse Channel	In for two-wire	Not available	Optional
Continuous Carrier	Not available	Out	Out

Table B-4. Recommended Options for Four-Wire Point-to-Point And Multi-point without Talkback Using Data Set 202T

Line Interface	Four-wire
Received Data Squelch	Out
Clear to Send Delay	8 milliseconds if remote data set is a 202T with Fast Mode Carrier Detection. 30 milliseconds if remote data set is Data Set 202T with Normal Mode Carrier Detection or Data Sets 202R, 202-D5, or 202-D6 with 20 millisecond carrier detector timing. 60 milliseconds if remote data set is Data Set 202C, 202-D3, or 202-D4; or if it is Data Set 202R, 202-D5, or 202-D6 with 40 millisecond carrier detector timing.
Fast Carrier Detection (Received Line Signal Detector Timing)	In (Fast Mode) if remote data set is Data Set 202T with 8 millisecond Clear to Send Delay. Out (Normal Mode) if remote data set is optioned for 30, 60, 180, or 200 millisecond Clear to Send Delay.
Soft Carrier Turnoff	24 milliseconds if remote data set is Data Set 202C; 202-D3, 4, 5, or 6; 202R; or 202T with Normal Mode Carrier Detection. 8 milliseconds if remote data set is Data Set 202T with Fast Carrier Detection option installed. Quick Turnoff if remote data set uses Carrier Detector Reset option.
Received Data Clamp	In
Carrier Detector Reset	In at master station of Broadcast Polling or Bridge Multi-point System when remote data sets use the Quick Carrier Turnoff and master station is able to implement this circuit. Out at all other times.
Continuous Carrier	In for point-to-point applications and for data set as Master Station of Split Bridge Multi-point Systems. Out may be used for above applications and should be used for data set at the Remote Station of Split Bridge Multi-point System and all stations on conference multi-point facilities.
Alternate Voice	Optional
Dial Backup	Optional
Grounding	AB connected to AA

Modem	Option	Description	Preferred Arrangement
208A	Grounding Option (AB Connected to AA/AB Not Connected to AA)	When provided, this option connects Protective Ground (Circuit AA, Pin 1) with Signal Ground (Circuit AB, Pin 7).	*AB Connected to AA* is the preferred arrangement unless local procedures and conditions dictate otherwise.
	Clock Source (Internal/ External)	When Internal clocking is selected, the modem supplies the clocking for data transfer between the data terminal equipment and the modem. When External clocking is selected, the data terminal equipment provides the clocking. When External clocking is used, the clock in the data terminal equipment must conform to the distortion accuracy of EIA RS-334, which requires peak individual distortion of no greater than 0.5 percent. Frequency accuracy must be ± 0.01 percent unless the one-second holdover option is being used at the distant modem, in which case the accuracy must be ± 0.005 percent.	*Internal* clocking is preferred for convenience.
	Carrier Control (Continuous/ Switched)	This option determines whether the modem transmitter operates all the time (Continuous) or whether it is under the control of the Request to Send lead.	For four-wire point-to-point circuits, choose *Continuous*. For multi-point configurations use *Continuous** or Request to Send Controlled at the master. For slave stations in multi-point or half-duplex service, use *Switched (Request to Send Controlled)*.
	CC Indication of Analog Loop (On/Off)	This option determines whether the Data Set Ready lead is asserted or negated when the modem is in the analog loop test mode. Some software systems require that Data Set Ready be asserted before data can be sent—in fact, some hardware has this requirement. Such systems require the On option.	*On* is preferred.

*The use of Continuous carrier at the master station eliminates the training sequence inherent in starting up the distant receiver (detecting carrier and operating the adaptive equalizer).

Modem	Option	Description	Preferred Arrangement
208A (Cont)	New Sync (With/ Without)	This option may be used on four-wire private multi-point lines, at the master station of a polling network, to assure rapid resynchronization of the receiver on a sequence of messages from several different remote transmitters. This feature is necessary because the receiver clock maintains the timing information of the previous message for some time interval (no more than 10 milliseconds) after it has ended and this may interfere with resynchronization on receipt of the next message. An On condition should be applied to this lead for a millisecond or more after detection of End of Message and after Received Line Signal Detect (Carrier Detect) has gone off. At all other times the data terminal equipment must hold New Sync Off. CAUTION Data terminal equipment which uses silo buffers or similar systems where characters are processed substantially after they are received must use New Sync very cautiously, as leaving it On too long will damage the next data message which may arrive within 7 milliseconds of the previous message.	*Without* is preferred unless one has both the exact application described at left and a modem control which can control this lead. In the application described, this option is required in those cases where intermessage intervals of incoming messages at the master station are 10 milliseconds or less. The intermessage interval consists of the time from the end of one message to the beginning of the next. It is thus the sum of the Request to Send/Clear to Send delay of the master station as it prepares its next poll, the length of time to transmit that poll, and the Request to Send/Clear to Send delay of the remote station as it begins its reply to the poll. If the Request to Send/Clear to Send delay in the master station is 7 milliseconds and the delay used in the remote station is also 7 milliseconds, the master station will not require the New Sync option, as the intermessage interval will be at least 14 milliseconds. If the master station uses a 0 millisecond Request to Send/Clear to Send delay, New Sync will be required.
	Alternate Voice Capability (Yes/No)	This option is applicable only in dedicated private wire service. It permits the use of the line for voice communication or data communication but not simultaneously.	*Yes* is preferable, because it could be of assistance to maintenance personnel. This is not a strong preference, and many users may prefer *No*.

Modem	Option	Description	Preferred Arrangement
208A (Cont)	Switched Network Backup (Yes/No)	This option provides some additional hardware to allow use of the modem to be transferred from the private line to the DDD network in case of a private line failure. Two calls are required to provide four-wire backup.	*Yes* is preferable if the criticality of the application and the anticipated failure rate of the private line overcome the additional costs; otherwise, *No*.
	Request to Send Operation in Continuous Carrier Mode (Continuous/ Switched)	This option permits a master station in a multi-point network to appear to be operating in switched carrier mode when in fact it is operating in continuous carrier mode. With the Continuous option, Clear to Send is returned to the data terminal equipment 8 ± 0.5 milliseconds after the data terminal equipment asserts Request to Send.	When the Carrier Control option is *Switched*, the Request to Send Operation option must also be *Switched*. When the Carrier Control option is *Continuous*, either Request to Send Operation option may be chosen. Switched is preferable if the software is going to control Request to Send; otherwise *Continuous* is preferable.
	One Second Holdover at Receiver on Line Dropout (Provided/Not Provided)	With this option the Received Line Signal Detector circuit is kept On up to one second beyond the time that carrier signal is lost, permitting the receiving modem to maintain timing synchronization during momentary line dropouts. The loss of carrier will be indicated by the Signal Quality Detector circuit's turning Off after a carrier loss of greater than two milliseconds and back On after return of carrier for more than four milliseconds. Without this option, negation of Received Line Signal Detector and clamping of the Received Data lead to MARK occurs after two milliseconds.	This option is recommended for use in modems receiving continuous carrier from a distant transmitter. *Provided* is preferred in that case. *Not Provided* is preferred when the distant transmitter uses switched carrier operation.
208B	CC Indication of Analog Loop (On/Off)	This option determines whether the Data Set Ready lead is asserted or negated when the modem is in the analog loop test mode. Some software systems require that Data Set Ready be asserted before data can be sent—in fact, some hardware has this requirement. Such systems require the On option.	*On* is preferred.

Modem	Option	Description	Preferred Arrangement
208B (Cont)	Grounding Option (AB Connected to AA/AB Not Connected to AA)	When provided, this option connects Protective Ground (Circuit AA, Pin 1) with Signal Ground (Circuit AB, Pin 7).	*AB Connected to AA* is the preferred arrangement unless local procedures and conditions dictate otherwise.
	Clock Source (Internal/ External)	When Internal clocking is selected, the modem supplies the clocking for data transfer between the data terminal equipment and the modem. When External clocking is selected, the data terminal equipment provides the clocking. When External clocking is used, the clock in the data terminal equipment must conform to the distortion accuracy of EIA RS-334 which requires peak individual distortion of no greater than 0.5 percent. Frequency accuracy must be ±0.01 percent.	*Internal* clocking is preferred for convenience.
	Automatic Calling Unit (Yes/No)	If this modem is used in conjunction with a Bell System 801 Automatic Calling Unit, certain wiring changes must be made within the modem and a cable to the 801 installed.	*No*, unless an automatic calling unit is being used, in which case, *Yes*.
	Automatic Answer (Yes/No)	The Automatic Answer option provides the appropriate wiring so that the modem will automatically answer any calls received while Data Terminal Ready is asserted.	*Yes*, unless one wants *all* calls to be answered manually.
	Request to Send, Clear to Send Delay (50 msec/ 150 msec)	This option is controlled by a button marked "50" on the front of the modem. When the button is depressed, there will be a *50 Millisecond Delay* between the time that the data terminal equipment asserts Request to Send and the time that the modem asserts Clear to Send. This will provide satisfactory service on most switched network connections, except those where the route of the call exceeds 2000 miles. The 2000 miles may either be the length of the direct route from the calling place to the called place or may be accumulated if the call is alternately routed by the telephone system during periods of heavy traffic. In the case of long connections, echos may occur which cause received data errors at the beginning of a data reception due to an echo returning from the previous transmission. In this case, the *150 Millisecond Delay* should be used, although system throughput will be reduced as a result.	

Modem	Option	Description	Preferred Arrangement
209A	Multiplex (1,2,3,4,5)	A customer accessible switch provides five different arrangements: 1) 9600 baud on Connector #1 2) 7200 baud on Connector #1, 2400 on Connector #2 3) 4800 baud on Connector #1, 4800 on Connector #2 4) 4800 baud on Connector #1, 2400 on Connectors #2 and #3 5) 2400 baud on Connectors #1, #2, #3, and #4 A sixth position is provided for factory testing.	
	Clock Source (Internal/ External)	When the Internal clocking is selected, the modem supplies the clocking for the data transfer between the data terminal equipment and the modem. When External clocking is selected, the data terminal equipment provides the clocking. When External clocking is used, the clock in the data terminal equipment must conform to the distortion accuracy of EIA RS-334 which requires peak individual distortion of no greater than 0.5 percent. Frequency accuracy must be ± 0.0025 percent. The external timing signal is to be provided by the data terminal equipment associated with Connector #1. If the other data terminal equipment associated with Connectors #2, #3, and/or #4 provide clocking also, the modem must be optioned with an elastic store for each connector so used.	*Internal* clocking is preferred for convenience.
	Carrier Control (Continuous/ Switched)	This option determines whether the modem transmitter operates all the time (Continuous) or whether it is under the control of the Request to Send leads.	For four-wire, point-to-point circuits, choose *Continuous*. For multi-point configurations, use *Continuous** or Request to Send Controlled at the master station. For slave stations in multi-point or for half-duplex service, use *Switched (Request to Send Controlled)*.

*The use of Continuous carrier at the master station eliminates the training sequence inherent in starting up the distant receiver (detecting carrier and operating the adaptive equalizer).

Modem	Option	Description	Preferred Arrangement
209A (Cont)	Request to Send Operation in Continuous Carrier Mode (Continuous/ Switched)	This option permits the master station in a multi-point network to appear to be operating in continuous carrier mode. With the Continuous option, Clear to Send is constantly On. With the Switched option, Clear to Send is returned to the data terminal equipment 8 ± 0.5 milliseconds after the data terminal equipment asserts Request to Send.	When the Carrier Control option is *Switched*, the Request to Send Operation option must also be *Switched*. When the Carrier Control option is *Continuous*, either Request to Send Operation option may be chosen. *Switched* is preferable if the software is going to control Request to Send; otherwise *Continuous* is preferable.
	Elastic Store (In/Out)	An elastic store option is associated with each of the four connectors. It is used to provide buffer storage for connectors used in many-point or one-to-many multiplexing extension service or where data terminal equipment supplying clocking is used on Connectors #2, #3, and/or #4.	*Out* is preferred for simple point-to-point applications. For other applications, refer to the Technical Reference (PUB41213).
	CC Indication of Analog Loop (On/Off)	This option determines whether the Data Set Ready lead is asserted or negated when the modem is in the analog loop test mode. Some software systems require that Data Set Ready be asserted before data can be sent—in fact, some hardware has this requirement. Such systems require the On option. On the other hand, the modem is not really ready when in test mode, so others prefer Off, which meets the provisions of the RS-232-C specification for Data Set Ready.	*On* is preferred.
	Grounding Option (AB Connected to AA/AB Not Connected to AA)	When provided, this option connects Protective Ground (Circuit AA, Pin 1) with Signal Ground (Circuit AB, Pin 7).	*AB Connected to AA* is the preferred arrangement unless local procedures and conditions dictate otherwise.

Modem	Option	Description	Preferred Arrangement
209A (Cont)	Slaved Transmitter Timing by Receiver (In/Out)	This option allows a 209A transmitter to be timed by its receiver based on signals from a far-end 209A which serves as a master timing source for the system. It is used in one 209A in many-point or one-to-many multiplexing configurations involving extension service on either modem.	*Out* is preferred for simple point-to-point applications. For other applications, refer to the Technical Reference (PUB41213).

Figure B-1 is presented to indicate typical examples of "many-point" and "one-to-many" multiplexing extension services using elastic store options and slaved transmitter timing options. For further details, refer to the Bell System Technical Reference on the 209A (PUB41213).

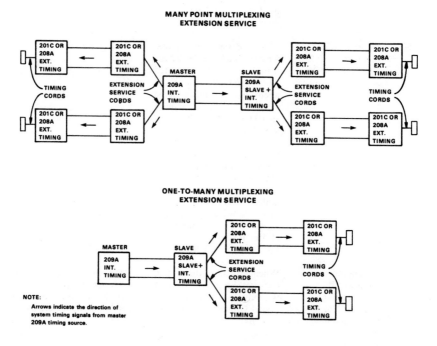

Figure B-1. Timing Synchronization Arrangements for Extension Service Configurations

Modem	Option	Description	Preferred Arrangement
212A	Receive Space Disconnect (Yes/No)	With this option installed, the modem will disconnect a call after receiving a SPACE signal of approximately two seconds duration.	*Yes* is preferred.
	Send Space Disconnect (Yes/No)	With this option installed, the modem, upon receiving a negation of Data Terminal Ready, sends approximately four seconds of SPACE signal and then disconnects. Without this option, the modem, upon receiving a negation of Data Terminal Ready, disconnects immediately.	*Yes* is preferable. This permits the modem at the distant end to disconnect from the line without special action by the modem control. It insures that the distant modem will be available for future calls and will not appear "off-hook" to the telephone switching equipment.
	Loss of Carrier Disconnect (Yes/No)	With this option installed, a loss of received carrier for 175–307 milliseconds will cause the modem to terminate the call.	*Yes*, except that some operating systems, such as Digital's RSTS-11, prefer to do their own timing. In those cases, *No* is preferred.
	CB and CF Indication (Common/ Separate)	When the CB/CF Separate option is provided, Clear to Send remains On despite loss of carrier. With CB/CF Common, performance mimics the early models of the 103, such as the 103A2, and Clear to Send turns Off if Carrier Detect turns Off. On the other hand, when the call is being established, the CB/CF Common options will not allow either to turn on until carrier has been received *and* the Clear to Send timer has run out.	*CB/CF Common* is preferred to make the newer modems appear the same to the software as the 103A2. Some operating systems, such as those for Digital's PDP-11, prefer the added flexibility of *CB/CF Separate*.
	CC Indication for Analog Loop (On/Off)	This option determines whether Data Set Ready is asserted or negated when the modem is in analog loop test mode.	*On* is preferred because some software and some hardware requires that Data Set Ready be asserted before data can be sent.
	Automatic Answer (Yes/No)	The Auto-Answer option provides the appropriate wiring for the modem to answer any calls received while Data Terminal Ready is asserted.	*Yes* unless it is desired that all calls be answered manually.

Modem	Option	Description	Preferred Arrangement
212A (Cont)	Common Grounds (Yes/No)	When the Common option is provided, Protective Ground (Circuit AA, Pin 1) is connected to Signal Ground (Circuit AB, Pin 7).	*Yes* is the preferred arrangement unless local procedures and conditions dictate otherwise.
	Speed Control (Interface/ HS Button)	When the 212A is used to originate calls (manually or with an ACU), it is necessary to specify whether the modem should operate the high speed (1200 baud) mode or in low speed (300 baud) mode. The speed may be controlled by means of an interface lead (CH–Pin 23) or via a front panel pushbutton (HS). This option selects the control method used.	*HS Button* is preferred unless the interface has control of Pin 23 and appropriate software has been written or Pin 23 is held in the desired state, in which case *interface* control could be used.
	Interface Controlled Make Busy, Analog Loop (In/Out)	If this option has been installed, an assertion, ground, or open condition of the CN lead will place the modem in Make Busy state, or, if Data Terminal Ready (CD) is also asserted, in Analog Loop State. If this option has not been installed, CN is strapped Off inside the modem.	Unless the data terminal equipment has control of Pin 25 (or 18 depending upon the pinning option chosen) *and* appropriate software has been written, *Out* must be selected due to the modem feature of interpreting an open circuit as an On condition.
	Transmitter Timing (Internal/ External/ Slave)	This option applies only to the use of the 212A as a synchronous modem. If Internal Timing is chosen, Transmitter Signal Element Timing (DB) is produced on Pin 15 from a clock within the modem. If External Timing is chosen, the Transitter Signal Element Timing (DB) on Pin 15 is phase-locked to a signal supplied to the modem on Pin 24 (DA) by the data terminal equipment. If Slave Timing is chosen, the Transmitter Signal Element Timing (DB) on Pin 15 is phase-locked to the clocking of the receiver section of the modem. The Slave Timing option can only be chosen for one end of a connection	*Internal Timing* is preferred for convenience.

Modem	Option	Description	Preferred Arrangement
212A (Cont)		between two modems and interferes with the Remote Digital Loop Test.	
	1200 BPS Operation (Asynchronous/ Synchronous)	This option determines whether the modem is used with asynchronous or synchronous data terminal equipment.	The choice depends upon the type of data terminal equipment being used.
	Character Length (9 bit/10 bit)	This option determines the character length in asynchronous operation. The number of bits includes the START bit and the first STOP bit.	For eight bit characters with a START bit and and one or two STOP bits, *10 bits* is preferred.
	Response to Digital Loop (In/Out)	When this option is installed, and the modem is in high speed mode, another 212A can send signals to this modem which will put it in loop (test) mode.	If an automatic remote test system is to be used, *In* would be preferred. If manual operation of the test capabilities is preferred to guard against false operation, select *Out*. The front panel pushbutton (DL) is operative regardless of which option is selected.
	Interface Controlled Remote Digital Loop (In/Out)	This option allows assertion of Pin 21 to cause the modem to initiate the remote digital loop feature, placing the remote modem in digital loop mode.	If the data terminal equipment can control Pin 21 and appropriate software exists, *In* would provide a valuable maintenance aid. Otherwise, select *Out*.
	Answer Mode Indication (On/Off)	With this option installed, the Ring Indicator (CE) circuit remains asserted after an incoming call has been answered and drops only when the connection has been broken.	*Off* is preferred, allowing CE to return to the Off state after the call has been answered.
	Speed Mode (High/Dual)	With the High Speed option installed, the modem only passes data on calls from other 212-type modems. In the Dual Speed mode, data is also passed on calls from 103-type modems. Calls from both types of modems are answered regardless of option choice. The option determines from which calling modems data is passed.	*Dual* would provide more functionality, unless there is a specific desire to exclude calls from low speed modems, in which case, select *High*.

Modem	Option	Description	Preferred Arrangement
212A (Cont)	Interface Speed Indication (In/Out)	If this option is installed, the Speed Mode Indicator (CI) circuit is connected to Pin 12.	If the data terminal interface can monitor Pin 12 and appropriate software exists, select *In*. Otherwise, *Out*.
	CN and TM Assignments (CN25, TM NC/ CN18, TM NC/ CN18, TM25)	This option determines the pinning for Make Busy/Analog Loop and for Test Mode. NC means Not Connected.	*CN25, TM NC* is the US common usage. *CN18, TM 25* corresponds to the recommendations of the International Organization for Standardization. To use CN, the "Interface Controlled Make Busy/ Analog Loop option must also be *In*.

Appendix C
Codes

The charts on the following pages are taken from information provided by Allan R. Kent of Digital Equipment Corporation. They are arranged in order by the number of bits used in the individual codes. In five bit ("five unit") codes and some six bit codes, the meaning of a particular bit combination is dependent upon whether the transmitting and receiving stations are operating in the "figures" shift mode or the "letters" shift mode, sometimes referred to as "shift" and "unshift" respectively. The shifting operation would be analogous to the shifting operation in a conventional office typewriter if the typewriter had only a "shift lock" facility. In other words, one depresses a key (shift lock on a typewriter, FIGS on a teleprinter) to enter the shifted state. From then on all characters typed are "upper case" on a typewriter or "figures" on a teleprinter. To leave the shifted state, one depresses another key: shift on a typewriter, LTRS on a teleprinter.

To facilitate comparison of the various five unit codes, the first section of the five unit code chart presents the "letters" shift characters that are common to all of the codes listed, showing those characters along the left hand edge of the chart. The next column in the chart shows the CCITT Alphabet Number 2 standard for the "figures" shift characters corresponding to the bit combinations. Finally, the remaining columns of the chart show the "figures" shift characters and symbols used in the various codes enumerated along the top edge of the chart.

In the seven unit code example shown, there are sufficient bits to represent various characters and symbols without the need of shifting.

Table C-1.   Five Unit Codes

Octal	Letters (common to all codes on this page)	CCITT Alphabet #2	American Communications Variant of CCITT #2	Western Union "A" Keyboard	Western Union Telex	Western Union Telegraph	United Press International
00	Blank	Blank	Blank	Blank	Blank	Blank	Blank
01	E	3	3	3	3	3	3
02	LF	LF	LF	LF	LF	LF	LF
03	A	—	—	—	—	—	—
04	Space	Space	Space	Space	Space	Space	Space
05	S	'	BELL	'	'	THRU	BELL
06	I	8	8	8	8	8	8
07	U	7	7	7	7	7	7
10	CR	CR	CR	CR	CR	CR	CR
11	D	WRU	$	$	WRU	$	$
12	R	4	4	4	4	4	4
13	J	BELL	'	BELL	BELL	BELL	'
14	N	,	;	'	,	,	;
15	F		!		$	CITY	!
16	C	:	:	:	:	:	∴
17	K	(	(	(	(	(	(
20	T	5	5	5	5	5	5
21	Z	+	"	"	"	"	"
22	L	)	)	)	)	)	)
23	W	2	2	2	2	2	2
24	H		STOP#	#	#	£	£
25	Y	6	6	6	6	6	6
26	P	0	0	0	0	0	0
27	Q	1	1	1	1	1	1
30	O	9	9	9	9	9	9
31	B	?	?	?	?	?	?
32	G		&	&	&	&	&
33	FIGS	FIGS	FIGS	FIGS	FIGS	FIGS	FIGS
34	M	.	.	.	.	.	.
35	X	/	/	/	/	/	/
36	V	=	;	;	;	;	;
37	LTRS	LTRS	LTRS	LTRS	LTRS	LTRS	LTRS

Note: The symbols shown for codes 05 and 13 are apostrophes; those for code 14 are commas.

Table C-2. Five Unit Codes

Octal	Letters (common to all codes on this page)	CCITT Alphabet #2	Australian Post Office Telex	American Weather Variant of CCITT #2	Danish Weather Bureau*	American 60 wpm TWX
00	Blank	Blank	Blank	—	Blank	Blank
01	E	3	3	3	3	3
02	LF	LF	LF	LF	LF	LF
03	A	—	—	↑	—	—
04	Space	Space	Space	Space	Space	Space
05	S	'	'	BELL	'	BELL
06	I	8	8	8	8	8
07	U	7	7	7	7	7
10	CR	CR	CR	CR	CR	CR
11	D	WRU	WRU	↗	"	$
12	R	4	4	4	4	4
13	J	BELL	BELL	∕		'
14	N	,	,	⊕	,	
15	F		%	→	F	1/4
16	C	:	:	○	:	WRU
17	K	(	(	←	(	1/2
20	T	5	5	5	5	5
21	Z	+	+	+	+	"
22	L	)	)	\	)	3/4
23	W	2	2	2	2	2
24	H		£	↓	H	#
25	Y	6	6	6	6	6
26	P	0	0	0	0	0
27	Q	1	1	1	1	1
30	O	9	9	9	9	9
31	B	?	?	⊕	?	5/8
32	G		$	\	%	&
33	FIGS	FIGS	FIGS	FIGS	FIGS	FIGS
34	M	.	.	.	.	.
35	X	/	/	/	/	/
36	V	=	=	①	=	3/8
37	LTRS	LTRS	LTRS	LTRS	LTRS	LTRS

Note: The symbols shown for codes 05 and 13 are apostrophes; those for code 14 are commas.

*The Danish Weather Bureau uses number groups in a specified format to identify locations in a symbol containing meteorological symbols.

Table C-3. Five Unit Codes, Elliot 803 Telecode

Octal	Letters (Unshift)	Figures (Shift)
00	Blank	Blank
01	A	1
02	B	2
03	C	8
04	D	4
05	E	&
06	F	=
07	G	7
10	H	8
11	I	'
12	J	,
13	K	+
14	L	:
15	M	−
16	N	.
17	O	%
20	P	0
21	Q	(
22	R	)
23	S	3
24	T	?
25	U	5
26	V	6
27	W	/
30	X	@
31	Y	9
32	Z	£
33	FIGS	FIGS
34	Space	Space
35	Return	Return
36	Linefeed	Linefeed
37	LETTERS	LETTERS

Table C-4. Six Unit Codes, PDP-8® Typesetting

Octal	(Unshift)	(Shift)	Octal	(Unshift)	(Shift)
00	Tape Feed		40	t	T
01	Thin Space		41	5	5/8
02	e	E	42	z	Z
03	3	3/8	43	)	(
04	Word Delete		44	l	L
05	With Leaders	WX	45	Tab Left	
06	a	A	46	w	W
07	$	!	47	2	1/4
10	Space Bar		50	h	H
11	Justify	TA	51	Em Leader	
12	s	S	52	y	Y
13	Quad Middle		53	6	3/4
14	i	I	54	p	P
15	8	—(Dash)	55	0	?
16	u	U	56	q	Q
17	7	7/8	57	En Leader	
20	Return		60	o	O
21	'(Quote)	'(Quote)	61	9	fi
22	d	D	62	b	B
23	-(Hyphen)	@	63	Tab Right	
24	r	R	64	g	G
25	4	1/2	65	;	:
26	j	J	66	Shift	
27	Call		67	Tab Center	
30	n	N	70	m	M
31	,(Comma)	,(Comma)	71	.(Period)	.(Period)
32	f	F	72	x	X
33	Quad Left		73	1	1/8
34	c	C	74	v	V
35	En Space		75	Quad Center	
36	k	K	76	Unshift	
37	Quad Right		77	Rub Out	

Table C-5. Six Unit Codes, New York Stock Exchange

Octal		Octal	
00	Null	40	■
01	E	41	5
02	■	42	c
03	A	43	l
04	Pr	44	■
05	S	45	s
06	I	46	q
07	U	47	Spare#4
10	W	50	0
	I	51	4
11	D	52	■ End Ann
12	R	53	■ Beg Ann
13	J	54	Space
14	N	55	6
15	F	56	3
16	C	57	Spare#3
17	K	60	1/8
20	T	61	7/8
21	Z	62	S
22	L		S
23	W	63	1/2
24	H	64	8
25	Y	65	3/4
26	P	66	S
27	Q		T
30	O	67	1/4
31	B	70	Spare#2
32	G	71	2
33	&	72	7
34	M	73	b
35	X	74	$
36	V	75	5/8
37	R	76	3/8
	T	77	Rubout

Table C-6. Seven Unit Codes, ASCll—1968*

Octal			Octal		
000	NUL	(Blank)	055	-	(Hyphen)
001	SOH	(Start of Header)	056	.	(Period)
002	STX	(Start of Text)	057	/	
003	ETX	(End of Text)	060	0	
004	EOT	(End of Transmission)	061	1	
005	ENQ	(Enquiry)	062	2	
006	ACK	(Acknowledge(Positive))	063	3	
007	BEL	(Bell)	064	4	
010	BS	(Backspace)	065	5	
011	HT	(Horizontal Tabulation)	066	6	
012	LF	(Line Feed)	067	7	
013	VT	(Vertical Tabulation)	070	8	
014	FF	(Form Feed)	071	9	
015	CR	(Carriage Return)	072	:	
016	SO	(Shift Out)	073	;	
017	SI	(Shift In)	074	<	(Less Than)
020	DLE	(Data Link Escape)	075	=	
021	DCI	(Device Control 1)	076	>	(Greater Than)
022	DC2	(Device Control 2)	077	?	
023	DC3	(Device Control 3)	100	@	
024	DC4	(Device Control 4—Stop)	101	A	
025	NAK	(Negative Acknowledge)	102	B	
026	SYN	(Synchronization)	103	C	
027	ETB	(End of Text Block)	104	D	
030	CAN	(Cancel)	105	E	
031	EM	(End of Medium)	106	F	
032	SUB	(Substitute)	107	G	
033	ESC	(Escape)	110	H	
034	FS	(File Separator)	111	I	
035	GS	(Group Separator)	112	J	
036	RS	(Record Separator)	113	K	
037	US	(Unit Separator)	114	L	
040	SP	(Space)	115	M	
041	!		116	N	
042	"		117	O	
043	#		120	P	
044	$		121	Q	
045	%		122	R	
046	&		123	S	
047	'	(Closing Single Quote)	124	T	
050	(		125	U	
051	)		126	V	
052	*		127	W	
053	+		130	X	
054	,	(Comma)	131	Y	

*This code is often sent with parity and is thus often referred to as an eight bit code.

Table C-6. Seven Unit Codes, ASC11—1968* (Continued)

Octal			Octal		
132	Z		155	m	
133	[	(Opening Bracket)	156	n	
134	\	(Reverse Slant)	157	o	
135	]	(Closing Bracket)	160	p	
136	∧	(Circumflex)	161	q	
137	—	(Underline)	162	r	
140	'	(Opening Single Quote)	163	s	
141	a		164	t	
142	b		165	u	
143	c		166	v	
144	d		167	w	
145	e		170	x	
146	f		171	y	
147	g		172	z	
150	h		173	{	(Opening Brace)
151	i		174	I	(Vertical Line)
152	j		175	}	(Closing Brace)
153	k		176	~	(Overline Tilde)
154	l		177	DEL	(Delete/Rubout)

Appendix D

Universal Asynchronous Receiver Transmitter (UART)

This appendix provides a functional description of the UART. It includes a table of UART signal functions and simplified block diagrams and timing diagrams of the UART receiver and transmitter.

The UART is a MOS/LSI device packaged in a 40-pin DIP. It is a complete subsystem that transmits and receives asynchronous data in duplex or half-duplex operation. The receiver and transmitter can operate simultaneously. The transmitter accepts parallel binary characters and converts them to a serial asynchronous output.

The receiver accepts serial asynchronous binary characters and converts them to a parallel output. The receiver and transmitter clocks are separate and must be 16 times the desired baud rate.

Control bits are provided to select character length of five, six, seven, or eight bits (excluding parity); odd, even or no parity; and one or two stop bits for six, seven or eight-bit characters. For five-bit characters, 1 or 1-1/2 start bits are used. The format of a typical input/output serial word is shown in Figure D-1.

Both the receiver and transmitter have double character buffering so that at least one complete character is always available. A register is also provided to store control information.

A block diagram and simplified timing diagram for the UART transmitter are shown in Figure D-2. The transmitter data buffer (holding) register can be loaded with a character when the TBMT (Transmitter Buffer Empty) line goes high. Loading is accomplished by generating a short negative pulse on the DS (Data Strobe) line. The positive-going trailing edge of the DS pulse performs the load operation. The character is automatically transferred to the UART transmitter Shift Register when this register becomes empty. The

This appendix was written by John Sullivan for Digital Equipment Corporation.

Figure D-1.   Format of Typical Input/Output Serial Character

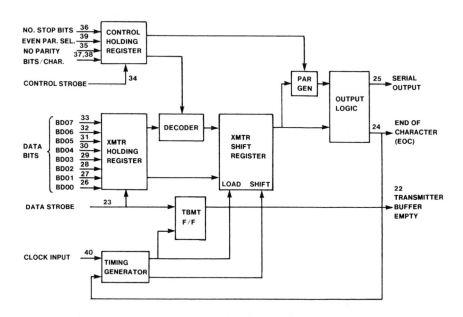

Figure D-2.   UART Transmitter, Block Diagram, and Simplified Timing Diagram

desired START, STOP, and parity bits are added to the data and transmission begins. One sixteenth of a bit time before a complete character (including stop bits) has been transmitted, the EOC (End of Character) line goes high and remains in this state until transmission of a new character begins.

A block diagram and simplified timing diagram for the UART receiver are shown in Figure D-3. Serial asynchronous data is sent to the SI (Serial Input) line. The UART searches for a high to low (MARK to SPACE) transition on the SI line. If this transition is detected, the receiver looks for the center of the start bit as the first sampling point. If this point is low (SPACE), the signal is assumed to be a valid start bit and sampling continues at the center of the subsequent data and stop bits. The character is assembled bit by bit in the receiver Shift Register in accordance with the control signals that determine the number of data bits and stop bits and type of parity, if selected. If parity is selected and does not check, the PER (Receive Parity Error) line goes high. If the first stop bit is low, the FER (Framing

Error) line goes high. After the stop bit is sampled, the receiver transfers in parallel the contents of the receiver Shift Register into the receiver Data Buffer (Holding) Register. The receiver then sets the DA (Received Data Available) line and transfers the state of the framing error and parity error to the Status Holding Register. When the computer interface accepts the receiver output, it drives the RDA (Reset Data Available) line low which clears the DA line. If this line is not reset before a new character is transferred to the receiver Holding Register, the OR (Overrun) line goes high and is held there until the next character is loaded into the receiver Holding Register.

Figure D-4 is a pin/signal designation diagram for the UART. The function of each signal is given in Table D-1. In the Function column, the references to high and low signals are with respect to the pins on the UART. This information is used during servicing of the device. Programmers should refer to the register descriptions for the interface being used to obtain information concerning the function of these signals.

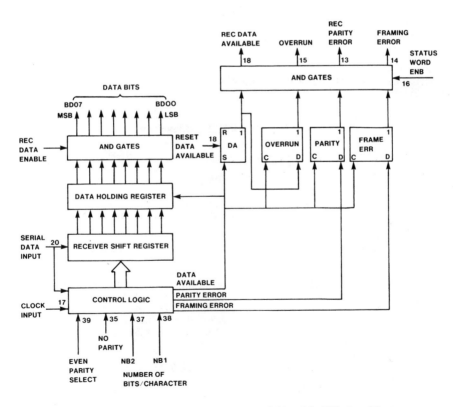

Figure D-3. UART Receiver, Block Diagram, and Simplified Timing Diagram

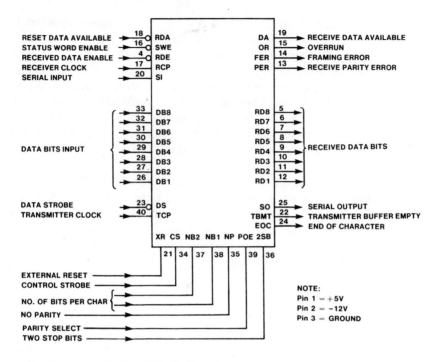

Figure D-4.   UART Signal Pin Designations

Table D-1.   UART Signal Functions

Pin No.	Mnemonic	Name	Function
1	+5	+5	Power
2	−12*	−12*	Power
3	GND	Ground	Ground
4	RDE	Received Data Enable	When low, gates the received data onto leads RD1–RD8.
5–12	RD1–RD8	Received Data	Eight data out lines that can be wire ORed. RD8 (pin 5) is the MSB and RD1 (pin 12) is the LSB. When five, six, or seven bit character is selected, the most significant unused bits are low. Character is right justified into the least significant bits.
13	PER	Receive Parity Error	Goes high if the received character parity does not agree with the selected parity.

*Many UARTs are available which do not require −12.

Table D-1. UART Signal Functions (Continued)

Pin No.	Mnemonic	Name	Function
14	FER	Framing Error	Goes high if the received character has no valid stop bit.
15	OR	Overrun	Goes high if the previously received character is not read (DA line not reset) before the present character is transferred to the receiver Holding Register.
16	SWE	Status Word Enable	When low, places the status word bits PER, OR, TBMT, FER, and DA) on the output lines.
17	RCP	Receiver Clock	Input for external clock whose frequency must be 16 times the desired receiver baud rate.
18	RDA	Reset Data Available	When low, resets the received DA (Data Available) line.
19	DA	Received Data Available	Goes high when an entire character has been received and transferred to the receiver Holding Register.
20	SI	Serial Input	Input for serial asynchronous data.
21	XR	External Reset	After power is turned on, this line should be pulsed high, which resets all registers, sets serial output line high, sets end of character line high, and sets transmitter buffer empty line high.
22	TBMT	Transmitter Buffer Empty	Goes high when the transmitter Data Holding Register may be loaded with another character.
23	DS	Data Strobe	Pulsed low to load the data bits into the transmitter Data Holding Register during the positive-going trailing edge of the pulse.
24	EOC	End of Character	Goes high each time a full character, including stop bits, is transmitted. It remains high until transmission of the next character starts. This is defined as the MARK (high) to (SPACE) low transition of the start bit. This line remains high when no data is being transmitted. When full speed transmission occurs, this lead goes high for 1/16 bit time at the end of each character.
25	SO	Serial Output	Output for transmitted character in serial asynchronous format. A MARK is high and a SPACE is low. Remains high when no data is being transmitted.
26–33	DB1–DB8	Data Input	Eight parallel Data In lines. DB8 (pin 33) is the MSB and DB1 (pin 26) is the LSB. If five, six, or seven bit characters are selected, the least significant bits are used.

Table D-1. UART Signal Functions (Continued)

Pin No.	Mnemonic	Name	Function
34	CS	Control Strobe	When high, places the control bits (POE, NP, SB, NB1, and NB2) into the control bits Holding Register.
35	NP	No Parity	When high, eliminates the parity bit from the transmitted and received character and drives the received parity error (PER) line low. As a result, the receiver does not check parity on reception and during transmission the stop bits immediately follow the last data bit.
36	2 SB	Two Stop Bits	Selects the number of stop bits that immediately follow the parity bit. A low inserts one stop bit and a high inserts two stop bits.
37,38	NB2, NB1	Number of Bits per Character (Excluding Parity)	Selects five, six, seven, or eight data bits per character as follows.
39	POE	Even Parity Select	Selects the type of parity to be added during transmission and checked during reception. A low selects odd parity and a high selects even parity.
40	TCP	Transmitter Clock	Input for an external clock whose frequency must be 16 times the desire transmitter baud rate.

Bits/ Char	NB2 (37)	NB1 (38)
5	L	L
6	L	H
7	H	L
8	H	H

Appendix E

Format and Speed Table for Asynchronous Communications

The tables that follow are arranged so that there is one table for codes with five information bits, one table for codes with six information bits, one table for codes with seven information bits, and one table for codes with eight information bits. For the purposes of these tables, a parity bit is considered to be an information bit.

In each of the codes, there is a single start bit followed by the designated number of information bits. The information bits are followed by a stop time equivalent to the number of bit times shown in the "Stop Units" column.

Within each table, entries are arranged according to baud rate, in ascending order. Where there are several entries for the same baud rate, those entries are arranged in ascending order by character rate.

From each table entry, other information can be derived. For example, to derive the total number of bits per character, take the number of information bits specified for that table (for example: 5), and 1 for the start bit, and then add the designated number of stop bits (for example: 1.42). The answer obtained in this example would be 7.42-bit characters. To obtain the bit length in milliseconds, divide 1 by the baud rate and divide the answer by 1000. For example, for 45.45 baud, divide 1 by 45.45 to get 0.0220022. Dividing that by 1000 produces the correct answer, which is that each bit is 22 milliseconds long.

To obtain the character length in milliseconds, take the result obtained in the bit time calculation and multiply that by the number of bits per complete character. Using the results of the previous two examples, one would multiply 22 milliseconds by 7.42 bits per character and obtain 163.24 milliseconds per character. Dividing 1 second by that number produces the character rate in characters per second, which in this case would be 6.126. In the chart for five unit codes, this entry has been rounded off to give (60 × 6.13) = 367.8 characters per minute or 61.3 words per minute, assuming an average word has six characters.

Table E-1.   Five Unit Codes

Baud Rate	Stop Units	Six-Character Words Per Minute	Usage
45.45	1.5	60.6	CCITT 60 wpm
45.45	1.42	61.3	US Government and Bell System 60 wpm
45.45	1.0	64.8	US Obsolete Western Union
50	1.5	66.67	CCITT #2, Western Union Telex
50	1.42	67.3	Some Western Union Telex
50	1.0	71.4	CCITT #1, Obsolete
56.86	1.42	76.6	US Standard 75 wpm
74.2	1.5	99	
74.2	1.42	100	US Standard 100 wpm
74.2	1.0	107	US Military
75	1.5	101	CCITT Standard 100 wpm
91	1.42	122.7	Teleprinter Duplex

Table E-2.   Six Unit Codes

Baud Rate	Stop Units	Six-Character Words Per Minute	Usage
45.45	1.42	54	Friden Teledata System 60 wpm
48.0	1.0	60	IBM 60 wpm
49.1	1.0	61.3	Teletypesetter
55.21	2.0	61.35	US M35 Teletype® (optional)
56.86	1.5	66.9	US Teletypesetter
60.6	2.0	67.3	
56.75	1.42	68.1	Friden Teledata System 75 wpm
69.25	2.0	76.6	US M35 Teletype® (optional)
66.67	1.0	83.3	Western Union #5A Stock Ticker
74.2	1.42	88.2	Friden Teledata System 100 wpm
80.0	1.5	100	NYSE Stock Ticker (obsolete)
135.0	2.0	150	NYSE 900 Stock Ticker

Table E-3.   Seven Unit Codes

Baud Rate	Stop Units	Six-Character Words Per Minute	Usage
45.45	1.42	48.2	Friden Teledata System 60 wpm
56.75	1.42	60.2	Friden Teledata System 75 wpm
61.35	2.0	61.35	US M35 Teletype® (optional) and Teletypesetter
67.34	2.0	67.3	
76.92	2.0	76.6	US M35 Teletype® (optional)
74.2	1.42	78.8	Friden Teledata System 100 wpm
75	1.0	83.3	IBM Model 1050 (optional)
100	2.0	100	IBM & M35 Teletype® (optional)
134.5	1.0	148	IBM Models 2740, 2741, 1050 standard speed
600	1.0	666.67	IBM System 1030

Table E-4. Eight Unit Codes

Baud Rate	Stop Units	Six-Character Words Per Minute	Usage
45.45	1.5	43.3	IBM Transceiver 60 wpm
45.45	1.42	43.6	Friden Teledata System 60 wpm
56.75	1.5	54.0	IBM Transceiver 75 wpm
56.75	1.42	54.5	Friden Teledata System 75 wpm
67.58	2.0	61.35	US M35 Teletype® (optional)
73.33	2.0	66.7	US M35 Teletype® (optional)
74.07	2.0	67.3	US M35 Teletype® (optional)
74.1	1.5	70.4	IBM Transceiver 100 wpm
74.2	1.42	71.3	Friden Teledata System 100 wpm
84.61	2.0	76.6	US M35 Teletype® (optional)
100	1.0	100	US M37 Teletype® (optional)
110	2.0	100	US M35 Teletype® (standard)
135.0	2.0	122.5	
150	2.0	136.4	
150	1.0	150	Standard Computer Terminal Speed
165	2.0	150	US M37 Teletype® Western Union
300	1.0	300	Standard Computer Terminal Speed
600	1.0	600	Standard Computer Terminal Speed
1200	1.0	1200	Standard Computer Terminal Speed
2400	1.0	2400	Standard Computer Terminal Speed
4800	1.0	4800	Standard Computer Terminal Speed
9600	1.0	9600	Standard Computer Terminal Speed

Appendix F

Channel Conditioning

Many modems operated on private line facilities require that those facilities be conditioned to control their electrical properties before the modems will operate at their advertised speed in a satisfactory manner. The information which follows pertains to the conditions of private line facilities provided by the Bell System companies and is extracted from Bell System Technical Reference PUB 41004, "Data Communications Using Voiceband Private Line Channels." This Technical Reference contains more than 50 pages of rather technical discussion of private line channels and is highly recommended to those desiring further knowledge of the subject.

The channel conditioning which will be discussed concerns the "type 3002 channel," which is the basic Bell System voice bandwidth private line channel. Some of the conditioning types mentioned, however, can also be obtained for type 2001 alternate voice/data channels. The relationship between channel conditioning and modem data rate can best be appreciated by referring to Table F-1. Note that the 202 series of modems is particularly sensitive to line conditioning. It should also be noted, however, that the newer modems, such as the 201C and the 208A, will operate at their rated speed on unconditioned ("basic") lines. This reflects a general trend in the modem industry away from a requirement for conditioned lines.

Table F-2 lists the various parameters that characterize a private line. These parameters are discussed in great detail in the PUB 41004 Technical Reference; they are listed here only as a reminder that the two variables specified for the various types of line conditioning, attenuation distortion and envelope delay distortion, are but two of a great many parameters. The other parameters are the same for all types of conditioning C1 through C5. A new type of conditioning, High Performance Data Conditioning Type D-1, specifies tighter limits on two of the transmission facility parameters listed in

**Table F-1. Error Performance Supported Using Bell System
200-Series Modems on Two-Point, Multi-point*
and Central Office Switched Channels**

CAUTION

The Bell System Technical Reference from which these tables are taken (PUB 41004) is being revised. This information will not be current after Fall 1982. Readers should obtain a copy of the Technical Reference Catalog dated January 1983 or later to obtain ordering information for the revised copy of PUB 41004. The catalog and the revised Technical Reference may be obtained from Publishers' Data Center, Inc. P.O. Box C738, Pratt Street Station, Brooklyn, New York 11205.

Data Set	Speed	Channel Conditioning	Minimum Performance Supported
201A	2000 bps	Basic	One 1000-bit block error per 100 blocks transmitted (Note 1)
201C	2400 bps	Basic	One 1000-bit block error per 100 blocks transmitted (Note 1)
202C,D,E,R	Up to 1200 bps	Basic	One bit error per 100,000 bits transmitted (Note 3)
	Up to 1400 bps	C1	
	Up to 1800 bps	C2	
203 four-level	3600,4800 bps	C2	One 1000-bit block error per 100 blocks transmitted (Note 2)
four-level	6400,7200 bps	C2	(Note 4)
eight-level	5400, 7200, 9600, 10,800 bps	C2	None supported
208A	4800	Basic	One 1000-bit block error per 100 blocks transmitted.

NOTES

1. Approximately equivalent to one bit error per 100,000 bits transmitted.
2. Approximately equivalent to one bit error per 10,000 bits transmitted.
3. Bit error rate specifications are used because these data sets are typically used for asynchronous transmission of characters and other very short blocks.
4. Limit not established.

*There are some restrictions on multi-point channels.

© American Telephone and Telegraph Company.

Table F-2, C-notched noise and harmonic distortion. Type D-1 conditioning will be discussed shortly.

Table F-3 lists the bandwidth parameters for the various types of channel conditioning, C1 through C5. The columns in the table are self-explanatory. Attenuation distortion is the frequency response and means the same thing in

Table F-2. Classification of Parameters

CAUTION

The Bell System Technical Reference from which these tables are taken (PUB 41004) is being revised. This information will not be current after Fall 1982. Readers should obtain a copy of the Technical Reference Catalog dated January 1983 or later to obtain ordering information for the revised copy of PUB 41004. The catalog and the revised Technical Reference may be obtained from Publishers' Data Center, Inc. P.O. Box C738, Pratt Street Station, Brooklyn, New York 11205.

Interface Parameters

1. Terminal Impedance and Balance
2. Isolation from Ground
3. In-Band Data Signal Powers
4. Test Signal Power
5. Distribution of In-Band Transmitted Signal Power (300 to 3000 Hz Nominal)
6. Out-of-Band Transmitted Signal Power
    (a) Above the Voiceband (3995 Hz and above)
    (b) Below the Voiceband (Below 300 Hz)

Bandwidth Parameters

1. Attentuation Distortion (Loss vs. Frequency)
2. Envelope Delay Distortion

Transmission Facility Parameters

1. 1004 Hz Loss Variation
2. C-Message Noise
3. C-Notched Noise
4. Impulse Noise
5. Single Frequency Interference
6. Frequency Shift
7. Phase Intercept Distortion
8. Phase Jitter
9. Nonlinear Distortion (Harmonic Distortion)
10. Peak-to-Average Ratio (P/AR)
11. Echo
12. Phase Hits
13. Gain Hits
14. Dropouts

© American Telephone and Telegraph Company, 1973.

this table as it does when one talks about high fidelity equipment for one's home (except that the fidelity is not very high here). Envelope delay distortion requires a bit more explanation.

Telephone transmission facilities propagate signals of various frequencies at different rates. For example, signals at 1800 Hertz propagate through such facilities faster than those at 600 Hertz. If data transmission involved signaling which contained both of these frequencies, the 1800 Hertz signal

Table F-3. Bandwidth Parameter Limits[1,2]

CAUTION

The Bell System Technical Reference from which these tables are taken (PUB 41004) is being revised. This information will not be current after Fall 1982. Readers should obtain a copy of the Technical Reference Catalog dated January 1983 or later to obtain ordering information for the revised copy of PUB 41004. The catalog and the revised Technical Reference may be obtained from Publishers' Data Center, Inc. P.O. Box C738, Pratt Street Station, Brooklyn, New York 11205.

Channel Conditioning	Attenuation Distortion (Frequency Response) Relative to 1004 Hz		Envelope Delay Distortion	
	Frequency Range (Hz)	Variation (dB)[3]	Frequency Range (Hz)	Variation (Microseconds)
Basic	500–2500[4] 300–3000[4]	−2 to +8 −3 to +12	800–2600[4]	1750
C1	1000–2400[4] 300–2700[4] 300–3000[4]	−1 to +3 −2 to +6 −3 to +12	1000–2400[4] 800–2600[4]	1000 1750
C2	500–2800[4] 300–3000[4]	−1 to +3 −2 to +6	1000–2600[4] 600–2600[4] 500–2800[4]	500 1500 3000
C3 (access line)	500–2800[4] 300–3000[4]	−0.5 to +1.5 −0.8 to +3	1000–2600[4] 600–2600[4] 500–2800[4]	110 300 650
C3 (trunk)	500–2800[4] 300–3000[4]	−0.5 to +1 −0.8 to +2	1000–2600[4] 600–2600[4] 500–2800[4]	80 260 500
C4	500–3000[4] 300–3200[4]	−2 to +3 −2 to +6	1000–2600[4] 800–2800[4] 600–3000[4] 500–3000[4]	300 500 1500 3000
C5	500–2800[4] 300–3000[4]	−0.5 to +1.5 −1 to +3	1000–2600[4] 600–2600[4] 500–2800[4]	100 300 600

[1]C-conditioning applies only to the attenuation and envelope delay characteristics.

[2]Measurement frequencies will be 4 Hz above those shown. For example, the basic channel will have −2 to +8 dB loss, with respect to the 1004 Hz loss, between 504 and 2504 Hz.

[3](+) means loss with respect to 1004 Hz. (−) means gain with respect to 1004 Hz.

[4]These specifications are tariffed items (FCC Tariff 260)

© American Telephone and Telegraph Company, 1973.

would reach the receiving station before the 600 Hertz signal, possibly causing some confusion at the receiver. This frequency dependent property of the propagation delay is called "envelope delay distortion." The figures given in Table F-3 for envelope delay distortion indicate that conditioning the channel can control the maximum time differential between the arrival of simultaneously generated signals of differing frequency at the receiving station. For both frequency response and delay distortion, it should be noted that, advancing from C1 to C5, each grade of conditioning represents progressively tighter tolerances for circuit performance.

The three most commonly used grades of circuit conditioning are C1, C2, and C4.

Recently a new grade of conditioning, called D-1, has become available (for two point 3002 channels only). Unlike the C1 through C5 conditioning, the bandwidth parameters are not affected by D-1 conditioning, and D-1 conditioning is not achieved by placing equalizers in the line as is done for the C types of conditioning. Rather, the facilities used to provide the service are chosen to minimize C-notched noise (no relation to the "C" type conditioning), and to minimize the harmonic distortion.

All channels have a certain amount of noise and some of that noise may increase when there is a signal present. Thus, to obtain a more accurate signal to noise ratio, a 1004 Hertz signal is placed on the line when the noise is to be measured, and the 1004 Hertz is filtered out at the receiver while the noise around it is measured. This is the basic principle of the C-notched noise measuring system.

Harmonic distortion refers to the tendency of certain types of telephone equipment to generate harmonics (multiples) of the frequencies being transmitted through them.

A question may arise as to the possible need for both a C type of conditioning and a D type. First of all, the D type of conditioning is only needed for transmissions in the vicinity of 9600 bits per second, and is required for 9600 bit per second operation of the Bell System 209 modem. The D type of conditioning is, however, the only type of conditioning required for the 209, as the bandwidth parameters are taken care of by a sophisticated adaptive equalizer in the modem. For non-Bell modems operating at 9600 bits per second, the modem manufacturer may well recommend that both D-1 type conditioning and some C type of conditioning be used, and such combinations of conditioning are indeed available.

A final note of caution on conditioning is that one should follow the modem manufacturer's recommendation fairly carefully. While there is a temptation to save money by ordering an unconditioned line and seeing how things work, the Telephone Company may change the facility some time and the new line may not necessarily be as good. You may have by chance received more than you paid for the first time and not the second time. With conditioned lines, the electrical characteristics are guaranteed, although Bell System does not certify the suitability of such lines for use with non-Bell modems.

Appendix G

Interface
Connector Pinning

A 25-pin connector with pins arranged as shown in Figure G-1 is the most widely used connector for EIA RS-232-C and Recommendation V.28 interfaces. A male connector is used on the Data Terminal Equipment and a female connector is used on the Data Circuit-Terminating (Communications) Equipment.

For about half of the pins there is an internationally accepted circuit assignment which is used by all modems which implement that circuit. These assignments are shown in Table G-1 below and in Reference 1.

For the pins that do not have an internationally accepted circuit assignment, there are variations between different modems. The variations are described in Reference 1.

No one should use the pins that are unassigned unless it is for a purpose described in the reference. Many manufacturers have put 20 milliampere interfaces on the "unused" pins of acoustic couplers (Data Circuit-Terminating Equipment). Many manufacturers of terminals (Data Terminal Equipment) have put TTL-level test points on the "unused" pins. Both companies have supplied cables which are wired appropriately for these com-

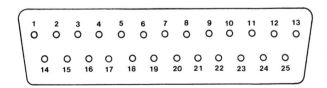

Figure G-1. View of Face of Connector on Data Terminal Equipment

297

Table G-1. Internationally Accepted Circuit Assignments for DTE/DCE Interface Using a 25-Pin Connector

Pin	CCITT	EIA	Circuit Name
1	Often used for 101/AA Protective Ground		
2	103	BA	Transmitted Data
3	104	BB	Received Data
4	105	CA	Request to Send
5	106	CB	Clear to Send
6	107	CC	Data Set Ready
7	102	AB	Signal Ground
8	109	CF	Received Line Signal (Carrier) Detector
9	Often used for modem power test point—do not connect		
10	Often used for modem power test point—do not connect		
11			
12			
13			
14			
15	114	DB	Transmit Signal Element Timing—DCE Source (Synchronous Modems Only)
16			
17	115	DD	Received Signal Element Timing—DCE Source (Synchronous Modems Only)
18			
19			
20	108	CD	Data Terminal Ready
21			
22	125	CE	Ring/Calling Indicator
23			
24			
25			

promised purposes. When the customer buys a cable from a third party, a cable with all 25 conductors wired, the 20 milliampere interface in the acoustic coupler blows up the TTL logic in the terminal.

For those using the 37-pin and 9-pin connectors associated with RS-422, RS-423, and RS-449 and the 15-pin connector associated with CCITT Recommendations X.20 and X.21, References 2 and 3 will be of assistance.

References

1. "Data Communication—25-pin DTE/DCE Interface Connector and Pin Assignments," (ISO/DIS 2110) International Organization for Standardization (ISO).
2. "Data Communication—37-pin and 9-pin DTE/DCE Interface Connectors and Pin Assignments," (ISO/DIS 4902) International Organization for Standardization (ISO).
3. "Data Communication—15-pin DTE/DCE Interface Connector and Pin Assignments," (ISO/DIS 4903) International Organization for Standardization (ISO).

Glossary

ACK0, ACK1 (affirmative acknowledgement) These replies (DLE sequences in binary synchronous communications) indicate that the previous transmission block was accepted by the receiver and that it is ready to accept the next block of the transmission. Use of ACK0 and ACK1 alternately provides sequential checking control for a series of replies. ACK0 is also an affirmative (ready to receive) reply to a station selection (multi-point), or to an initialization sequence (line bid) in point-to-point operation.

Acoustic coupler A device that converts electrical signals into audio signals, enabling data to be transmitted over the public telephone network via a conventional telephone handset.

Alternate route A secondary path used to reach a destination if the primary path is unavailable.

Amplitude modulation (AM) A method of transmission whereby the amplitude of the carrier wave is modified in accordance with the amplitude of the signal wave.

ASCII American Standard Code for Information Interchange. This is a seven-bit-plus-parity code established by the American National Standards Institute (formerly American Standards Association) to achieve compatibility between data services. Also called USASCII.

Asynchronous transmission Transmission in which time intervals between transmitted characters may be of unequal length. Transmission is controlled by start and stop elements at the beginning and end of each character. Also called Start-Stop transmission.

Audio frequencies Frequencies which can be heard by the human ear (usually between 15 cycles and 20,000 cycles per second).

Automatic calling unit (ACU) A dialing device supplied by the communications common carrier. This device permits a business machine to automatically dial calls over the communications network.

Bandwidth The range of frequencies assigned to a channel or system; the difference expressed in Hertz between the highest and lowest frequencies of a band.

Baseband signaling Transmission of a signal at its original frequencies, i.e., unmodulated.

Baud A unit of signaling speed equal to the number of discrete conditions or signal events per second. In asynchronous transmission, the unit of signaling speed corresponding to one unit interval per second; that is, if the duration of the unit interval is 20 milliseconds, the signaling speed is 50 baud. Baud is the same as "bits per second" only if each signal event represents exactly one bit. A baud is the reciprocal of the Unit Interval. See also: *Unit Interval.*

Baudot code A code for the transmission of data in which five bits represent one character. It is named for Emile Baudot, a pioneer in printing telegraphy. The name is usually applied to the code used in many teleprinter systems, which was first used by Murray, a contemporary of Baudot.

Binary digit (bit) In the binary notation either the characters 0 or 1. "Bit" is the commonly used abbreviation for binary digit.

Binary synchronous communications (BSC) A uniform discipline, using a defined set of control characters and control character sequences, for synchronized transmission of binary coded data between stations in a data communications system. Also called BISYNC.

Bit Abbreviation for *binary digit.*

Bit transfer rate   The number of bits transferred per unit time, usually expressed in bits per second (bps).

Block   A group of digits transmitted as a unit, over which a coding procedure is usually applied for synchronization or error control purposes. See also: *packet*.

Block check character (BCC)   The result of a transmission verification algorithm accumulated over a transmission block, and normally appended at the end; e.g., CRC, LRC.

Broadband   See *wideband*.

Buffer   A storage device used to compensate for a difference in the rate of data flow when transmitting data from one device to another.

Busy hour   The peak 60-minute period during a business day when the largest volume of communications traffic is handled.

Byte   A binary element string operated upon as a unit and usually shorter than a computer word, e.g., six bit, eight bit, or nine bit bytes.

Carrier   A continuous frequency capable of being modulated or impressed with a signal.

Carrier system   A means of obtaining a number of channels over a single path by modulating each channel upon a different "carrier" frequency, and demodulating at the receiving point to restore the signals to their original form.

Cathode-ray tube (CRT)   A television-like picture tube used in visual display terminals.

CCITT   Comite Consultatif Internationale de Telegraphie et Telephonie. An international consultative committee that sets international communications usage standards.

Central office   The place where communications common carriers terminate customer lines and locate the equipment that interconnects those lines.

Channel   That part of a communications system that connects a message source to a message sink. A path for electrical transmission between two or more points. Also called a circuit, facility, line, link, or path.

Channel capacity A term which expresses the maximum baud rate that can be handled by the channel.

Circuit In communications the complete electrical path providing one- or two-way communication between two points comprising associated go and return channels. Compare: *channel*.

Circuit switching A method of communications, where an electrical connection between calling and called stations is established on demand for exclusive use of the circuit until the connection is released. See also: *packet switching, message switching*.

Code 1) A set of unambiguous rules specifying the way in which data may be represented, e.g., the set of correspondences in the Standard Code for Information Interchange. 2) In data communications, a system of rules and conventions according to which the signals representing data can be formed, transmitted, received, and processed. 3) In data processing, to represent data or a computer program in a symbolic form that can be accepted by a data processor.

Common carrier In data communications, a public utility company that is recognized by an appropriate regulatory agency as having a vested interest and responsibility in furnishing communication services to the general public, e.g., Western Union, The Bell System. See also: *specialized common carrier, value added service*.

Communication control character A functional character intended to control or facilitate transmission over data networks. There are 10 control characters specified in ASCII which form the basis for character-oriented communications control procedures. See also: *control character*.

Communications computer A computer that acts as the interface between another computer or terminal and a network, or a computer controlling data flow in the network. See also: *front end processor, concentrator*.

Computer network An interconnection of assemblies of computer systems, terminals, and communications facilities.

Concentrator A communications device that provides communications capability between many low speed, usually asynchronous channels and one or more high speed, usually synchronous channels. Usually different speeds, codes, and protocols can be accommodated on the low speed side. The low speed channels usually operate in contention requiring buffering. The concentrator may have the capability to be polled by a computer, and may in turn poll terminals.

Conditioning   The addition of equipment to leased voice-grade lines to provide specified minimum values of line characteristics required for data transmission, e.g., equalization and echo suppression.

Connect time   A measure of system usage by a user, usually the time interval during which the user terminal was on-line during a session. Also, the amount of time it takes a switching system to connect the calling party to the called party.

Console   1) A part of a computer used for communication between operator or maintenance engineer and the computer. 2) Part of a terminal providing user input and output capability.

Contention   A condition on a communications channel when two or more stations try to transmit at the same time.

Control character   1) A character whose occurrence in a particular context initiates, modifies, or stops a control function. 2) In the ASCII code, any of the 32 characters in the first two columns of the standard code table. See also: *communications control character*.

Control procedure   The means used to control the orderly communication of information between stations on a data link. Also called: line discipline. See also: *protocol*.

Control station   The station on a network which supervises the network control procedures such as polling, selecting, and recovery. It is also responsible for establishing order on the line in the event of contention, or any other abnormal situation, arising between any stations on the network. Compare: *tributary station*.

Crosstalk   The unwanted transfer of energy from one circuit, called the disturbing circuit, to another circuit, called the disturbed circuit.

Cyclic redundancy check (CRC)   An error detection scheme in which the check character is generated by taking the remainder after dividing all the serialized bits in a block of data by a predetermined binary number.

Data access arrangement (DAA)   Data communication equipment furnished or approved by a common carrier, permitting attachment of privately owned data terminal and data communication equipment to the common carrier network.

Data collection   The act of bringing data from one or more points to a central point.

Data communication   The interchange of data messages from one point to another over communications channels. See also: *data transmission.*

Data communication equipment (DCE)   The equipment that provides the functions required to establish, maintain, and terminate a connection, the signal conversion, and coding required for communication between data terminal equipment and data circuit. The data communication equipment may or may not be an integral part of a computer (e.g., a modem). See also: *terminal installation.*

Data concentration   Collection of data at an intermediate point from several low and medium speed lines for retransmission across high speed lines.

Data integrity   A performance measure based on the rate of undetected errors.

Data-Phone   A trademark as well as a service mark of the AT&T Company. As a trademark, it identifies the data sets or modems manufactured and supplied by the Bell System for use in the transmission of data over the regular telephone network. As a service mark, it identifies the transmission of data over the regular telephone network.

Data-Phone 50   A public switched communications service of the Bell System featuring high-speed data communications at 50 kbps.

Data-Phone Digital Service (DDS)   A communications service of the Bell System in which data is transmitted in digital rather than analog form, thus eliminating the need for modems.

Data set   1) A modem. 2) A collection of data records, with a logical relation of one to another. See also: *Data-Phone, modem.*

Data terminal equipment (DTE)   1) The equipment comprising the data source, the data sink, or both. 2) Equipment usually comprising the following functional units: control logic, buffer store, and one or more input or output devices or computers. It may also contain error control, synchronization, and station identification capability. See also: *data communications equipment, terminal installation.*

Data transmission   The sending of data from one place for reception elsewhere. Compare: *data communication.*

DDCMP (Digital Data Communications Message Protocol) A uniform discipline for the transmission of data between stations in a point-to-point or multi-point data communications system. The method of physical data transfer used may be parallel, serial synchronous, or serial asynchronous.

Delay distortion Distortion resulting from non-uniform speed of transmission of the various frequency components of a signal through a transmission medium.

Delimiter A character that separates and organizes elements of data.

Demodulation The process of retrieving an original signal from a modulated carrier wave. This technique is used in data sets to make communications signals compatible with computer signals.

Dial-up line A communications circuit that is established by a switched circuit connection.

Direct Distance Dialing (DDD) A telephone exchange service which enables a user to directly dial telephones outside his local area without operator assistance.

Direct memory access (DMA) A facility that permits I/O transfers directly into or out of memory without passing through the processor's general registers; either performed independently of the processor or on a cycle-stealing basis.

DLE (data link escape) A control character used exclusively to provide supplementary line-control signals (control character sequences or DLE sequences). These are two-character sequences where the first character is DLE. The second character varies according to the function desired and the code used.

Duplex Simultaneous two-way independent transmission in both directions. Also referred to as full-duplex.

EBCDIC (Extended Binary Coded Decimal Interchange Code) An eight bit character code used primarily in IBM equipment. The code provides for 256 different bit patterns.

Echo A portion of the transmitted signal returned from the distant point to the source with sufficient magnitude and delay so as to cause interference.

Echo check A method of checking the accuracy of transmission of data in which the received data are returned to the sending end for comparison with the original data.

Echo suppressor A device used to suppress the effects of an echo.

Electronic Industries Association (EIA) A standards organization specializing in the electrical and functional characteristics of interface equipment.

Electronic switching system (ESS) The common carrier communications switching system which uses solid state devices and other computer-type equipment and principles, in particular, such systems provided by the Bell System.

ENQ (enquiry) Used as a request for response to obtain identification and/or an indication of station status. In binary synchronous (BSC) transmission, ENQ is transmitted as part of an initialization sequence (line bid) in point-to-point operation, and as the final character of a selection or polling sequence in multi-point operation.

EOT (End of Transmission) Indicates the end of a transmission, which may include one or more messages, and resets all stations on the line to control mode (unless it erroneously occurs within a transmission block).

Error Any discrepancy between a computed, observed, or measured quantity and the true, specified, or theoretically correct value or condition. Systematic Error: A constant error or one that varies in a systematic manner (e.g., equipment misalignment). Random Error: An error that varies in a random fashion (e.g., an error resulting from radio static).

Error control An arrangement that detects the presence of errors. In some systems, refinements are added that will correct the detected errors, either by operations on the received data or by transmission from the source.

Equalization Compensation for the increase of attenuation with frequency. Its purpose is to produce a flat frequency response.

ETX (End of Text) Indicates the end of message. If multiple transmission blocks are contained in a message in BSC systems, ETX terminates the last block of the message. (ETB is used to terminate preceding blocks). The block check character is sent immediately following ETX. ETX requires a reply indicating the receiving station's status.

Exchange   A defined area, served by a communications common carrier, within which the carrier furnishes service at the exchange rate and under the regulations applicable in that area as prescribed in the carrier's filed tariffs.

Facility   See *channel.*

Facsimile (FAX)   Transmission of pictures, maps, diagrams, etc. The image is scanned at the transmitter, reconstructed at the receiving station, and duplicated on some form of paper.

FIFO   See: *silo.*

Foreign exchange line   A line offered by a common carrier in which a termination in one central office is assigned a number belonging to a remote central office.

Forward channel   A data transmission channel in which the direction of transmission coincides with that in which information is being transferred. Compare: *reverse channel.*

Frame   See: *block.*

Frequency division multiplexing (FDM)   Dividing the available transmission frequency range into narrower bands, each of which is used for a separate channel.

Frequency modulation (FM)   A method of transmission whereby the frequency of the carrier wave is changed to correspond to changes in the information signal wave.

Frequency shift keying (FSK)   Also called frequency shift signaling. A method of frequency modulation in which frequency is made to vary at significant instants by smooth as well as abrupt transitions. Typically a data "1" bit is represented as one frequency and a data "0" as another frequency.

Front end processor   A communications computer associated with a host computer. It may perform line control, message handling, code conversion, error control, and applications functions such as control and operation of special-purpose terminals.

Full-duplex   See: *duplex*

Fully connected network A network in which each node is directly connected with every other node.

Half-duplex A circuit designed for transmission in either direction but not both directions simultaneously.

Hardware Physical equipment, as opposed to a computer program or method of use, e.g., mechanical, electrical, magnetic, or electronic devices.

Header The control information prefixed in a message text, e.g., source or destination code, priority, or message type. Also called: heading, leader.

Hertz A unit of frequency equal to one cycle per second. Cycles are referred to as Hertz in honor of the experimenter Heinrich Hertz. Abbreviated Hz.

Holding time The length of time a communication channel is in use for each transmission. Includes both message time and operating time.

Host computer A computer attached to a network providing primarily services such as computation, data base access, or special programs, or programming languages.

Host interface The interface between a communications processor and a host computer.

Hunt group An arrangement of a group of telephone lines such that a single telephone number is listed in the directory. A person dialing that listed number is automatically connected by the telephone switching equipment to an available line in that group. Only if all lines in the group are busy does the caller get a busy signal.

Information bit A bit which is generated by the data source and which is not used for error control by the data transmission system. Compare: *overhead bit*.

Information path The functional route by which information is transferred in a one-way direction from a single data source to a single data sink.

Information (transfer) channel 1) The functional connection between the source and the sink data terminal equipments. It includes the circuit and the associated data communications equipments. 2) The assembly of data communications and circuits including a reverse channel if it exists.

Interchange point   A location where interface signals are transmitted between equipment by means of electrical interconnections. See also: *interface.*

Interface   1) A shared boundary defined by common physical interconnection characteristics, signal characteristics, and meanings of interchanged signals. 2) A device or equipment making possible interoperation between two systems, e.g., a hardware component or a common storage register. 3) A shared logical boundary between two software components.

ITB (intermediate text block)   In binary synchronous communications, a control character used to terminate an intermediate block of characters. The block check character is sent immediately following ITB, but no line turnaround occurs. The response following ETB or ETX also applies to all of the ITB checks immediately preceding the block terminated by ETB or ETX.

Leased line   A line reserved for the exclusive use of a leasing customer without interexchange switching arrangements. Also called: private line.

Line   1) The portion of a circuit external to the apparatus consisting of the conductors connecting a telegraph or telephone set to the exchange or connecting two exchanges. 2) The group of conductors on the same overhead route in the same cable.

Link   1) Any specified relationship between two nodes in a network. 2) A communications path between two nodes. 3) A data link. See also: *line, circuit, virtual circuit.*

Load sharing   The distribution of a given load among several computers on a network.

Local exchange   An exchange in which subscribers' lines terminate. Also called: end office.

Longitudinal redundancy check (LRC)   An error checking technique based on an accumulated exclusive-OR of transmitted characters. An LRC character is accumulated at both the sending and receiving stations during the transmission of a block. This accumulation is called the Block Check Character (BCC), and is transmitted as the last character in the block. The transmitted BCC is compared with the accumulated BCC character at the receiving station for an equal condition. An equal comparison indicates a good transmission of the previous block.

MARK Presence of a signal. In telegraphy, MARK represents the closed condition or current flowing. Equivalent to a binary one condition.

Master station See: *primary station.*

Message switching A method of handling messages over communications networks. The entire message is transmitted to an intermediate point (i.e., a switching computer), stored for a period of time, perhaps very short, and then transmitted again towards its destination. The destination of each message is indicated by an address integral to the message. Compare: *circuit switching, packet switching.*

Modem (modulator-demodulator) A device that modulates signals transmitted over communications circuits. Also called: data set.

Multiplexing A division of a transmission facility into two or more channels. See also: *frequency division multiplexing, time division multiplexing.*

Multiplexer A device used for multiplexing. It may or may not be a stored program computer. Also a device for connecting a number of communications lines to a computer.

Multi-point line A single communications line to which more than one terminal is attached. Use of this type of line normally requires some kind of polling mechanism, addressing each terminal with a unique ID. Also called: multi-drop.

Narrowband channels Sub-voice grade channels characterized by a speed range of 100 to 200 bits per second.

Negative acknowledgement (NAK) Indicates that the previous transmission block was in error and that the receiver is ready to accept a retransmission of the erroneous block. NAK is also the "not ready" reply to a station selection (multi-point) or to an initialization sequence (line bid) in point-to-point operation.

Noise Undesirable disturbances in a communications system. Noise can generate errors in transmission.

Non-switched line A communications link which is permanently installed between two points. Also called: leased line or private line.

Non-transparent mode   Transmission of characters in a defined character format, e.g., ASCII or EBCDIC, in which all defined control characters and control character sequences are recognized and treated as such.

Null modem   A device which interfaces between a local peripheral that normally requires a modem, and the computer near it that expects to drive a modem to interface to that device; an imitation modem in both directions.

One-way only operation   A mode of operation of a data link in which data are transmitted in a preassigned direction over one channel. Also called: simplex operation.

Operating system   Software that controls the execution of computer programs and that may provide scheduling, debugging, input and output control, accounting, storage assignment, data management, and related service. Sometimes called supervisor, executive, monitor, or master control program depending on the computer manufacturer.

Overhead bit   A bit other than an information bit, e.g., check bit, framing bit.

Packet   A group of bits including data and control elements which is switched and transmitted as a composite whole. The data and control elements and possibly error control information are arranged in a specified format.

Packet switching   A data transmission process, utilizing addressed packets, whereby a channel is occupied only for the duration of transmission of the packet. NOTE: In certain data communication networks the data may be formatted into a packet or divided and then formatted into a number of packets (either by the data terminal equipment or by equipment within the network) for transmission and multiplexing purposes. See also: *circuit switching, message switching.*

Parallel transmission   Method of data transfer in which all bits of a character or byte are transmitted simultaneously either over separate communication lines or on different carrier frequencies on the same communication line.

Parity check   Addition of non-information bits to data, making the number of ones in each grouping of bits either always odd for odd parity or always even for even parity. This permits single error detection in each group.

Phase modulation (PM) A method of transmission whereby the angle of phase of the carrier wave is varied in accordance with the signal.

Point-to-point connection 1) A network configuration in which a connection is established between two, and only two, terminal installations. The connection may include switching facilities. 2) A circuit connecting two points without the use of any intermediate terminal or computer. Compare: *multi-point connection.*

Polling The process of inviting another station or node to transmit data. Compare: *selecting.*

Primary station 1) The station which at any given instant has the right to select and to transmit information to a secondary station, and the responsibility to insure information transfer. There should be only one primary station on a data link at one time. 2) A station which has control of a data link at a given instant. The assignment of primary status to a given station is temporary and is governed by standardized control procedures. Primary status is normally conferred upon a station so that it may transmit a message, but a station need not have a message to be nominated primary station.

Protocol A formal set of conventions governing the format and relative timing of message exchange between two communicating processes. See also: *control procedure.*

PTT (Post, Telephone and Telegraph Authority) The governmental agency that functions as the communications common carrier in most areas of the world except North America.

Pulse code modulation (PCM) Modulation of a pulse train in accordance with a code.

Redundancy In a protocol the portion of the total characters or bits that can be eliminated without any loss of information.

Regulatory agency In data communications, an agency controlling common and specialized carrier tariffs, e.g., the Federal Communications Commission and the State Public Utility Commissions.

Remote station (Multi-point) synonymous with tributary station. (Point-to-point switched network) a station that can be called by the central station, or can call the central station if it has a message to send.

Reperforator   A device that automatically punches a paper tape from received signals.

Response time   The elapsed time between the generation of the last character of a message at a terminal and the receipt of the first character of the reply. It includes terminal delay, network delay, and service node delay.

Reverse channel   A channel used for transmission of supervisory or error-control signals. The direction of flow of these signals is in the direction opposite to that in which information is being transferred. The bandwidth of this channel is usually less than that of the forward channel, i.e., the information channel.

Reverse interrupt (RVI)   In binary synchronous communications, a control character sequence (DLE sequence) sent by a receiving station instead of ACK1 or ACK0 to request premature termination of the transmission in progress.

Ring network   A computer network where each computer is connected to adjacent computers.

SDLC (synchronous data link control)   A uniform discipline for the transfer of data between stations in a point-to-point, multi-point, or loop arrangement, using synchronous data transmission techniques.

Secondary station   A station that has been selected to receive a transmission from the primary station. The assignment of secondary status is temporary, under control of the primary station, and continues for the duration of a transmission. Compare: *primary station.*

Selecting   A process of inviting another station or node to receive data. Compare: *polling.*

Serial transmission   A method of transmission in which each bit of information is sent sequentially on a single channel rather than simultaneously as in parallel transmission.

Signal element   Each of the parts of a digital signal, distinguished from oth-'ers by its duration, position, and sense, or by some of these features only. In start-stop operation a signal element has a minimum duration of one unit interval. If several unit intervals of the same sense run together, a signal element of duration of more than one unit element may be formed. Signal elements may be start elements, information elements, or stop elements.

Signal-to-Noise Ratio (SNR)   Relative power of the signal to the noise in a channel, usually measured in decibels.

Silo   A first-in/first-out (FIFO) hardware buffer used with multiplexers.

Simplex mode   Operation of a channel in one direction only with no capability of reversing.

Slave   A remote system or terminal whose functions are controlled by a central "master" system. It is similar in concept to a host system in that it responds to remotely generated requests, but unlike a host system is usually capable of performing a limited range of operations.

Software   A set of computer programs, procedures, rules, and associated documentation concerned with the operation of network computers, e.g., compilers, monitors, editors, utility programs. Compare: *hardware*

Specialized common carrier   A company that provides private line communications services, e.g., voice, teleprinter, data, facsimile transmission. See also: *common carrier, value added service.*

Start element   In start-stop transmission, the first element in each character, which serves to prepare the receiving equipment for the reception and registration of the character.

Start of Header (SOH)   A communication control character used at the beginning of a sequence of characters which constitute a machine-sensible address or routine information. Such a sequence is referred to as the heading.

Start of Text (STX)   A communication control character which precedes a sequence of characters that is to be treated as an entity and entirely transmitted through to the ultimate destination. Such a sequence is referred to as text. STX may be used to terminate a sequence of characters (heading) started by SOH.

Start-stop transmission   Asynchronous transmission in which a group of code elements corresponding to a character signal is preceded by a start element and is followed by a stop element.

Station   That independently controllable configuration of data terminal equipment from or to which messages are transmitted on a data link. It includes those elements which serve as sources or sinks for the messages, as well as those elements which control the message flow on the link, by means of data communication control procedures. See also: *terminal installation.*

STD (Subscriber Trunk Dialing)   European version of Direct Distance Dialing.

Stop element   In start-stop transmission, the last element in each character, to which is assigned a minimum duration, during which the receiving equipment is returned to its rest condition in preparation for the reception of the next character.

Stunt-box   A device to control the nonprinting functions of a teleprinter terminal. Control characters can be sent to it over the communications channel.

Supervisory programs   Computer programs that have the primary function of scheduling, allocating, and controlling system resources rather than processing data to produce results.

Supervisory sequence   In data communication, a sequence of communication control characters, and possibly other characters, that perform a defined control function.

Switched line   A communications link for which the physical path may vary with each usage, e.g., the dial-up telephone network.

Synchronous idle (SYN)   Character used as a time fill in the absence of any data or control character to maintain synchronization. The sequence of two continuous SYNs is used to establish synchronization (character phase) following each line turnaround.

Synchronous transmission   Transmission in which the data characters and bits are transmitted at a fixed rate with the transmitter and receiver synchronized. This eliminates the need for start-stop elements, thus providing greater efficiency. Compare: *asynchronous transmission.*

Tandem exchange   A telephone switching office that handles traffic between local exchanges.

Tariff   1) A published rate for services provided by a common or specialized carrier. 2) The means by which regulatory agencies approve such services. The tariff is a part of a contract between customer and carrier.

Teletype   Trademark of Teletype Corporation. Usually refers to one of their series of teleprinters.

Teletypewriter Exchange Service (TWX)   A public teletypewriter exchange (switched) service in the United States and Canada formerly belonging to AT&T Company which is now owned by the Western Union Telegraph Company. Both Baudot and ASCII-coded machines are used.

Telex Service   A Western Union world-wide teletypewriter exchange service that uses the public telegraph network. Baudot equipment is used.

Telpak   The name given to the pricing arrangement by AT&T in which many voice-grade telephone lines are leased as a group between two points.

Temporary text delay (TTD)   In binary synchronous communications, a control character sequence (STX . . . ENQ) sent by a transmitting station either to indicate a delay in transmission or to initiate an abort of the transmission in progress.

Terminal   A device or computer which may be connected to a local or remote host system, and for which the host system provides computational and data access services. Two common types of terminals are timesharing (typically interactive keyboard terminals) and remote batch.

Terminal installation   1) The totality of equipment at a user's installation including data terminal equipment, data communication equipment, and necessary support facilities. See also: *terminal, station.* 2) A set composed of data terminal, a signal converter, and possibly intermediate equipment; this set may be connected to a data processing machine or may be part of it.

Text   1) A sequence of characters forming part of a transmission which is sent from the data source to the data sink, and contains the information to be conveyed. It may be preceded by a header and followed by an "End of Text" signal. 2) In ASCII as well as in general communications usage, a sequence of characters treated as an entity if preceded by a "Start of Text" and followed by an "End of Text" control character.

Tie line   A private line communications channel of the type provided by communications common carriers for linking two or more points together.

Time-division multiplexing   A system of multiplexing in which channels are established by connecting terminals one at a time at regular intervals by means of an automatic distribution.

Time-sharing   A method of operation in which a computer facility is shared by several users for different purposes at (apparently) the same time. Although the computer actually services each user in sequence, the high speed of the computer makes it appear that the users are all handled simultaneously.

Torn-tape switching center   A location where operators tear off incoming printed and punched paper tape and transfer it manually to the proper outgoing circuit.

Touch Tone   AT&T registered trademark for pushbutton dialing. The signaling form is multiple tones.

Transit exchange   European version of *tandem exchange*.

Transparent mode   Transmission of binary data with the recognition of most control characters suppressed. In binary synchronous communications, entry to and exit from the transparent mode is indicated by a sequence beginning with a special Data Link Escape (DLE) character.

Tributary station   A station, other than the control station, on a centralized multi-point data communications system, which can communicate only with the control station when polled or selected by the control station.

Trunk   A single circuit between two points, both of which are switching centers or individual distribution points.

Turnaround time   1) The elapsed time between submission of a job to a computing center and the return of results. 2) In communications, the actual time required to reverse the direction of transmission from sender to receiver or vice versa when using a two-way alternate circuit. Time is required by line propagation effects, modem timing, and computer reaction.

Two-way alternate operation   A mode of operation of a data link in which data may be transmitted in both directions, one way at a time. Also called: half-duplex operation (US).

Two-way simultaneous operation   A mode of operation of a data link in which data may be transmitted simultaneously in both directions over two channels. NOTE: One of the channels is equipped for transmission in one direction while the other is equipped for transmission in the opposite direction. Also called: full-duplex, duplex.

TWX   See: *Teletypewriter Exchange Service.*

Unattended operation The automatic features of a station's operation which permit the transmission and reception of messages on an unattended basis.

Unit element A signal element of one unit element duration.

Unit interval A unit interval is the duration of the shortest nominal signal element. It is the longest interval of time such that the nominal durations of the signal elements in a synchronous system or the start and information elements in a start-stop system are whole multiples of this interval. The duration of the unit interval (in seconds) is the reciprocal of the telegraph speed expressed in baud.

USASCII See *ASCII.*

Value added service A communication service utilizing communications common carrier networks for transmission and providing added data services with separate additional equipment. Such added service features may be store and forward message switching, terminal interfacing, and host interfacing.

Vertical redundancy check (VRC) A check or parity bit added to each character in a message such that the number of bits in each character, including the parity bit, is odd (odd parity) or even (even parity).

Virtual circuit A connection between a source and a sink in a network that may be realized by different circuit configurations during transmission of a message. Also called: logical circuit.

Voice-grade channel A channel used for speech transmission usually with an audio frequency range of 300–3400 Hertz. It is also used for transmission of analog and digital data. Up to 10,000 bits per second can be transmitted on a voice-grade channel.

WACK (Wait Before Transmitting Positive Acknowledgement) In binary synchronous communications, this DLE sequence is sent by a receiving station to indicate that it is temporarily not ready to receive.

WATS (Wide Area Telephone Service) A service provided by telephone companies in the United States that permits a customer to make calls to or from telephones in specific zones for a flat monthly charge. The monthly charges are based on size of the zone instead of number of calls. WATS may be used on a measured-time or full-time basis.

Wideband Communications channel having a bandwidth greater than a voice-grade channel characterized by data transmission speed of 10,000–500,000 bits per second.

Word 1) In telegraphy, six characters (five characters plus one space). 2) In computing, an ordered set of characters that is the normal unit in which information may be stored, transmitted, or operated upon within a computer.

Index

Abandon Call (ACR), *see* Interface leads
Abort, 167, 172
Acoustic couplers, 223–224, 297, 299,
  (defined) 300
Active Interface, *see* Interface
ADCCP (American National Standards
  Institute protocol), 147, 169–172
ACK0, ACK1 (affirmative
  acknowledgment), defined 300
Alloter (hunt-group) device, 69. *See also*
  Telephone
ALOHA network, 228–229
Alternate route, (defined) 300
AM, *see* Amplitude Modulation
American National Standards Institute, 147
Amplitude Modulation (AM), 126–127,
  131, (defined) 300
Analog systems, 193, 194, 225
Answer mode, *see* Modems
ARPANET (packet-switching network),
  197
ASCII (American Standard Code for
  Information Interchange), 3, 124, 148,
  149, 151, 160, 281–282 (table),
  (defined) 300
Associative memory, 177. *See also* Direct
  Memory Access (DMA)
Asynchronous Time Division Multiplexing,
  199
Asynchronous transmission, *see*
  Transmission
AT&T (American Telephone and Telegraph
  Company), 28, 32, 73, 203, 205. *See
  also* Bell System
Attenuation distortion, 293

Audio frequencies, *see* Frequencies
Australian Post Office, 277
Automatic calling (X.21 interface), 216,
  220
Automatic calling units, 93–99, 105,
  (defined) 301
  801A, 93–94, 97, 99
  801C, 93, 95, 97, 99
Automatic dialing units, 68, 69, 96, 206
Automatic Electric Company, 65
AUTOVON (military voice network),
  203–204

Backward channel, *see* Reverse channel
Bandpass filter, 89
Bandwidth
  channel conditioning and, 292–294, 296
  defined, 301
  local area network, 225
Baseband signaling, (defined) 301
Baud, (defined) 301
Baudot (five-bit) code, 3, 101
Baud rate, 191, 241
  limitation of (hardware and), 14, 23, 222,
  224
  in phase modulation, 130, 131
  for switched network modems, 80–81, 83,
  84–85, 92, 193
  See also Speed
BCC, *see* Block Check Character
Bell System, 65, 68
  Technical Reference PUBs, 27, 66, 67,
  131, 195, 243–244, 270, 292
Bell System modems, 12n, 32, 80, 244–274,
  296